ALL HIS BRIGHT LIGHT GONE

The Death of John F. Kennedy and The Decline of America

PETER McKENNA

When we go back to the
sea . . . we are going back
from whence we came.
— John F. Kennedy

ALL HIS
BRIGHT LIGHT
GONE

The Death of John F. Kennedy and
The Decline of America

PETER MCKENNA

NEW FRONTIER PUBLISHING

NEW YORK CITY, NEW YORK

ALL HIS BRIGHT LIGHT GONE: The Death of John F. Kennedy and The Decline of America
by Peter McKenna

ISBN 978-0-9971372-0-0

Book Designer: Robert L. Lascaro
LascaroDesign.com

New Fronter Publishing
New York City, New York
HTTP://allhisbrightlightgone.com

Front Cover Photo: portrait of President Kennedy by Jacques Lowe

Back Cover Photo: Eternal Flame at President Kennedy's gravesite,
Arlington National Cemetery, by Larry Downing

Printed in the United States
on acid-free paper

This book is dedicated to my wife, Perrin.

CONTENTS

This is the first of two books about the influence of the Kennedy family on the United States, focusing on the economic, political, and social changes that occurred after the assassination of President John F. Kennedy. An upcoming book will cover the impact of losing Robert and Ted Kennedy.

AUTHOR'S NOTE:

Four months after President Kennedy's death, Jacqueline Kennedy appeared in a newsreel shown in movie theaters across the country and on television. She thanked the American people for their expressions of sympathy. One sentence of her remarks read simply, "All his bright light gone from the world." The title of this book comes from that sentiment.

The soft, the complacent, the self-satisfied societies will be swept away with the debris of history.—John F. Kennedy

PROLOGUE

THE SINS OF THE COLD-BLOODED

TOO MANY YEARS have gone by for me to recall exactly what I said in class that awful Friday morning. I remember only that it was my nature then to be arrogant and rude, that the classroom erupted in raucous laughter, and that the teacher, normally a placid man, angrily slammed a book on his desk and shouted for quiet. He glared at me for a moment, but just as he began to speak, the bell rang, cutting him off, and I bolted out the door to avoid his reprimand.

The passage of time, however, will never dull my memory of what happened next. In the hallway, students who should have been walking casually to their next class were instead gathering in small groups. The girl in front of me screamed and covered her face with her hands. A teacher wrapped her arms around the girl and drew her close.

Clearly, something was terribly wrong. I stood for a moment in utter confusion, unable to make sense of the nervous chatter that filled the hallway. Then from across the hall a friend noticed my bewilderment. He shouted: "It's Kennedy. He was riding in a convertible in Dallas and somebody shot him in the head!"

In my mind's eye, I saw Kennedy's face. I could not understand why anyone would want to hurt this man. When I pictured the damage a bullet to the head would cause, I went weak in the knees, and for a moment, I was unable to form a coherent thought.

I cut my afternoon classes and went home to watch television. Before long, I heard Walter Cronkite say that Kennedy was dead, his words catching in his throat as he reported this shattering news. Immediately, I lapsed into denial, conjuring fantastic scenarios in which Cronkite was wrong and that Kennedy was still alive. It had all been a mistake.

As I awoke the next morning, I somehow sensed that once fully awake, I would have to admit that there had been no mistake, that my denial had been absurd, and that Kennedy was gone. So I tossed and turned, fighting desperately to remain under the protective blanket of sleep. But as sunlight brightened my bedroom, the events of the previous day came flooding back. I sat upright in bed, shuddered, and finally, I began to cry.

There was a reason for my intense reaction to Kennedy's death. I grew up in a lower-middle-class Irish family. My father was a cynical, irresponsible man, quick with his fists and his caustic tongue. He often called me "a dumb mick" and said that college "was for rich kids and Jews." I should be content, he insisted, with a lifetime of menial jobs and weekends sitting on a barstool.

I modeled my behavior on these low expectations. In high school, I was a habitual truant, contemptuous of the adults who tried to force me to care about things that did not matter. It took me five years to graduate dead last in my class. Like my father, I was a cynic, eager to find the worst in everyone.

One day in 1962, all this began to change. I picked up a newspaper and read an article about a White House dinner honoring Nobel Prize winners. President Kennedy began the evening by saying, "This is the most extraordinary collection of talent, of human knowledge, that has ever been gathered together at the White House, with the possible exception of when Thomas Jefferson dined alone."

At the time, I was unaware that it was possible to convey a complex, meaningful thought with a mere handful of words. As I read and reread the article, I could see that Kennedy's purpose was not political; he was not pandering to voters. Instead, he was inspiring the citizens of this country to admire men who used their minds to improve the human condition. He was celebrating intellect and accomplishment, attributes that I had never considered important.

Kennedy's idealism, expressed so briefly and so beautifully, to borrow a phrase from Emily Dickinson, "took the top of my head off." I became enchanted by the English language.

It occurred to me that a president who possessed both the ability and the inclination to heighten our awareness of intellectual brilliance was unique. I began to follow his progress by reading newspapers and watching his press conferences. To gain a better understanding of the issues he discussed, I read books about history, politics, and current events. And I read everything I could find about Thomas Jefferson.

One day, in study hall, a teacher accustomed to my disdain for anything in print snatched a book out of my hands, no doubt expecting something pornographic. The book, *Rendezvous with Destiny*, was about Franklin Delano Roosevelt. We fell into a discussion of the Roosevelt years, and then I recited for him a short biography of each member of Kennedy's cabinet. His stunned disbelief was proof of my change. I had to build a makeshift bookshelf to hold the growing number of books I now eagerly consumed.

As I followed Kennedy, I also came to admire his idealistic approach to government. At a press conference, he said politics was a "noble profession," the mechanism used to fashion policies that make the United States a magnificent country. I thought of Washington, D.C., as an almost sacred place. I vowed to visit that city one day.

THEN CAME THAT AWFUL FRIDAY in November when I stood in the hallway at school, struck dumb by a thunderbolt of shock and sadness. Two days later, I stood on line for six hours, waiting to walk by Kennedy's flag-draped coffin in the Rotunda of the Capitol. My pilgrimage to Washington had come far sooner than I expected.

I had gained enough self-respect to understand that spending my life working menial jobs would be unproductive, wasteful, certainly not a life that Kennedy would approve of. It was too late to undo my appalling performance in high school, so I took night courses to prove to college admissions officers that I was not an imbecile, that I was serious about getting a degree. Eventually, I graduated from college and then earned a master's degree in journalism. Because John Kennedy awakened my interest in language, I have worked as a writer for more than 25 years.

While Kennedy was alive, I was elated just knowing that such an enlightened man was leading the country. But after he was gone, in the decades after Dallas, I slowly lost the thread of what he meant to me. For a few years, on each anniversary of his death, I would listen to replays of his speeches, and old emotions would be rekindled.

But those moments gradually fell away, as did my interest in politics and history. The presidents who followed Kennedy in office seemed one-dimensional, so different from Kennedy; they spoke with passion only about the issues that promoted their narrow political agendas. Politics no longer seemed like a noble profession, and John Kennedy faded from my thoughts.

I now realize that a countless number of Americans experienced Kennedy in a similar manner. He inspired them to improve their lives, making his death particularly shattering. But as the shock of his death wore off, the best parts of him, his intelligence and uplifting spirit, became less immediate, and his impact on their lives gradually dissipated.

My indifference to politics lasted more than 40 years, until midway through the presidency of George W. Bush, when I could no longer ignore what was happening in this country. Bush was making a colossal mess of things, almost as if he spent each day trying to find ways to weaken our economy, our political system, and our morale.

In 2008, as the economy faltered and nearly collapsed, costing countless Americans their jobs, their homes, their health care, and their pride, Kennedy again became an important figure in my life. The economy had become my specialty as a writer. It occurred to me that this misery would not have occurred on Kennedy's watch. He was simply too intelligent to have promoted policies capable of tearing our economic system to shreds.

Could this vague feeling be true? Under John Kennedy's leadership, would the nation have suffered a crisis comparable to the horrific meltdown of 2008?

My search for an answer to this question became an obsession. I studied Kennedy's life and presidency in detail. To put his presidency into context, I also studied this nation's economic and political history, from its founding to the present day.

During this research, I discovered that Kennedy was indeed too sophisticated to have allowed a massive collapse of the U.S. economy. But this was just the beginning, the proverbial tip of the iceberg. As improbable as it sounds, the loss of Kennedy's overall approach to government has changed this country more profoundly than is commonly believed. Without his leadership, the United States has become a bewildered nation, awash in childish political bickering and unable to resolve or even intelligently address the political and social issues that determine the quality of our lives.

You will find the reasoning behind these assertions in the body of this book. As a prelude, however, I offer the following: Our current understanding of Kennedy, who he was and what he meant to this country, even with five decades of hindsight to draw from, is immature and incomplete.

THIS NATION BEGAN AS A DEMOCRATIC REPUBLIC. If it is to succeed, it must remain a democratic republic. Kennedy governed through the lens of this sentiment. He did everything he could to preserve and protect the principles of government that make this republic strong; he brought them to life for the American people. This was his genius.

After Kennedy's death, his approach to government slowly disappeared and the United States became a hollowed-out version of the country he had left behind. Less competent presidents ignored the principles that Kennedy honored, replacing them with a system that slowly destroyed the values of a republic. Their desperate attempts to perpetuate this system have created a form of government-by-ideology that would make the Founding Fathers and John Kennedy apoplectic with rage.

Here is an unconventional way of making the same point. In filmmaking, there is a mechanism called "the inciting incident," an event that determines what will happen during the remainder of the film. In the first minutes of a film, for example, if a man leaps from a tall building, we understand that all that follows will be devoted to explaining why he jumped. Everything evolves from this incident.

The film, *Hud*, was released the year Kennedy died. It explores the ethical dilemma faced by an elderly cattle rancher in the Texas Panhandle. The "inciting incident" occurs when he unknowingly buys a herd of cattle infected with a fatal disease. He faces two options: He can have the ranch quarantined and the cattle destroyed before the disease spreads, driving the ranch into bankruptcy, or he can quickly sell the cattle to unsuspecting buyers.

The rancher decides not to sell the infected cattle to others, an act of honesty that infuriates his son, who will now inherit a worthless ranch. The son berates his father, saying that he is out of touch with reality, too old to understand that turning a profit is all that matters.

The old man endures his son's tirade and finally defends his ethical stance by saying: "Little by little, the look of the country changes because of the nature of the men we admire."

The loss of John Kennedy's influence on our society was an inciting incident. In 1963, the nation did not admire men who believed that the accumulation of wealth was more important than integrity. Instead, we admired and often tried to emulate a president who urged us to heighten our sense of accomplishment, our respect for government, and our feelings of empathy for others.

But after Kennedy's death, we began to admire political leaders who, like the son in the scenario above, believed the accumulation of wealth should be our guiding principle. They told us that greed was good. We gave them respect and political power, and little by little, the look of this nation began to change.

Kennedy was once asked to contrast his style of leadership with that of his political opponents. Quoting Franklin D. Roosevelt, he said:

> We have all made mistakes. But Dante tells us that divine justice weighs the sins of the cold-blooded and the sins of the warm-hearted on different scales. Better the occasional faults of a party living in the spirit of charity than the consistent omissions of a party frozen in the ice of its own indifference.

In this book, we are going on a journey through the life and times of John Kennedy. We will learn that he possessed the intelligence and vision to promote the values that make us an honorable people and an honorable nation.

We will learn that in the absence of this type of leadership, the quality of our lives has declined. We will learn that Kennedy's focus on improving the common good rather than individual greed was based on principles passed down to us from the Founding Fathers.

We will learn that it is time to return to the type of government he so briefly gave us, a government that weighs the sins of the cold-blooded and the sins of the warm-hearted on different scales.

And we will learn that to repair the damage inflicted on our democracy after 1963, we must acknowledge the following: President Kennedy gave us a prototype of what government in America should be. If we have the courage, we can use this prototype to ensure that "Government of the people, by the people, for the people, shall not perish from the Earth."

Finding the courage to make this change, to use Kennedy as our teacher, is what this book is all about.

Peter McKenna
May 2016

John Kennedy arriving in Southampton, England with his father and older brother in July 1938. He visited nearly every continent on the globe to see firsthand how foreign nations managed various political and economic situations. This relentless travel was the foundation of the foreign policy he would adopt as president.

PART ONE

THE FORMATIVE YEARS

CHAPTER ONE

A New Appreciation of John Kennedy

We are creating a culture that is not conducive to good policy or good politics. — President Barack Obama.

A HALF-CENTURY AGO, on a cool November evening, an enormous jet landed at an airport near Washington, D.C., and taxied into the harsh glare of klieg lights. A truck with a hydraulic cargo lift mounted on the back sped across the tarmac to an open door at the rear of the plane. In the doorway, several men in dark suits struggled with the weight of an ornate wooden coffin as they carried it onto the lift and set it down at their feet.

Almost immediately, someone threw a switch and the lift began to move down to the tarmac. But after it had gone just a few feet, it stopped and would go no farther, forcing the men in suits to jump down and remove the coffin by hand. They moved quickly, almost frantically, knowing that each moment of delay was an eternity for Jacqueline Kennedy, the bewildered young woman who stood at the edge of the lift, her eyes locked on the coffin.

Unobserved, Robert Kennedy had galloped up a boarding ramp and pushed his way through the plane to be with her. Now they stood together on the lift, holding hands as they watched the manic frenzy on the ground below them. The men in suits swarmed around the coffin and pushed it into the rear of an ambulance. Jacqueline Kennedy fell forward into the outstretched arms of a man in military uniform, and he gently lifted her down to the ground. There were dark stains on her skirt and stockings. She walked to the ambulance and tried to open the door. When it would not open, she stepped back, confused, unsure of what to do next. After several uncomfortable seconds, someone unlocked the door from the inside. Jacqueline Kennedy took a seat behind a curtained window, and the ambulance disappeared into the night shadows.

Millions of Americans watched this macabre homecoming on black and white televisions. Unheard was their collective gasp the instant the coffin came into view. Unheard was the skipped beat of their hearts when Jacqueline and Robert Kennedy held hands, a small moment of tenderness that for a fleeting moment softened the raw grief that was spreading across the nation. Unheard was their muffled cries when they realized the dark stains on Jacqueline Kennedy's clothing were remnants of her husband's destruction.

Three days of elegant solemnity would follow: a tribute from the woman who loved John Fitzgerald Kennedy and sat beside him when he died. But on this night, those who brought him home were engulfed by anguish so raw that it could be endured only if their emotions were temporarily shut down. The friends, aides, and political leaders who came to the airport to show their respect found themselves incapable of speech. A journalist who stood among them would later write, "One wished for a cry, a sob, any human sound" to break the desperate silence.

Lyndon Baines Johnson and his wife came down a stairway at the head of the plane and walked to a microphone. The new president spoke with little emotion; his words were neither profound nor comforting. He said the nation had suffered a loss that could not be weighed, that the assassination was a deep personal tragedy for him, and that he would do his best. Then he asked the nation, and God, to help him in the days ahead.

It was about him; not once did he mention the name of the extraordinary leader who moments before had been removed from Air Force One on a cargo lift and hauled away like excess baggage.

Nor did he tell us how to deal with the awful questions that were beginning to tear at our guts.

For a brief time, the nation had been under the spell of an eloquent, idealistic man who spoke with passion about our history and culture. He challenged us to meet our civic responsibilities and spoke about the joy that comes with "the pursuit of excellence." We had come to rely on his ability to make us proud of our country and of ourselves.

Now, suddenly, he was gone. How could something like this happen in the most civilized country on earth? What would become of us without him? Why had he died?

Kennedy had himself wrestled with the "why" of senseless death many times. His brother, a bomber pilot during World War II, had died when his plane exploded. A few years later, his sister died in a plane crash, and he slid into a deep, paralyzing grief, crying for days and endlessly re-reading her letters. Men he had come to love died under his command in combat. He stood in stunned silence over the grave of a friend killed during the bloody fighting on Guadalcanal, unable to comprehend why such a good man was destined to meet such a gruesome end.

Later, to help others cope with their own times of loss, Kennedy spoke about what grief had taught him. "There is always inequity in life," he said. "Some men are killed in a war, and some men are wounded, and some men never leave the country. It is very hard in military or in personal life to assure complete equality. Life is unfair."

Now, on this cool November evening, as the nation began to realize that he was gone forever, the harsh truth of his own words became the only possible explanation for the "why" of his death: "Life is unfair."

What should we make of him now, after all this time, this man whose death so devastated this country? A half-century after Dallas, we are still struggling with that question, still coming to terms with John Kennedy, his life and presidency. Did he leave behind enduring gifts or merely a few years of style and glamor? Was he a great president or, as some have argued, a great pretender?

The American people have never wavered in their estimation that Kennedy was a great president. In one poll, they ranked him as the second greatest president in history, a few percentage points behind Abraham Lincoln, an astonishing statement of respect. When asked in polls to name the past president they would like to see returned to office today, the people have consistently answered overwhelmingly, John Kennedy.

The historians, political scientists, and pundits who assess the performance of presidents, however, believe the people love Kennedy because his brutal death broke their hearts. They argue that he was not in office long enough to be considered great. To them, his legacy will forever be what he could have done had he lived. He was "a work in progress."

In 1968, when he eulogized his slain brother Robert, Ted Kennedy said that he need not be "idealized in death beyond what he was in life." According to the academics, the people have done exactly that with John Kennedy; they have irrationally elevated him to a status that he does not deserve.

James MacGregor Burns, a respected historian and Kennedy biographer, questioned the perception that Kennedy was a great president as follows:

> His actual tangible material impact on history was not enough to justify this. After all, he was not a Churchill, he was not a Roosevelt. He didn't have time to be these people. Why did he have this kind of impact on the world? Was it a fabrication? Was it that he was handsome, his wife and kids? Was it civil rights?

There is some merit to this view. Only four presidents have been considered truly great: Washington, Lincoln, and Theodore and Franklin D. Roosevelt. George Washington led the revolution that created this nation and then set a high standard for future presidents. Abraham Lincoln transcended the presidency, preserving our unique system of democracy with his humanity and eloquence during a gruesome civil war that could have permanently torn the nation in two. Teddy Roosevelt ended years of government-sanctioned corporate greed and made this country a global power. Over a period of 12 years, Franklin Roosevelt, from his wheelchair, led us through the Great Depression and successfully fought a catastrophic world war.

Without the towering leadership of these men, the United States would be a vastly different country today. It is indeed irrational to rank Kennedy among these leaders. He was president for just 1,037 days, 103 days shy of a full term. Only five presidents in history served less time in office. He did not lead the nation through a prolonged crisis that tested his leadership abilities. He was Washington without the American Revolution, Lincoln without the Civil War, Franklin Roosevelt without the Great Depression or World War II.

Why, then, do the people insist, year after year, that Kennedy was a great president?

A researcher who examines attitudes toward the presidency told the author, "I wish I had a dollar for every time someone told me that things were never the same after Kennedy died. They cannot explain exactly what changed, but they believe things went downhill after he died, and they miss him."

The emotional trauma caused by his death, as the academics contend, is certainly a factor. It is impossible to minimize the anguish the nation endured when Kennedy was murdered. If the shooting in Dealey Plaza occurred today, it would be captured by cell phone cameras and immediately uploaded to the Internet. We would be able to watch endless replays until we became numb to the horror.

But in 1963, we knew only that Kennedy had been shot in the head by a man using a high-powered rifle. This fate was too violent and hideous to comprehend. Our only recourse was to wrap Kennedy in a blanket of unconditional reverence.

The public may also believe that Kennedy was a great president because he possessed qualities often associated with great presidents. He could explain complex issues with the type of soaring eloquence that captivates and motivates people.

Having this ability, however, does not automatically elevate a president to greatness. Despite his charm and eloquence, Kennedy had not passed a prolonged test of his leadership. According him the mantle of greatness, under traditional standards, is impossible.

Should we say with finality that ordinary citizens are simply not as objective as historians, that their opinion of Kennedy is based on raw emotion rather than logic? Kennedy was a very good president who simply did not have the time to earn the greatness the people have bestowed on him. Would it be best to just let the matter rest with this assessment?

To do so would be a mistake. Kennedy's legacy is not what he could have accomplished if he had more time. It is instead what he accomplished in the short time he was given. His "actual tangible material impact on history" was enormous. His true legacy is the difference between the type of country he was building during his presidency and the type of country we became after his death.

What exactly is this "difference"? Consider the following: When a president enters the White House, he brings with him the characteristics that will shape his time in office. His genetic inheritance, family background, intelligence, education, and life experiences will determine his view of America and the methods he uses to promote this view.

A CHILD PRODIGY

IN THIS REGARD, KENNEDY WAS UNIQUE in our history. His early life was a perfect training ground for the presidency. He was, in fact, a child prodigy. As a boy, he spent countless hours reading about history, government, and world affairs, acquiring an adult's understanding of the very issues a good president should master. At boarding school, he read the *New York Times* every day. Then he would lie in bed and think about what he had just learned. A Kennedy family friend who visited him in the hospital said, [I found him] "so surrounded by books I could hardly see him. I was very impressed, because at that point this very young child was reading *The World Crisis* by Winston Churchill."

Kennedy was also no stranger to the brutal side of life. He endured the deaths of loved ones, the horror of war, and unrelenting physical illness and pain. He was rushed to a hospital, clinic, or infirmary, sometimes in a desperate attempt to save his life, 43 times in his 46 years. He received the last rites three times. He lived with the expectation that his life would be short.

Thus, by the time he reached the White House in 1960, Kennedy had lived through more intense, formative experiences than most people encounter in a lifetime. They endowed him with a sophisticated knowledge of government and a sense of empathy for the suffering of others. As president, he merged these attributes into a single, uplifting force that was unlike anything this country had ever seen. His goal was to use government to make our lives worth living during the short time we spend on earth.

STUDY AND TRAVEL

HISTORIANS TEND TO OVERLOOK the importance of the experiences that shaped John Kennedy. They are, however, the key to understanding what he accomplished as president. He studied government and political theory at Harvard, where he encountered the works of the great political and social philosophers, such as Aristotle, Thomas Hobbes, John Locke, and Jean Jacques Rousseau. One of his professors, Payson S. Wild, observed that he "had the ability to think deeply and in theoretical terms."

Then, to supplement his study, between 1937 and the outbreak of war in Europe in 1939, he traveled to nearly every continent on the globe, visiting France, England, Germany, Belgium, Italy, the Netherlands, Scotland, Austria, Russia, Hungary, Czechoslovakia, Poland, the Baltic Republics, Turkey, Egypt, Palestine, and eight countries in Central and South America.

As he traveled, he probed the minds of both those in high office and ordinary citizens, anxious to learn about the politics and economies of each country. It was during this study and travel that he began to develop the principles of government that he would bring to the presidency.

He came to believe, for example, that effective political leadership was a matter of intellectual and political courage. He felt that leaders in prewar Europe had lacked the courage to tell their people the truth about Adolf Hitler's intention to start another war in Europe.

Because their leaders had withheld this vital information, Kennedy reasoned, the citizens of England and France had been unable to comprehend the urgent need to prepare for war. They changed their views slowly, trapped by what Kennedy called "the inertia of human thought."

Based on what he had observed, Kennedy concluded that "for a free society to survive, to successfully compete, the leaders have to tell the truth." He believed that it was the duty of world leaders to urge people to confront reality.

Later, during his time in the House and Senate, Kennedy became contemptuous of political leaders who made decisions based on "doctrinaire beliefs" and ignored their obligation to promote the common good. In his view, political leaders must objectively diagnose problems and offer solutions based on facts, not on a predetermined set of beliefs or an overarching ideology.

Thus, Kennedy based his presidency on three basic principles, the product of his relentless study and travel:

1. It is the president's responsibility to identify threats to the nation's welfare.
2. It is the president's responsibility to inform the people about these threats truthfully, so they are prepared to react to them effectively.
3. It is the president's responsibility to provide the people with facts, not biased information clouded by "predetermined beliefs."

The purpose of this approach was to prevent the people from becoming uninformed and complacent. To reach this goal, Kennedy deliberately governed as if the nation faced a never-ending series of threats, and he deliberately involved the people in the process of dealing with these threats. In less than three years in office, he held more than 60 press conferences. Today, the media often recounts the humor he displayed during these televised meetings. More important, however, is that he used them to treat the people as if they were an essential component of government, elevating them to the status of concerned and involved citizens. He gave them the capacity to understand and embrace the need for action and change.

He also did something that few presidents have even attempted: He used the presidency to bring out the best aspects of human nature. He once described his vision of America as follows:

> If we can make our country one of the great schools of civilization, then on that achievement will surely rest our claim to the ultimate gratitude of mankind...I am certain that after the dust of centuries has passed over our cities, we will be remembered not for victories or defeats in battle or in politics but for our contributions to the human spirit.

To elevate the human spirit, Kennedy cultivated the interior aspects of our lives, the qualities that make us better people, and thus better citizens. He challenged young people to join the Peace Corps, to begin their lives by leaving the comfort of their homes and traveling abroad to help the impoverished people of other nations.

With this approach, Kennedy tapped into something science has long known: human beings thrive when they are inspired and encouraged. Inspiration contains the kindness we all crave. It can lift people out of apathy and allow them to contribute to society.

Unlike any president who followed him in office, Kennedy had the capacity and the will to build a responsive government. During his time in office, there was a bond between government and the people; in fact, government actually nurtured them on a personal level. This is the real meaning of "Camelot," the term often used to describe the Kennedy years.

GOVERNMENT BECOMES A SCAPEGOAT

KENNEDY'S DEATH DEPRIVED THE NATION of this nurturing. Our presidents no longer speak about making America one of the great schools of civilization, nor do they seek to make us better citizens. A president who spoke in such terms today would draw blank stares from the people and ridicule from his opponents.

In the years after Dallas, the nation was led by presidents who had little comprehension of the principles that Kennedy brought to the White House. Both Lyndon Johnson and Richard Nixon lied to the people. Johnson lied to escalate the war in Vietnam. Nixon, among other things, lied about the Watergate burglary in a desperate attempt to hang on to his presidency.

They embedded in the nation's consciousness the demoralizing notion that presidents will do anything to get what they want or to protect themselves. And they trampled upon Kennedy's dictum that for this nation to flourish, our leaders must tell the truth.

Damaged and disillusioned, America suffered through years of bitterness, a needless war, and the social conflict it caused. The people became cynical and uncertain about the honesty and objectives of their leaders. Without Kennedy to inspire them, they eventually succumbed to the complacency, "the inertia of human thought," that he had tried to prevent.

Into this vacuum in 1981 stepped a man who tragically reversed Kennedy's view of government. In the mind of Ronald Reagan, government was not a noble, time-tested system in which men like Jefferson and John Adams addressed the needs of the people with reason and intellect.

Instead, he told the nation that government, because it collects taxes, spends money on the poor, regulates business, and is too large, is the enemy of the people and should be feared and distrusted. "The best minds are not in government," he declared. "If any were, business would hire them away."

The United States, Reagan believed, should be guided by special interests and the wealthy, because they possess the capacity to generate massive amounts of wealth. Brimming with contempt, Reagan said, "Government is not the solution to the problem; government *is* the problem." This, as historian Thom Hartman has pointed out, is like saying that

"America is not the solution to the problem; America *is* the problem."

Reagan's bizarre, self-destructive philosophy would have enraged Kennedy, who felt that presidents should strengthen, not destroy or mock, the principles that tie the people and government together.

Kennedy acknowledged the wastefulness of big government, but rather than making it the enemy, he urged the people to work with him to make it more effective and responsive to their needs.

As we will see, Reagan's willingness to make government a scapegoat in order to promote a flawed ideology has been disastrous for the United States. The growth of special interests, entities greatly feared by the Founding Fathers, has become the driving force in America, while John Kennedy's idealistic view of government has been shoved to the side.

Here is just one example of the damage caused by government-by-ideology. Just hours after Obama took the oath of office in 2009, a group of 15 House Republicans met for a secret dinner in a restaurant in Washington, D.C.

Their purpose was not to explore ways to to work with Obama. Most political scientists believe that, for the good of the nation, competing political parties must compromise on the issues that divide them. Liberals and conservatives can resolve their differences and move forward only if each side is willing to make concessions in the name of progress.

But over the next four hours, the 15 men instead devised ways to obstruct every move Obama made. No matter what he proposed, no matter how important the issue he raised, they agreed to oppose everything he said or did. If he said black, they would say white.

The objective of the Republicans was to defeat Obama in the next election by creating a firestorm of controversy in the media over every issue he addressed. A Democrat, Obama was a threat to conservative ideology, particularly that part of its belief system that says the private sector, not government, should be the dominant force in America. Above all else, their philosophy had to be preserved; they would not give an inch to a president who likely would favor liberal attitudes and policies.

When news of the meeting became public, three years after it occurred, there was mock outrage in the media, but little effort was made to condemn the Republicans for purposely creating political gridlock in a country of 315 million people. Something that under Kennedy would have been called treason is today an accepted part of the political process.

This is not the type of government Kennedy wanted for this country. In 1962, he warned the nation about the danger of allowing ideologues like Reagan to take control of government. He particularly feared the damage their rigid policies would inflict upon the economy. He said the nation's economic policy should never be determined by

> some grand warfare of rival ideologies which will sweep the country with passion... but with the practical management of a modern economy. What we need are not labels and clichés but more basic discussion of the sophisticated and technical questions involved in keeping a great economic machinery moving ahead.

We have yet to confront the long-term consequences of losing John Kennedy. The harm inflicted on the nation by some of the men who came after him has gone largely unaddressed. Without much opposition, his successors have transformed the United States into a nation controlled by the wealthy, a plutocracy in which corporations are considered the equal of human beings. In the process, the political system bequeathed to us by the Founding Fathers has become secondary and dysfunctional.

The purpose of this book is to discover how John Kennedy gained the wisdom to make America an enlightened nation. This knowledge, perhaps, will help give the people the courage to demand that we return to the type of responsible government the Founders established and Kennedy brought to life.

We begin with the events and experiences that made John Kennedy the man, and the president, that he was.

CHAPTER TWO

TRAGEDY AND MAGIC IN HIS SOUL

Though I may not be able to remember material things such as tickets, gloves and so on... I can remember things like Ivanhoe.
—John Kennedy

THE YEAR 1917 HAD ITS SHARE OF IMPORTANT EVENTS. Tsar Nicholas II of Russia was forced to abdicate and the Russian Revolution began. Albert Einstein published his first paper on cosmology. In October, Congress declared war on Germany and more than 100,000 young men were sent to their deaths.

And on May 29 of that year, John Fitzgerald Kennedy was born in Brookline, Massachusetts, the second son of Joseph Patrick Kennedy and Rose Elizabeth Fitzgerald.

From the start, there was tragedy and magic in his soul. As a baby, he was sick so often that his mother worried that something might be terribly wrong with her son. When he was two, he came down with measles and then whooping cough and chicken pox, but he did not shrug off these diseases as most children do; instead, they left him weak and racked by constant fever. At two years and nine months, he almost died from scarlet fever, spending two months in a hospital and another two weeks convalescing in a sanatorium. A doctor who treated him warned his parents that Jack could succumb to the strain of the disease.

But Jack was a fighter and he survived. Even so, over the next ten years it became apparent that he had no resiliency; an ear infection or fever would keep him in bed for weeks, and he remained thin and fragile, never able to stay healthy long enough to put on weight. Every so often, his body would completely break down, draining his reserves of strength and bringing him perilously close to death. Despite his family's wealth, they could do nothing to lessen his suffering.

While he did not have good health, Jack possessed other gifts. Adults remarked that he seemed more evolved than other boys his age. The nurse who took care of him as he recovered from scarlet fever was so captivated by his endearing ways that she successfully begged to care for him when he was sent home.

Jack was devoid of self-pity and never whined or complained. He refused to use his illness to extract special treatment from adults, which was part of his appeal, as was his natural, self-deprecating wit.

As he grew older, Jack became a voracious reader. He had a little boy's need for heroes, and he devoured books about the Founding Fathers and presidents and famous leaders. He read *The Knights of the Round Table* over and over, constructing in his mind a world in which he was not a sickly child but rather a man of strength and honor who lived in a time of service to others.

At boarding school, he read *Ivanhoe* by Sir Walter Scott, a tale of allegiance and chivalry. In a letter to his mother he said, "though I may not be able to remember material things such as tickets, gloves and so on I can remember things like Ivanhoe." His attachment to chivalry stayed with him for the rest of his life, through his travels and the war and political battles and during his short time in the White House.

Jack's parents encouraged his love of learning and idealism. In the Kennedy household, each child was encouraged to read about history and current events, then challenged to use what they learned to form opinions about important issues.

Years later, Jack's brother Robert would say, "I can't remember a dinner when the conversation was not dominated by what Franklin Roosevelt was doing or what was happening around the world."

To foster this atmosphere, Jack's mother hung a bulletin board in the kitchen and pinned to it newspaper and magazine articles. The children were expected to discuss the articles at the dinner table. Joe Kennedy wanted his children to be informed, useful citizens. He told them, "To those to whom much is given, much is expected."

Joe Kennedy did not expect his children to endorse his political views; rather, he encouraged them to form their own opinions. During the dinnertime discussion of politics, according to a family friend, Joe "would encourage [his children] to disagree with him, and of course, they did! Mr. Kennedy is, I'd say, far right of his children, yet he certainly didn't try to influence them that way."

The Great Depression of 1929 had little impact on the Kennedy family. Joe, who eventually amassed a fortune estimated at between $200 and $400 million, anticipated the stock market collapse, and positioned himself to make money while others watched their fortunes evaporate.

When Jack was 12, his father moved the family into a mansion on six acres of land in Bronxville, New York. Jack's life was one of comfort and privilege; he would later recall arriving at school in a chauffeur-driven Rolls Royce and spending summers at the vacation estate his father had purchased in Hyannis Port on Cape Cod.

Of the Depression, he said:

> My family had one of the great fortunes of the world and it was worth more than ever then. We had bigger houses, more servants, we traveled more. About the only thing I saw directly was when my father hired some extra gardeners just to give them a job so they could eat.

UNREMITTING ILLNESS

IT WAS EXPECTED THAT JACK WOULD OUTGROW his illnesses as he matured, but the opposite occurred. As he entered adolescence, he was plagued by a series of mysterious and frightening physical breakdowns. In 1930, when he was 13, Jack was sent to the Canterbury School in New Milford, Connecticut, a Catholic academy, to begin the ninth grade. He hated being cut off from his family and friends at the austere school. "You have a whole lot of religion and the studies are pretty hard," he told a friend. "This place is freezing at night and pretty cold in the daytime."

Shortly after the first term began, while attending a chapel service, Jack became dizzy and disoriented and stumbled from the room. He lost consciousness and fell, but was caught by the headmaster just before he hit the ground. No cause for this alarming incident could be found.

A few months later, he again collapsed, this time with acute abdominal pains, which proved to be appendicitis. He endured an operation and a painful recovery.

Jack begged his father not to send him back to the grim atmosphere at Canterbury. He much preferred Choate, a private boarding school in Wallingford, Connecticut, where he would be with his older brother, Joe Jr. He got his wish, but his health continued to plague him. At Choate, he suffered from colds that became serious enough to require hospitalization. He was still unable to put on weight. At age 15 he weighed just 117 pounds. He was always tired, his blood pressure was low, his glands were often swollen, and he had constant pain throughout his body, particularly in his knees.

Joe Kennedy sent his son to the best doctors at the best hospitals in the country, but extensive tests found nothing. One doctor said he did not drink enough milk, and another, at the Mayo Clinic, said he had leukemia. Doctor after doctor solemnly told his parents that no cause could be found for his illnesses, and that he could die young. His brothers and sisters joked that if a mosquito bit Jack, the insect would die.

Jack dealt with his illnesses by pretending they did not exist. He used his humor to deflect questions about his frequent absences from school. Jack told his friends he had come home from the hospital with an unusually large rectum, because it had been probed by "everything from rubber tubes to iron pipes."

Behind the humor, however, Jack was acutely insecure about his appearance. He was not proud of his thin, at times emaciated, body, which he felt made him look weak and effeminate. He tried to cover the hives and blotches that sometimes marked his skin by always having a tan. The glow of a tan, he said, "gives me confidence; it makes me feel strong, healthy, attractive." To bulk up, he lifted weights and threw himself into sports, but then he would become sick again, sometimes for months at a time, and his pale, skeletal look would return.

In time, Jack would become a scholar, perhaps the most widely-read political leader in U.S. history. As a boy, however, he earned Bs in subjects he liked, such as English, math, and history, and Cs in Latin and science, subjects that bored him.

He was also habitually late, careless, and sloppy. He made targets of teachers and headmasters who he felt were austere or excessively strict. When he convinced a group of boys to blow-up a toilet, he was almost expelled. Biographers would later argue that Jack's rebellious nature was a reaction to his mother's strict, unemotional parenting.

At Choate, while he ignored subjects that did not hold his interest, he still read voraciously, particularly about current events. When he became ill, he took with him to his sickbed newspapers and books to feed his curiosity.

Jack's endearing qualities did not desert him as he matured. He was widely admired at Choate, where a teacher described him as "an exuberant, joyous, intelligent boy who everyone wanted to be around."

When he became seriously ill, the headmaster, despite his frustration with Jack's sloppiness and acts of defiance, could not contain his sorrow. He wrote to his father that, "Jack is one of the best people who ever lived. . . one of the most able and interesting. I could go on about Jack! To see how sorry everyone is when Jack is ill proves the kind of fellow he is."

Jack spent six years at boarding schools, a rebellious student with an adult's sense of humor and intellectual ability.

Despite his youth, Jack understood his family's strengths and weaknesses. He had three brothers and five sisters. Joe Jr. was born first, followed by Jack, Rosemary, Kathleen, Eunice, Patricia, Robert, Jean, and Edward. As a boy he had been eternally at war with Joe, who was brawny and vigorous, his father's favorite.

Joe was the Kennedy who was destined to accomplish great things. Jack was the Kennedy, because he was so sickly and undisciplined, who was expected to do little with his life.

Aware of this perception, Jack assumed the role of the detached intellectual, a boy who displayed both an impressive command of history and political issues and a sharp wit that expressed his rebellious nature. Jack, said biographer Nigel Hamilton, "was the family joker: witty, irresponsible, irreverent, careless, and tardy, refusing to conform like the other children to Rose's pathetic preoccupation with manners."

When he was 17, Hamilton discovered, Jack submitted to a psychological evaluation by Dr. Prescott Lecky, a psychologist at Columbia University. Lecky concluded that Jack had an exceptional mind, but clung to his reputation as a sloppy, thoughtless boy as a defense mechanism, a way of defining himself in comparison with his brother.

Dr. Lecky pointed this out to Jack, asking, "How are you going to amount to anything if you have to be thoughtless and sloppy to be true to your role?" Jack took the question seriously, saying, "My brother is the efficient one in the family, and I am the boy that doesn't get things done. If my brother were not so efficient, it would be easier for me to be efficient."

After graduating 65th in a class of 110 at Choate, Jack was accepted at Harvard in 1935. His father had graduated from Harvard in 1912, and his older brother, Joe Jr., was in his second year at the school. So his family name, more than his grades, paved the way for Jack.

For two years at Harvard, Jack continued the pattern he had established at Choate, spending his time pursuing social activities and ignoring his studies. "His focus," said Robert Dallek, in *An Unfinished Life:*

> remained on the extracurricular and social activities he found more enjoyable (than study), and stamped him as one of the many students at Harvard more interested in earning the social standing that attendance and graduation provided than in the book learning needed to advance a career.

Despite his frail body, Jack became powerfully attractive to women. His endearing qualities, his humor and his self-deprecating wit, made him nearly irresistible. Sex became an obsession, as it is for many teenage boys; for Jack, however, it was also a way to prove his virility, to ward off his feelings of inferiority. For a time, he also became a bit of an elitist, fully aware and proud of his family's wealth and his elevated social standing. He was not immune from the arrogance that comes with wealth.

But slowly, using the insight he displayed during his talk with Dr. Lecky, Jack began to mature, to demand more of himself than his role as the irreverent but gifted rebel. He began to take seriously his father's admonition that, "to those to whom much is given, much is expected."

Jack Kennedy was a gifted, rebellious young man. Now he would begin to develop the insights into government and world affairs that he would bring to the presidency.

CHAPTER THREE

THINKING OUT THE PROBLEMS OF THE WORLD

The trip to Europe schooled him in the satisfaction of forming independent judgments rather than giving in to easier clichés.
— Robert Dallek

HOW DIFFERENT OUR HISTORY MIGHT HAVE BEEN if Joe Kennedy had been worth $4,000 rather than $400 million. As his wealth grew, Joe started trust funds for each of his nine children to assure their financial independence for the rest of their lives. When the funds matured, Joe said, his children would have enough money, "to spit in my eye."

Jack Kennedy would never have to punch a time clock or worry about paying the rent. Instead, as Joe wanted, he was free to pursue the aspects of life that gave him the most satisfaction. He did not squander this priceless opportunity, but instead chose a life of travel and intellectual inquiry that would forever set him apart from so many other sons of wealthy men.

During his last two years at Harvard, Jack displayed what Lem Billings, his best friend, described as "a desire to think out the problems of the world." Why, Jack wondered, were countries in Europe turning toward fascism? What were the benefits and drawbacks of this form of government? Why did a man in Germany named Adolf Hitler have such a hold on the citizens of that country? What effects would these events have on the United States in the years to come?

THE SOPHISTICATION TRAVEL PROVIDES

TO FIND THE ANSWERS HE SOUGHT, Jack studied and traveled. With his father footing the bill, from 1935 to 1945, he made three trips abroad, eventually traveling to nearly every continent on the globe. He learned that history is not a series of static dates and events to be memorized and filed away. It is, rather, a series of events that can be used to foretell the future.

His first trip overseas at age 18 was brief. Joe had made millions by exploiting the lack of regulation in the stock market, mastering a scheme that years later would be known as "pump and dump." This was the practice of buying a low-priced stock, colluding with other traders to drive up the price, and then selling before the real value of the stock became known and the price plummeted.

During the 1920s, fueled by visions of great wealth in the galloping stock market, banks, investment firms, and small investors began to buy stocks on margin, meaning they would put up a portion of the cost and pay the rest later, a very risky practice. When the market crashed in 1929, those investors went broke and the Great Depression began.

Reportedly, one morning in 1929, Joe stopped for a shoeshine and was given a stock tip by the boy who shined his shoes. He went immediately to his office and sold every share of stock he owned, explaining that when shoeshine boys give stock tips, it is time to get out of the market. Two days later the market crashed. Joe not only survived the crash, he made money buying greatly depressed stocks that would someday rebound.

Joseph Kennedy's wealth and his rapidly growing family made him a public figure, featured in newsreels and magazine articles. He spoke forcefully on political issues, acquiring a reputation as a pundit. When Franklin Roosevelt ran for president in 1932, Joe publicly supported his candidacy. Two years later, Roosevelt made him the first head of the Securities and Exchange Commission, with a mandate to find ways to outlaw the very practices he had used to make millions. When asked why he had appointed a crook to reform the financial markets,

Roosevelt replied that, "It takes one to catch one."

Kennedy did an admirable job. His signature achievement was instituting a rule that required companies to file detailed financial statements with the SEC, making it difficult for them to hide shady dealings.

By 1935, however, disappointed that Roosevelt had not offered him a more prestigious post, Kennedy resigned and went to London, taking Jack with him. Jack was sent to study at the London School of Economics, but he contracted hepatitis and was sent home after just one week.

THE GRAND TOUR WITH LEM

JACK'S TRAVELS ABROAD began in earnest in September, 1937. He traveled with Lem Billings. They spent ten weeks touring France, England, Italy, Germany, and Holland, traveling much of the time in Jack's Ford Cabriolet convertible, which they brought with them on the ship that took them to the French port of Le Havre.

Lem's father was a physician. But the family had little money, so the two friends stayed at the cheapest hotels and pinched pennies, haggling endlessly with clerks and attendants over prices.

Jack was 20 and had just completed his freshman year at Harvard, which he had devoted to seducing women and high times with his friends. When an exam approached, he told Lem, "I'll have to crack the book and see what the fucking course is about."

He ended up hiring tutors to help him learn what he had been too busy socializing to absorb.

Jack met Lem at Choate when he was 14, and the two hit it off immediately. As their friendship progressed, Lem confessed that he was homosexual and wanted a sexual relationship with Jack.

This was in 1934, when homosexuality, as described by David Pitts in his book, *Lem and Jack,* was considered "as almost subhuman, certainly sinful and degenerate. A gigantic taboo."

Lem expressed his desire in a note written on toilet paper, a common practice among homosexuals at boarding schools. Pitts explained that notes on toilet paper "could easily be swallowed or discarded to eliminate any paper trail."

From a hospital, Jack replied, "Please don't write to me on toilet paper anymore. I'm not that kind of boy." Then he changed the subject and the two continued their friendship.

"That John Kennedy maintained a deep friendship with a man whom he knew to be gay and did so in an age of homophobia," David Pitts wrote, "was an extraordinary demonstration of loyalty and commitment."

In France, Jack and Lem traveled to the required cathedrals, museums, and World War I monuments. While he found sightseeing a valuable experience, it was the French people, particularly their views on important topics, that truly piqued Jack's interest. "While we were in France," Lem recalled, "Jack spent a great deal of time talking to the French as to how they felt about Germany, and whether there was going to be a war; and if so, could Germany invade France again."

The answer he most often received was that Germany would not dare move on France. The nation had built a concrete wall along its border with Germany called the Maginot Line. It was defended by heavy artillery and thousands of troops living in underground bunkers. Trams moving along railroad tracks could quickly bring them to any area of the border the Germans attempted to breach. The heavily fortified Maginot Line made a German invasion unlikely.

In his diary, Jack noted that, "the general impression... seems to be that there will not be a war in the near future and that France is much too well prepared for Germany."

A few years later, however, the Nazis stormed through a weak section of the wall in Belgium and raced through France, bringing the country to its knees in just six weeks. Jack Kennedy had personally observed the public complacency that led to the collapse of that great nation, learning in the process an important lesson about the tendency of the public to overlook and deny impending danger.

After France, Jack badly wanted to cross the border into Spain, where a year earlier a military revolt led by future dictator General Francisco Franco had sparked a civil war. In 1931, leaders in Spain established a republican government and enacted a series of reforms to make the government more responsive to the people. Conservatives like Franco feared this change, viewing the measures as a prelude to social revolution.

With aid pouring in from fascist governments in Germany and Italy, Franco started a bloody civil war against the republican government, using brutality and mass slaughter to impose his will on the nation.

Alarmed that word of his atrocities would be observed and reported, Franco kept tourists out of Spain during the civil war. Jack, however, had other ideas, and before leaving the states, he asked his father to find a way to get him into Spain, as a correspondent or a member of the Red Cross. Joe, fearing for his son's safety, did nothing.

Jack and Lem instead went to the Spanish border to interview citizens streaming into France. Jack "spent a great deal of time talking to the refugees, making notes and writing a great deal," Lem recalled.

Billings said the refugees that Jack interviewed:

> were probably the upper class refugees of the Franco group, so we heard some pretty blood-curdling tales of what the non-Franco's were doing in Spain. At the time, we were very much shocked, but I suppose this was because they were the only refugees we met. There were no refugees from the other side at all.

The two young men accepted the refugee's biased view of the situation in Spain and naively concluded that Franco was a strong leader capable of stabilizing Spain's fractured political and social systems.

Jack brought a trunk load of books with him on the trip. One of them, *Inside Europe*, by John Gunther, was his favorite and he carried it with him everywhere he went. After reading Gunther's harshly critical account of Franco, Jack changed his mind and championed the republican cause. He quickly realized that he had formed an opinion of the situation in Spain without first gathering all relevant facts.

"Not quite as positive now about Franco victory," he wrote in his diary. "Shows that you can be easily influenced by people around you if you know nothing and how easy it is for you to believe what you want to believe."

Moving on to Italy, Jack and Lem went to hear Mussolini speak at a rally in Rome. His pomposity made Jack squirm. As he had in France, he quizzed those he met on their political views and pondered the various scenarios that could arise during the upheavals sweeping across Central Europe. Then, the two friends crossed into prewar Germany, which they found clean and efficient, but utterly lacking in the civility they had discovered in France and Italy.

There was a side to the German people that both Jack and Lem found obnoxious. Billings said, "They were repulsive; they thought they were superior to everyone, so anti-everything and so snotty. We had just awful experiences there." The two often picked up hitchhikers, including Nazi soldiers, whom they pestered with questions about Hitler and his growing National Socialist movement.

Jack and Lem were annoyed when German citizens expected them to return their "Heil Hitler!" salutes and waved back at them, adding sarcastically, "Hi ya, Hitler!"

What Jack quickly came to despise was the enforced military regimentation and conformity that he witnessed in Germany. He realized that Hitler had skillfully used propaganda to gain his hold over Germany, recording in his diary that "Hitler seems to be as popular here as Mussolini in Italy, although propaganda is probably his most powerful weapon."

Years later, Ted Sorensen, President Kennedy's special counsel and speech writer, would observe that as he traveled, Kennedy had constantly compared the governments of other nations with the government of the United States. "He greatly preferred," Sorensen said, "our own" style of government.

THE DANGER OF DOCTRINAIRE BELIEFS

JACK HAD DEVELOPED a profound contempt for people who form unshakable beliefs without first gathering facts to support their point of view. At Harvard, the campus was alive with protests against the growing menace of fascism and communism overseas, but Jack stayed removed from them. He believed the protesters, whether right or wrong, lacked intellectual integrity and were driven by doctrinaire beliefs rather than facts.

In a letter to Lem, he ridiculed the students "who espouse their certitude" on developments in Europe from thousands of miles away, without, he felt, complete, on-the-spot knowledge of salient facts.

The importance of Jack's first trip to Europe, said Robert Dallek, was that it "schooled him in the satisfaction of forming independent judgments rather than giving in to easier cliché."

In 1939, Jack returned to Europe, this time without Lem. Again, he lugged around a trunk filled with books on political philosophy. On this trip, however, he was far from an ordinary tourist, as his father was now Roosevelt's Ambassador to Great Britain. Jack now had access to prominent journalists, diplomats, military leaders, and decision makers, who answered his questions about the momentous events sweeping across Europe on the eve of war.

In Great Britain, Jack observed that, as Hitler became more aggressive, the British government and the British people chose to retreat into denial. Few young men rushed to join the military; instead they waited to be drafted. British citizens believed the Royal Air Force should bomb Germany into submission, and get it over with. But government leaders demurred, saying that factories in Germany were private property, and that such an extreme act would cause the Germans to retaliate. Bombers instead dropped leaflets on German cities that called for peace between the two nations.

Ambassador Kennedy desperately wanted both Great Britain and America to avoid a second war with Germany. He believed Hitler's iron-willed ground troops and powerful air force would eventually defeat both Great Britain and the United States. It was a war we could not win, and one likely to claim the lives of his two eldest sons. He believed opposing Hitler would be suicidal, leading to, in his words, "the end of democracy."

Although warned by the State Department to keep his personal views to himself, Joe publicly endorsed the appeasement policies of Prime Minister Neville Chamberlain. In September 1938, amid great drama, Chamberlain flew to Munich and signed an agreement giving Hitler free rein in the Sudetenland region of Czechoslovakia. In exchange, Hitler pledged to back away from war.

Chamberlain arrived home to a hero's welcome, waiving the "Munich Pact" agreement in the air and declaring that he had secured "peace for our time." He was desperate to prevent another war just two decades after the obscene loss of life and suffering that occurred during World War I. "When I think of the seven million men cut down in their prime," Chamberlain said, "and the thirteen million maimed and mutilated, I realize that in war there are no winners, only losers."

What Chamberlain and many other British political leaders could not see, their judgment clouded by their terror of another war, was that Hitler was insane. His objective was not merely the acquisition of small territories in Czechoslovakia or the domination of Europe; he wanted to spill blood on a massive scale, for hate to prevail over good.

Some, such as Winston Churchill, First Lord of the Admiralty before the war began, had a more realistic understanding of Hitler's menace and exhorted the government to prepare for war. But these astute politicians were called alarmists and their warnings were ignored.

The flash point for the war Hitler longed to start was Poland. He insisted the Poles give up territory in the region of Danzig, on the Baltic coast, knowing that the Polish government would refuse his demands, leading to invasion and war.

As this process was playing out, 22-year-old Jack visited Danzig, where he managed to speak with both Nazi and Polish officials about the widening conflict between the two nations. He spent four weeks in Warsaw, watching events unfold and predicting accurately in a letter to his father that:

> Poland is determined not to give up Danzig... What Germany will do if she decides to go to war will be to try to put Poland in the position of being the aggressor, and then go to work. Poland has an army of 4,000,000 who are damn good but poorly equipped. The Poles are not Czechs and they will fight, but they will be alone.

During his seven-month-excursion, Jack visited Germany and the Soviet Union, making stops in Munich, Berlin, Hamburg, Moscow, Leningrad, Kiev, and the Crimea. He then went to Lithuania, Hungary, Latvia, Estonia, Romania, Turkey, Egypt, and Palestine. He left Germany for London the day before German troops marched into Poland, arriving in time to sit in the House of Commons in London just as Prime Minister Chamberlain finally declared war on Germany.

Both Chamberlain and Ambassador Kennedy were to pay a price for their support of appeasement. Before hostilities began, Joe Kennedy twice had tried to arrange a personal meeting with Hitler, without prior approval from Roosevelt. He also opposed Roosevelt's efforts to provide aid to Great Britain.

As the Nazi's began bombing London night after night, Kennedy told reporters that "democracy is finished in England." The day before German troops marched into Poland, Kennedy advised Chamberlain to offer even more concessions to Hitler. Chamberlain responded, "I have done everything I can think of, Joe, but it looks as if all my work has been of no avail."

The press in London attacked Ambassador Kennedy as an appeaser and isolationist. The criticism became almost savage after he retreated with his family to the countryside to avoid the London blitz. A member of Parliament said the ambassador was "a rich man, untrained in diplomacy, unlearned in history and politics, who is a great publicity seeker and who apparently is ambitious to be the first Catholic president of the U.S."

Neville Chamberlain resigned in May 1940, succeeded by Churchill, and died of cancer six months later. Joseph Kennedy resigned and returned home the same year, his long-held wish to one day run for president now in ruins.

As the war began, Jack returned to Harvard to write his senior thesis, a study of why the British had been so slow to confront Hitler. The original thesis was hardly a masterpiece. Written in three months, its 180 pages contained many spelling and grammatical mistakes; Jack had not yet become a polished writer. With professional editing, however, it was turned into a book, *Why England Slept,* which became a best-seller at a time when America was facing its own decision about whether or not to go to war with Germany.

After observing the failure of European leaders to confront fascism and national socialism, Kennedy concluded that true courage was found in a political leader's willingness to fight against the factors that make people complacent about important issues, particularly national security.

Why England Slept asserted that the British people, like the complacent French citizens Kennedy had spoken with during his first European trip in 1937, had failed to confront reality. "The great trouble was that few could think of England except as the Mighty Britain of the nineteenth century," Kennedy wrote. "Because of the inertia of human thought, nations, like individuals, change their ideas slowly."

The inertia of human thought, this tendency of people to resist change, alarmed Kennedy. In his view, a courageous political leader would force the issue, using fear if necessary to make the people confront their intellectual lethargy. The subjects of his later book, *Profiles in Courage,* were politicians who ignored harsh criticism and even the possible end of their careers in an effort to tell the truth as they saw it.

In a 1932 speech before Parliament, former Prime Minister Stanley Baldwin had said:

> I think it well also for the man in the street to realise that there is no power on earth that can protect him from being bombed. Whatever people tell him, the bomber will always get through.

This acceptance of defeat, in Jack's view, created a general feeling of hopelessness among the British people. Why make the sacrifices necessary to prepare for war if defeat is thought to be inevitable? A courageous leader, Jack believed, would not have been afraid to urge the people to confront serious issues head on.

"For a free society to survive, to successfully compete," he wrote, "the leaders have to tell the truth." If he had been in Baldwin's or Chamberlain's shoes, Kennedy would have pushed, even terrified, the complacent British people into preparing for Hitler's onslaught.

By the time he left Harvard in 1940, Kennedy had already concluded that a president must never lie to the people, that he must educate them about important events, and create a national feeling of hope rather than hopelessness.

Having gained a priceless education in world affairs, Jack Kennedy returned to the States and graduated cum laude from Harvard in 1940. What he had learned during these years would later form the heart of his presidency. But first, he would have to endure a period of physical and psychological torment that would have broken a lesser man.

CHAPTER FOUR

THE WARRIOR NO ONE WANTED

Those of you who want to come back after the war and raise families need not apply: PT boat skippers are not coming back.
— Commander John D. Bulkeley

ON SUNDAY, DECEMBER 7, 1941, as he drove home after playing touch football on the lawn in front of the Washington Monument, Jack Kennedy switched on the radio and heard about the Japanese sneak attack on Pearl Harbor.

A few days later, Adolf Hitler declared war on the United States, calling it a weak nation inhabited by an inferior race of people who would be too cowardly to fight.

Kennedy, now 24, badly wanted to join the military, partly to serve his country, partly to test his courage, and partly to keep pace with big brother Joe Jr., who had dropped out of Harvard Law School to become a Navy pilot.

Jack's poor health, however, would make service in the military difficult if not impossible. A Harvard friend, who mistakenly believed Jack had been drafted, wrote him a letter saying, "The only humorous thing in my life to date has been you getting drafted. I swear to God,

Jack, I thought I would die of exhaustion from laughing. Christ, of all the guys in the world..."

To everyone's surprise, Jack presented himself for examination by doctors in the army and navy, hoping to find his way into OCS (Officer's Candidate School). But after getting a look at his medical history, the doctors, surprised that he was still among the living, sent him home. If he had managed somehow to pass the physicals, it would have been wise for him to be stationed at a hospital, close to the emergency room.

THE ONLY HAPPINESS THAT LASTS

JACK DID NOT HAVE TO LOOK FAR for a solution to his problem. His father had powerful friends and he did not hesitate to ask them for favors, particularly involving his children. One of his friends was a high-ranking naval officer stationed in Washington, D.C. Joe prevailed upon him to have navy doctors overlook Jack's fragile health and certify him fit for duty.

It was surprising that Joe Kennedy was willing to fight to get his son into, not out of, the military. In 1917, when the United States entered World War I, Kennedy was known in Massachusetts as the youngest bank president in the country and as the Harvard man who had married Rose Fitzgerald, the daughter of the mayor of Boston.

Joe was different from the men who rushed to induction stations when the war began. He did not view war as a proving ground or a great crusade into manhood, and he scoffed at the use of patriotic sentiments to appeal to a young man's sense of duty and masculinity. He had been appalled, not proud and impressed, when his friends and peers left their families and careers and marched off to the killing grounds of Europe. He successfully avoided induction and rejected pleas from his family and friends to enlist.

In another time, Joe Kennedy may have been admired as the rare man who could rise above the lure of patriotism and see the carnage and futility of this "war to end all wars." Rose once said that after a sharp argument with friends about military service, her husband looked down at his first-born son, Joe Jr., asleep in his bed, and remarked, "This is the only happiness that lasts."

Joe Kennedy was not a committed pacifist; he simply did not understand why he should risk death or injury when he had a wife and two children to support and a fortune to amass. His goal was to elevate himself and his children above the prejudice that made the Irish in Boston second-class citizens. The only way he knew to reach this goal was to make money, a lot of money, and to someday see his eldest son elected president.

His opinion of war had not changed a quarter century later when Jack asked for his help. However, if Jack served honorably and survived the fighting, his service would soften the stigma of Joe's so-called cowardice. It would also allow Jack, if he ever decided to enter politics, to have a war record to wave before voters.

In September 1941, Jack was commissioned as an ensign in the U.S. Naval Reserve. A few weeks later, he was assigned to the Foreign Intelligence Branch of the Division of Naval Intelligence in Washington, D.C. His job was to distill convoluted reports and decryptions from overseas stations into concise reports for the Office of Naval Intelligence.

Kennedy was a recent Harvard graduate. His writing was clear and direct, and he impressed his superiors with his diligence and skill. He probably could have remained at this comfortable post, or one like it, for the duration of the war.

JACK AND KATHLEEN

THERE WAS ANOTHER BENEFIT of living in the nation's capital. His apartment was just a few blocks from his younger sister, Kathleen. He had a competitive, sometimes hostile relationship with Joe Jr., but from childhood, Jack and Kathleen had loved each other without reservation.

Lem Billings recalled meeting Kathleen when she attended a religious school close to Choate:

> God, was Kathleen a great girl. I can still remember how happy Jack was when she came to the convent at Noroton. The first week she was there, he insisted we sneak up and visit her and what fun we had! I think I probably fell in love with her right then and there. She opened up a side of me that no woman ever reached. Kathleen and Jack—they were the two people I loved more than anyone else in my life, and they in turn loved each other as much as any brother and sister I have ever seen.

A friend who observed the two said, "After parties, Kathleen liked nothing better than to sit up in her bathrobe with Jack, talking into the middle of the night about the personality of everyone who was there. They were so close I thought of them as twins."

For Jack, sitting at a desk in a small room typing out intelligence reports simply was an inadequate contribution to the nation's effort to defeat Japan and Germany. It was time for him to move as close to the action as he could and prove that he was not a delicate man who should be content with service at home.

After spending two months in navy hospitals during 1942, suffering from back problems and another illness that perplexed his doctors, Jack requested sea duty. He asked for a very dangerous type of sea duty, the command of a PT boat in the South Pacific. Once again, to get what he wanted, he went to his father for help.

The use of PT boats in World War II was championed by General Douglas MacArthur. Before the war, he had retired from the army to become a military adviser to the Philippine government. His mission was to modernize the nation's small army and establish defensive strategies in case war came. On a trip to Washington, D.C., in 1937, he lobbied for the construction of fast, highly maneuverable torpedo boats that could operate in the shallow waters of the Philippines.

The attack on Pearl Harbor brought MacArthur back to active service. He was given command of U.S. forces in the Far East and was assigned the impossible task of stopping the rampaging Japanese army when it reached the Philippines. His army of American and Filipino troops fought heroically, but they were ill equipped and badly outnumbered by the Japanese. MacArthur was forced to retreat to the peninsula of Bataan.

In March 1941, he was ordered to abandon his doomed command and make his way to Australia, leaving behind a broken army that would face the indignity of surrender and the brutality of the Bataan Death March.

To make his escape, MacArthur used the craft he had earlier believed vital to the defense of the Philippines, the PT boat. A swashbuckling PT boat commander named John D. Bulkeley took the general, his wife, and son, nearly 600 miles through enemy-controlled waters. They arrived at Mindanao, where the battered, seasick travelers gratefully took a plane to Australia.

This daring action electrified the public back home; PT boats were celebrated as swift, deadly warships on which exceptional young men sought fame and glory. Bulkeley returned to the States to select just 50 men for the navy's PT boat training program. More than 1,000 men, including Jack Kennedy, volunteered for the training.

Jack assumed that his poor health would disqualify him for such rigorous duty. "I have applied," he wrote to a friend, "for torpedo boat training under Lt. Bulkeley. The requirements are very strict physi- cally—you have to be young, healthy, and unmarried—and as I am young and unmarried, I'm trying to get in."

When Bulkeley arrived home he went to the nation's capital to be decorated by President Roosevelt, and then to ride in a ticker-tape parade in New York. There, Joe Kennedy took up his son's cause. He invited Bulkeley to lunch at the Plaza Hotel. "Joe wanted to know if I had the clout to get Jack into PT boats," Bulkeley said years later. "I told him that I did, and would interview his son. If I thought Jack could measure up, I would recommend his acceptance."

Although Jack impressed Bulkeley during his interview, he was probably given one of the few spots in the program because the Ken- nedy name would help glamorize PT boats. He was assigned to Offi- cer's Candidate School and then to the Motor Torpedo Boat Squadron Training Center in Rhode Island.

He left the safety of his desk job with the following admonition from Bulkeley ringing in his ears, "Those of you who want to come back after the war and raise families need not apply: PT boat skippers are not coming back."

For a scant eight weeks, Jack was taught how to make near-suicidal runs at enemy ships, launch his torpedoes and then turn and flee, us- ing the boat's three, powerful engines to dodge and outrun incoming shells. He spent another five weeks teaching other young men the same tactics, then pulled some strings of his own to get into combat in the Southwest Pacific.

On March 6, 1943, promoted to the rank of lieutenant, junior grade, Jack boarded the troopship *Rochambeau* in San Francisco, bound for Australia and then the Solomon Islands. He arrived in Espiritu Santo in the New Hebrides region of Melanesia on April 3, 1943. He then boarded a landing ship (LST) for a three-day trip to Guadalcanal, the scene of brutal fighting for the control of Henderson Field, the island's strategically important landing strip. From there he would proceed to Tulagi, a smaller island where his squadron was based.

Jack escaped death by just a few feet on the trip to Guadalcanal. His lumbering LST, laden with fuel and explosives, approached the island just as the Japanese mounted a massive bombing attack on Henderson Field. Some of the bombers attacked the harbor, and a bomb landed close enough to Jack's LST to lift it out of the water, badly injuring the captain.

Jack recounted his narrow escape in a letter to Billings:

> To give you an idea what we are against—the day I arrived, they had a hell of an attack. As we were carrying fuel oil & bombs—and on a boat that was a tub—I thought we might withdraw + return at some later date, but the captain thought he was in command of the USS North Carolina as he sailed right in. Well, they dropped all around us but we were O.K. During a lull in the battle—a Jap parachuted into the water—and we went to pick him up as he floated along—and got within about 20 yds of him. He suddenly threw aside his life jacket + pulled out a revolver and fired two shots at our bridge. I had been praising the Lord + passing the ammunition right along- side—but that slowed me a bit—the thought of him sitting in the wa- ter——battling an entire ship. We returned the fire with everything we had——the water boiled around him—but everyone was too surprised to shoot straight. Finally an old soldier standing next to me—picked up his rifle—fired once—and blew the top of his head off. He threw his arms up—plunged forward + sank—and we hauled our ass out of there. That was the start of a very interesting month—and it brought home very strongly how long it is going to take to finish the war.

This would not be his only brush with death. For Jack Kennedy, the war was just beginning.

CHAPTER FIVE

THE TESTING OF JACK KENNEDY

So this is how it feels to be killed.
—John F. Kennedy

THE PAINFULLY THIN YOUNG NAVAL OFFICER floating on his back under a pitch black sky was unconscious, his body miraculously carried in circles by the current rather than drifting toward the enemy. The water was cold and his ankles and legs were covered with deep cuts from sharp coral ridges. Before passing out, Jack Kennedy thought about the barracuda that he had been told would come up under a man swimming in the water and devour his testicles. Then he succumbed to fatigue, had visions, and fell into a trance a mile or so from the safety of a tiny island in the Southwest Pacific Ocean.

Kennedy had sensed this night was coming; he could feel it. In recent weeks, he had twice come close to death when attacked by Japanese planes while on patrol.

He had taken command of PT 109 shortly after arriving on Tulagi, replacing a skipper who had survived intense fighting and feared for the safety of any man who took his place. Jack was 25 and weighed 153 pounds. A crew member assigned to his boat had second thoughts when he saw his skipper for the first time, thinking this scrawny young man "was about fifteen."

The keel for the 80-foot boat, built by Elco, was laid in March 1942, and she was fitted out in the navy's shipyard in Brooklyn, New York. The hull was made of two layers of mahogany planking, each one-inch thick. She was powered by three 1,500 horsepower Packard engines, which ran on high octane aviation gasoline, giving the boat a top speed of 40 knots.

Bringing a PT boat into action against Japanese warships was not the glamorous adventure Jack had imagined. Some of his commanding officers were scandalously inept, insisting on dangerous missions that made little strategic sense. The wooden hulls of PT boats were easily penetrated, their engines were unreliable, and their torpedoes, built during World War I, were temperamental, sometimes running in circles after they were launched.

Most of the boats did not have radar and lacked adequate gunnery in a firefight. Their 30-caliber machine guns and 20-mm cannon could not match the heavier caliber weapons used by Japanese gunboats and barges. After a short time in the warm Pacific water, the hulls of PT boats would become coated with marine growth. This greatly reduced their maximum hull speeds and rendered them incapable of outrunning Japanese destroyers. With these limitations, operating during the day was risky, so Jack and his crew became night fighters.

THE OBLIGATIONS OF CITIZENS

L IFE ASHORE AT TULAGI WAS DISMAL. It rained for a few hours every day, turning the ground to mud that flowed into the tent Jack shared with other officers. During the day, he worked on the boat with his crew and every other night he went out on patrol. Free time was spent discussing two of Jack's favorite topics, politics and civic responsibility.

His commanding officer said, "We'd sit in a corner and I'd recall all the political problems in New Jersey and Long Island, where I come from. He did that with everybody—discussed politics."

Another of his friends said:

> He made us all conscious of the fact that we'd better be concerned about why the hell we're out here, or else what's the purpose of having the conflict, if you're going to come out here and fight and let the people that got us here get us back into it again. He made us all very

aware of our obligations as citizens of the United States to do something to be involved in the process.

Letter writing was another specialty for Jack. The men were required to run their letters past a censor, but since there was no official censor on the island, they did the job themselves, passing their letters to each other for review.

Everyone wanted a chance to read a letter written by Jack.

One of them, written to Inga Arvad, a Danish woman he had fallen in love with before shipping out for the Pacific, illustrated his facility with the theater-of-the-absurd humor later popularized in *Catch 22*, by Joseph Heller. It concerned a surprise inspection by an admiral:

He must have weighed over three hundred, and came bursting through our hut like a bull coming out of chute three. A burst of speed when he got into the clear brought him against the machine shop. He harrumphed a couple of times, and then inquired: "And what do we have here?"

"Well, General," was the answer, "this is our machine shop."

"Harrumph, and what do you keep in it—MACHINERY?"

After it was gently but firmly explained to him that machinery was kept in the machine shop and he had written that down on the special pad he carried for such special bits of information that can only be found "if you get right up to the front and see for yourself'," he harrumphed again, looked at the map, and wanted to know what we had there—"there" being a small bay some distance away. When we said nothing, he burst out with "Well, by God, what we need to do is build a dock. Well, someone said it was almost lunch and it couldn't be built before lunch... After a moment of serious consideration and a hurried consultation with a staff of engineers, he agreed and toddled off to stoke his furnace at the luncheon table.

The first sentence in the fourth paragraph is 75 words long, yet it hurtles the reader forward with considerable comedic skill.

Jack was, according to a crew member:

a fellow who made you feel good to be with—and you never would
have known about his personal, privileged life by visiting with him.
It was written all over the sky that he was going to be something big.
He just had that charisma.

The men also noticed the sense of kindness that others had observed in him. Jack and Jim Reed, along with an ensign who had just
arrived in the Solomon Islands, once brought a PT boat from Tulagi to
Rendova. Once ashore on Rendova, Reed mentioned that he had seen
the ensign in his tent, crying.

"Jack didn't say anything," Reed recalled, "but shortly after that I
looked for him, and he was gone. I looked everywhere, for two and
a half hours. Finally, I found him. He'd been with the ensign all that
time, talking to him, calming him down."

Jack was astounded when he discovered that some of the young
Melanesian boys who became friendly with the Americans on Tulagi were cannibals. He developed a fondness for one of them, named
Lani, who taught him simple words in his language. The authorities
eventually took Lani away, but the *pidgin* English he taught Jack would
later help him devise the rescue of the men of PT 109.

"LIKE BEING IN A CLOSET WITH THE DOOR CLOSED"

IN JULY 1943, FATE BEGAN CLOSING IN on Jack and his crew. During a routine patrol, a Japanese plane dropped bombs that landed
on either side of PT 109, so close that two of his crew were injured.
He again narrowly escaped a direct hit a few nights later.

On August 1, along with 14 other boats, operating out of a base on
Lumbari, Jack went out on patrol. The mission, to intercept Japanese
warships that were resupplying troops on New Georgia, was doomed
from the start. Visibility was near zero. Barney Ross, a crew member
on PT 109, would later describe conditions that night as "like being in
a closet with the door closed. No moon, no stars."

At about 2:30 a.m, Harold Marney, a gunner stationed on the starboard side, saw a dark shape hurtling toward him and shouted, "Ship
at two o'clock."

Marney had not seen the ship until it was on top of them. Jack Kennedy, at the helm, had been moving slowly, running on just one of the
boat's three engines. He swung the wheel and shouted, "Sound gen-

eral quarters!" and signaled the engine room to gun the engines, but these commands came too late to prevent what was about to happen. Not long after Marney's warning, the 2,000-ton Japanese destroyer *Amagiri*, traveling at 40 knots, sliced into PT 109, which carried 2,000 gallons of 100 octane fuel.

According to an after-action report written by Lieutenant Byron White, later a U.S. Supreme Court Justice, the *Amagiri* hit Kennedy's boat on the starboard side, "striking it forward of the forward starboard (torpedo) tube and shearing off the starboard side of the boat aft, including the starboard engine." The boat was sliced down the middle; later reports that it had been cut in half were incorrect.

The ship's fuel tanks split open and hundreds of gallons of fuel spilled out. Sparks from the collision ignited the fuel, and PT 109 exploded in a ball of flames that soared a hundred feet into the dark sky. Jack Kennedy was catapulted violently backward into a metal protrusion in the cockpit, permanently injuring his lower back.

As Jack lay on his back in agony, he looked up at the hull of the *Amagiri* as it sliced through his boat, so close that he could almost touch it. He later remembered thinking, "So this is how it feels to be killed."

When the shock wore off and he gathered his wits, Jack began to search for his crew. He ignored the searing pain in his back. There had been 13 men on the boat when it was rammed. Five of them clung to the port side of the boat, which remained afloat because its watertight compartments had been closed when the crash occurred. Mercifully, a gush of water from the *Amagiri's* wake had pushed the burning gasoline away from them.

One-by-one, Jack called out the names of the eight men who had been catapulted into the water. Two of them, Harold Marney, who had sounded the alarm, and Andrew Kirksey, who earlier had a premonition that he was about to die in battle, did not answer his call. They were never seen again.

The six survivors had drifted a hundred yards from the wreckage. Two were injured and helpless. Patrick McMahon had been down below when the collision occurred; he was badly burned, drifting in and out of consciousness. Charles Harris was dazed and badly bruised and his leg was broken.

Jack took off his shirt, shoes, and pistol and swam out to help them. Fighting a strong current, it took him more than an hour to shepherd them safely back to what was left of PT 109.

Some of the crew feared the *Amagiri* crew would circle back, turn on their searchlights, and machine gun them in the water. But the destroyer never altered course. Years later, Barney Ross would say the collision was "like what I would imagine it would be like to be hit by a train."

The explosion of PT 109 had been visible for miles and was clearly witnessed by the men on other PT boats. But the explosion had been so violent the skippers on those boats assumed all hands had been lost. Rescue efforts were limited, or, according to some, never took place at all. Jack and his crew were angry for years at those who left comrades-in-arms behind without being certain they were beyond rescue.

"We were waiting for the other PT boats to come back," said a PT 109 crewman. "Those sons of bitches ran away from us. We were left."

Days later, at the PT base on Lamburi, a memorial service was held for Jack and his crew. Some of his friends wrote letters home in which they expressed great sorrow for the loss of a man they had greatly admired.

THE FIGHT FOR SURVIVAL

WHEN THE SUN ROSE THE NEXT MORNING, only a few feet of the bow remained above the water. Jack and his men were shipwrecked between two islands, Kolombangara, three miles away, where 10,000 Japanese were stationed, and the much smaller Gizo, a mile away, with about 100 Japanese stationed at an anchorage. The floating hulk of PT 109 could easily be spotted by a Japanese pilot or by lookouts on either island.

By noon, it was apparent that the boat was sinking and would submerge in a few hours. Jack decided they would swim to the smallest island that appeared to be uninhabited and unlikely to be closely watched by the enemy. The island they selected, Barney Ross said:

> was three or four miles distant: a tiny little piece of land, like a New Yorker cartoon. It looked like about 12 feet across, which was exactly what we wanted. Just some place that would be dry land and wouldn't have a hostile group of Japs staring at it.

It was time to move. Jack put a life jacket around McMahon and stuck its strap in his mouth; he would literally tow the horribly burned man through the water. The nine others, the swimmers helping the non-swimmers, held on to a large piece of timber and paddled toward the island. The trip took four hours; Jack arrived first and collapsed on the beach.

The crew of PT 109 hid in the bushes of the tiny circle of land, known locally as Plum Pudding Island, keeping low to avoid showing their profiles. They had a few pistols and a battle lantern, but no food or water. McMahon was in agony, and most of the crew retched from having swallowed gasoline. They vowed that if the Japanese came for them, they would fight to the death rather than surrender.

Jack knew that PT boats returning from night patrols regularly passed through Ferguson Passage, which was about two miles from Plum Pudding. He told his men that when the sun went down, he would swim out to the passage, where he might be able to signal a PT boat with the lantern.

He left the island at dusk after tying a pistol and a pair of shoes around his neck and strapping a life belt around his waist. He took off his pants and wrapped the heavy lantern in a separate life jacket. As he walked into the water, he felt dizzy, but the feeling passed.

To reach Ferguson Passage, Jack would have to wade through shallow water and cross the coral reef that surrounded the island. His shoes protected his feet, but the coral left cuts on his ankles and shins. When he reached deeper water, he tied the shoes around his neck and swam for an hour, until he was well into the passage. Then he floated, listening for the deep-throated rumble of diesels driving a PT boat through the waves. Hours passed and there was nothing but silence. Jack could not know that the route home for the PT boats had been changed. The new route took them well beyond sight of Jack's lantern.

The realization that there would be no rescue this night drained Jack emotionally. Now, in the pitch black, he would have to swim back to the reef, cross into deeper water, and then swim about two miles to Plum Pudding Island.

He found his way back to the reef, but soon realized that the current was pushing him past his landing spot on the beach, not toward it. To reach safety, he would have to cross the coral and then swim against the swift current. In college, in a pool, he had been a powerful swimmer, but now he began to struggle as his body broke down. Suddenly, his strength was gone and he was unable to move. He had been in the water almost continuously since the previous morning. He flashed the lantern, fired the pistol, and yelled as loud as he could for help.

The crew of PT 109 had come out of hiding and gone to the beach, waiting for Jack to return. They saw his lantern and heard the shots, but could do nothing but call to him in hushed tones to avoid alerting the enemy. Sound carries on the water, particularly on a still night, and Gizo Island was very close. When there was no reply, after a few hours, they gave up and went back into the bushes.

In the cold and covered with deep cuts, Jack fought to stay alive. He was unable to focus his thoughts, seeing images that he could not comprehend. Before he passed out, he had the good sense to flip over on his back.

When he did not return the next morning, the men of PT 109 believed that Jack had perished, a victim of the sharks or that he had been blown to bits by a jumpy PT boat gunner who mistook the light of his lantern for an enemy ship. Jack's crew had already come to depend on his unbreakable spirit; he had made avoiding self-pity and thoughts of death a matter of pride, making them believe in themselves and their ultimate deliverance from this hell. Without him, they might lose hope. By noon, he had still not returned and the men grew more and more depressed.

Most of the men considered Jack's decision to make the swim into Ferguson Passage to be irrational, almost suicidal. "In the first place, it was a hell of a long way out to the passage," McMahon later recalled. It would also be a dangerous swim; if spotted by a lookout on a Japanese ship, he would be gunned down or taken prisoner.

However, to a man, they respected Jack's courage. "None of us felt the base had done enough to save us, but Kennedy had done everything he possibly could to save us," one of the crew said years later. "He had extraordinary energy. He just would not give up. That is what made him go out and try to flag down a PT boat."

Jack Kennedy regained consciousness as the sun rose. His fingers were still tightly wrapped around the battle lantern. As his mind cleared, he realized that the current had pushed his body in circles all night and that he had awakened close to the spot where he had passed out. He marveled at this coincidence, thankful that he had not drifted toward Kolombangara, infested with 10,000 Japanese soldiers.

The current had reversed direction and would now push him toward Plum Pudding. Still, he had to force himself to move. The shoes that he had tied around his neck had disappeared; crossing the sharp coral would be sheer hell. His mind blurred as he moved forward. Was he supposed to be heading back to his men or out to the passage to flag down a PT boat? He could not remember.

He kept moving, eventually feeling sand under his feet. He crawled ashore and passed out on the beach until noon. When he awoke, feverish and exhausted, he staggered back to the clump of bushes where his men had taken shelter. His skin had turned yellow and he could barely speak or move... but he was alive. As his jubilant crew surrounded him, he said, "Ross, you try it tonight." Then he vomited and passed out.

TOO WEAK TO CLIMB A TREE

THE NEXT MORNING, his strength returning, Kennedy reasoned that staying on Plum Pudding was certain death. His crew had become too weak to climb a tree and shake down a coconut. He reasoned, correctly, that PT boats were now taking a different route home through Ferguson Passage, and that he could get closer to this route by swimming from island to island, until he reached one that overlooked the new route.

He led them back into the water, cajoling and reassuring the desperate men, again towing McMahon behind him. It took three hours to reach Olsana Island, where they found coconuts, but not fresh water. The next stop was Naru, an island with a beach that faced the new PT route. Kennedy and Barney Ross reached the island in an hour, leaving the others on Olsana. The cuts on Jack's feet had become infected and grotesquely swollen; every step he took was an ordeal.

Were there Japanese stationed on Naru? Jack and Barney could not tell as they swam toward the beach, so once ashore they moved cautiously, darting in and out of cover. They found a small drum of water, some candy, and about 30 small packets of crackers left behind by the enemy. Jack triumphantly brought this stash back to his men on Olsana, using a small, rotting canoe he found on the beach.

There would be more drama. Jack convinced Barney to join him as he took the rotting canoe into Ferguson Passage to flag down a PT boat. A sudden squall drove the canoe onto a reef. It turned over and the pair exhausted themselves and nearly drowned getting it back upright. But they finally made it to shore.

In the end, it was the pidgin English Jack had learned from his friend Lani on Tulagi that led to his salvation. Jack and Barney met two natives on Naru. They worked as scouts for an Australian coast watcher stationed behind enemy lines on Kolombangara. It was their job to observe Japanese movements in the area and aid downed American aviators.

The natives kept their distance from Jack and Barney, fearing they might be Japanese soldiers who would execute them if they were caught helping Americans. When Jack approached them, they fled in panic, paddling their canoe to Olsana, where they encountered the crew of PT 109. Eventually, they went back to Naru, where Jack coaxed them to come close, using the pidgin English he had learned.

Years later, one of the natives said that Jack had been, "easy to communicate with because he spoke pidgin." If the natives had run away again, Jack and his crew would have died of hunger and thirst, 40 miles from safety.

Jack scratched a message into the husk of a green coconut with his jackknife and managed to make the natives understand that he wanted them to take the message to the PT base on Rendova. The message read: *NATIVE KNOWS POSIT HE CAN PILOT 11 ALIVE NEED SMALL BOAT KENNEDY.*

The message got through. The next day, a canoe was sent to bring Kennedy to safety. He hid under palm leaves as a Japanese plane came in low over the canoe. That night, several PT boats, with Kennedy showing the way, picked up the ten remaining crewmen on Olsana.

Joe Kennedy was driving home to Hyannis Port when he heard the news of Jack's rescue on the radio. Rose Kennedy heard the same broadcast. When Joe arrived, she ran to him, saying, "I just turned on a news broadcast. They said Jack has been saved. Saved from what?" Joe Kennedy knew that Jack was missing, but he had not yet told his family, hoping desperately that he would be found.

CHAPTER SIX

HUNGRY FOR REVENGE

"Whatever he does, he earns solely by his capabilities and not by the prestige of his name. People like that make me realize what an American is, something you find nowhere else in this world."
—Alvin Cluster's description of John Kennedy.

IN JANUARY 1944, newspapers across the nation carried the story of a PT boat skipper whose boat had exploded in a ball of flames in the South Pacific. He was thought to have been killed, along with his crew. Miraculously, six days later, the young skipper and all but two of his crew were found alive on a deserted island.

This was front-page news only because it concerned Jack Kennedy, Joe Kennedy's son. Hundreds of young men had survived far worse conditions and acted with more raw courage than Jack did. He had taken a PT boat on night patrols in the Solomon Islands. While dangerous, the risks of this duty paled in comparison with the bloody, hand-to-hand combat faced by the Marines and GIs on Guadalcanal and Tarawa.

Jack understood this distinction and made little of his heroics; embellishing his actions would cheapen the love he had developed for the men who fought with him and the abiding respect he had for all the men who fought in World War II.

He wrote to his best friend, Lem Billings, saying simply that he had "a bad time for a week on a Jap Island—but finally got picked up." When the writer John Hersey asked for his help researching a story about the saga of PT 109, Jack agreed as long as Hersey talked first with members of his crew and focused on their survival rather than on his personal heroics. Hersey later said that Jack's "insistence that I see the crew first struck me very favorably. It didn't seem to me to be self-serving. They were wildly devoted to him, all of them."

Jack realized, of course, that he had good reason to be proud of himself. Not many sons of millionaires who weighed 150 pounds and could become seriously ill at any moment had forced their way into combat in a remote area of the world when they would not have been blamed for staying at home.

Before the war, the most conspicuous elements of Kennedy's personality had been his intelligence and his insatiable need to learn about world affairs. Now, in war, Jack had discovered that he could be tough as nails when needed. He also discovered that he possessed the courage to put his life on the line for others.

In the years ahead, Jack would become seriously ill again and again, sometimes barely escaping death. But now he knew that he could rise above his illness and push himself to achieve things he never dreamed possible.

HUNTING THE ENEMY

FOR A TIME AFTER PT 109 WENT DOWN, Jack had been filled with rage, driven to find the enemy and exact revenge for the deaths of Harold Marney and Andrew Kirksey. His crew had been spirited and close-knit; they were his brothers. He had been in command that night and the responsibility for what had happened was his alone.

After his cuts healed and his strength returned, Jack resumed active duty. He had long resented the lack of firepower on PT boats, so he was delighted to discover that the navy had decided to re-arm some PTs, turning them into gunboats.

Jack spent five weeks on Guadalcanal, ripping the guts out of a PT boat so larger caliber guns could be installed. When finished, he would have command of a boat with enough firepower to slug it out with the Japanese. His gunboat had 40-caliber machine guns in the bow and stern, three 50-caliber machine guns on each side, and two 30-caliber machine guns in front of the cockpit. The boat also had armor plating around the guns and the gas tanks. This vessel was not designed to hit and run; it was designed to stand and fight the enemy.

Jack was driven; he wanted blood. Alvin Cluster, his squadron commander, said, "I don't think I ever saw a guy work harder, longer hours," [than Kennedy to get the boat ready for combat]. He admired Jack and wrote glowing fitness reports about his seamanship and leadership abilities. In a letter home, he addressed Jack's personal qualities:

> I've only know him about six months but I am proud to serve with him in my outfit. Whatever he does, he earns solely by his capabilities and not by the prestige of his name. People like that make me realize what an American is, something you find nowhere else in this world—men and women achieving ends in spite of their background. In fact, I'd say it would be just as hard for a boy like Jack to make good as it is for a kid from the slums. Both have disadvantages to overcome. No one out here has done a better job than Jack.

When the gunboat was ready for action, five crewmen from PT 109 appeared at the dock and told Jack they wanted to ship out with him again. Jack fought to beat back tears. This type of genuine loyalty was the highest compliment a boat captain could ever receive. He welcomed them aboard.

Jack was relentless in his pursuit of the enemy, and went out of his way to find action, extending patrols past their allotted time. Unable to find targets at night, he proposed a daring daytime raid on Japanese installations, but the attack would likely have been disastrous. Cluster, recognizing Jack's blind hunger for revenge, wisely vetoed the idea.

In October, Jack and his crew took part in the emergency evacuation of Marines surrounded by Japanese on the island of Choiseul. Ten of the men, some of them badly wounded, were taken aboard Jack's boat. One young Marine did not make it back to base; he died in Jack's bunk.

PT 109 sank three barges on one patrol and engaged in a firefight on another. Taking fire from gun emplacements on the shore, Jack ordered every gun on the boat to open up, destroying the enemy guns and likely killing several Japanese soldiers.

Jack was far too intelligent, however, to let revenge control him for long. He began to acknowledge the contempt for war that was building within him. His letters home expressed sorrow for the men he had seen injured and killed in action. In a letter to Inga Arvad, he said:

> I received a letter today from the wife of my engineer, who was so badly burnt that his face and hands were just flesh, and he was that way for six days. He couldn't swim, and I was able to help him, and his wife thanked me, and in her letter she said, "I suppose to you it was just part of your job, but Mr. McMahon is part of my life and if he had died I don't think I would have wanted to go on living."

> There are so many McMahons that don't come through. There was a boy on my boat, only twenty-four, had three kids, one night two bombs straddled our boat, and two of the men were hit, one standing right next to him. He never got over it. He hardly ever spoke after that. He told me one night that he thought he was going to be killed. I wanted to put him ashore to work, he wouldn't go. I wish I had, he was in the forward gun turret where the destroyer hit us. [Jack was speaking about Andrew Kirksey, who was killed when PT 109 collided with the *Amigiri*.]

> I don't know what this all adds up to, nothing I guess, but you said that you figured I'd go to Texas, and write my experiences... I wouldn't go near a book like that. This thing is so stupid, that while it has a sickening fascination for some of us, myself included, I want to leave it far behind me when I go.

Nigel Hamilton would later write: "Among his fellow PT officers, Jack was now a legendary figure. He impressed people neither through bravado or chumminess, but by a confident friendliness and courage." Some said that he had "a magical quality," and others talked about his lack of pretense and "absence of phoniness."

In the end, poor health brought Jack's hunt for revenge to an end. His back hurt constantly. Sent back to Tulagi for x-rays and an exam, he learned that, in addition to the damage from the collision, he had a degenerative disease in his spine and was developing an ulcer. Ordered home, he departed for the States aboard the carrier *U.S.S. Breton* and arrived in San Francisco on January 7, 1944. His weight had dropped to 145 pounds, and he was in a state of physical decline that frightened those who welcomed him home.

INGA

JACK'S FIRST STOP after San Francisco was Inga Arvad's home in Beverly Hills. His relationship with the Inga had been intense, yet troubled by an odd set of circumstances. Inga had come to the States from Denmark in 1940 to study at Columbia University School of Journalism. She was fluent in five languages, well-traveled, and highly intelligent, qualities that Jack prized. One day, she stopped *New York Times* correspondent Arthur Krock on the street and asked for his help finding a job. "I was so stupefied by the beauty of this creature that I said I would," Krock recalled.

She met Jack in Washington, D.C., in 1941, when he worked for Naval Intelligence and she, thanks to Krock, was a columnist for the *Washington Times Herald*. Inga's best friend, Jack's sister Kathleen, who also worked at the *Herald*, introduced them. They began an affair almost immediately.

Five years earlier, working for a newspaper in Copenhagen, Inga had interviewed Hitler. The dictator, intrigued by Inga's blonde hair and blue eyes, invited her back for another interview, telling her that she was the ideal Nordic woman. In the article she turned in, Inga said of Hitler, "[He] is not evil as he is depicted by enemies of Germany. He is without doubt an idealist; he believes that he is doing the right thing for Germany and his interests do not go any further."

Arvad's interview, while painfully naive, could have been written by dozens of journalists who would have jumped at the chance to talk with Hitler in 1936. But after 1941, with the world at war against Germany, any prior association with Hitler, no matter how innocent or remote, was cause for suspicion.

That Inga grew to detest Hitler's fascist government had no impact on J. Edgar Hoover, director of the FBI, who considered her a potential spy and had her followed. When he discovered that she was dating Joe Kennedy's son, who happened to be working with classified navy materials, he had wiretaps installed on her phone and in her Washington apartment. Jack and Inga were followed wherever they went.

Ultimately, Jack went off to the Pacific and Inga, her career in ruins, found work where she could. The two would continue to feel a powerful mutual attraction. When Jack finally returned home from the Pacific, he was eager to resume their relationship.

His visit to Beverly Hills, however, did not go well. Inga had found someone else. She brought the two men together at her home, and after chatting amiably for a bit, it became evident that one of the men should leave. Jack, exhausted and weak, excused himself and left. He gradually lost touch with a woman who was his perfect match. Inga eventually married another man.

That Inga and Jack could not stay together was a sour twist of fate. She had perceived that, deprived of his mother's affection, alone and sick for long periods of time, Jack had not matured emotionally. He would always be a charming, handsome, brilliant boy, particularly when it came to matters of the heart. She also knew that he would be a poor choice for a long-term relationship, and that as a twice-divorced woman, there was little chance that he would marry her.

Yet she loved him, saying that, "he's got a lot to learn and I'll be happy to teach him." Inga could indeed have taught her emotionally immature lover a great deal. She could have "completed" Jack Kennedy... but it was not to be.

Jack retreated to his father's oceanfront home in Palm Beach, where his depression over losing Inga became tangled in a new struggle to stay alive. A Kennedy house guest in Palm Beach said Jack:

> would go into a fever and he'd be shaking with cold and his face would go yellow. We all thought he might die. We'd call the ambulance and I'd go with him. They'd all be in the living room when we went out to the ambulance. But in three or four days he'd snap out of it.

At 26, Jack Kennedy had spent four years studying government at Harvard. He had already traveled to almost every continent on the globe and witnessed the spread of fascism and national socialism firsthand. He had watched the world erupt into war. He had the love of a beautiful, intelligent woman. He had a wide variety of friends who believed in him, and he had proved himself in combat.

The next few months, however, would be among the worst of his life. He would suffer horribly, both physically and emotionally. Still in the navy, Jack submitted to two back operations at the Naval

Hospital in Chelsea, Massachusetts. The doctors botched the surgeries, and his lengthy recovery was an ordeal worse than his time in the Pacific. Jack's friends were horrified by the trussed-up, skeletal man they saw in the hospital. He was six-foot-one and weighed 120 pounds. He was tormented by back and abdominal pain and by incredibly painful and violent colitis.

Yet when asked by a friend how he felt as he lay in deep pain in a hospital bed, he said, "Great." Seeing the perplexed look on his friend's face, he added, "Well, great considering the condition I'm in."

THE DEATH OF JOE JR.

IN JULY 1944, while he struggled to recover, Jack received the devastating news that Joe Jr., had been killed while flying a top-secret mission from a base in Great Britain.

He had graduated cum laude from Harvard in 1938 and left Harvard Law School before his final year to join the Navy Air Corps. In September, 1943, he was transferred to England to fly B-24s bombers. By July, 1944, he had completed 25 combat mission and was eligible to return to the States.

As they matured, Joe and Jack began to regard each other as brothers bound by love and respect, and they made efforts to dispense with their childish sibling rivalry. Jack suspected, however, that his brother would find it difficult to accept that he had not earned a medal in combat, while Jack had been decorated for bravery.

He desperately wanted his brother to come home without needlessly exposing himself to danger, simply to win a medal. In his letters, he told Joe that he had done enough, that he had admirably completed his responsibility to serve, and that it was time to get out of harm's way. Joe agreed and made plans to return to the states.

Then, at the last minute, fate provided Joe with a way to come home as a hero. The navy needed volunteers to fly a dangerous mission, and Joe took the risk.

Jack wrote the following about his brother:

> His squadron, flying in the bitter winter over the Bay of Biscay, suffered heavy casualties, and by the time Joe had completed his designated number of missions in May, he had lost his former co-pilot and a number of close friends.

Joe refused his proffered leave and persuaded his crew to remain on for D-day. They flew frequently during June and July, and at the end of July they were given another opportunity to go home. He felt it unfair to ask his crew to stay on longer, and they returned to the United States. He remained. For he had heard of a new and special assignment for which volunteers had been requested which would require another month of the most dangerous type of flying.

It may be felt, perhaps, that Joe should not have pushed his luck so far and should have accepted his leave and come home. But two facts must be borne in mind. First, at the time of his death, he had completed probably more combat missions in heavy bombers than any other pilot of his rank in the Navy and therefore was preeminently qualified, and secondly, as he told a friend early in August, he considered the odds at least fifty-fifty, and Joe never asked for any better odds than that.

Joe's mission was to get a B-24, laden with 22,000 pounds of explosives, into the air and bail out over Great Britain. The bomber would then be remotely controlled by a mother ship that would send it into a crash dive at a V-1 rocket-launching site in Normandy.

Joe Kennedy and his co-pilot flew the bomber over the English Channel. As the two prepared to bail out, the plane was torn apart by a massive explosion, killing Joe and his co-pilot instantly. The explosion was so violent that it shattered windows in a nearby coastal town.

Joe was awarded the Navy Cross, and in 1946, the navy named a destroyer after him. Many years later, it was revealed that British Intelligence had failed to notice that the German rocket base either had been abandoned or destroyed by an earlier bombing attack. Joe's death was pointless, one of countless deaths that resulted from military incompetence during the war.

To Jack, Joe's death would have been pointless no matter what the cause. All that mattered was that he would never come home; the war he hated had claimed another precious life.

Jack asked those who knew Joe best, his college teachers and friends, his girlfriend, his commanding officer, and several others, to sit down and commit their thoughts about Joe to paper. They submitted their work to Jack, and he set about shaping it into a book.

Eunice Kennedy later said, "It was Jack who disappeared every night from five to seven-thirty and wrote letters and made calls, and collected information, and wrote the book while the rest of us were still playing games."

Jack's own essay about Joe expressed admiration and respect. He pointed out that Joe had constantly encouraged his brothers and sisters to become productive and accomplished citizens. He demanded their best. Jack wrote:

> I think that if the Kennedy children amount to anything now or ever amount to anything, it will be due more to Joe's behavior and his constant example than to any other factor. His worldly success was so assured and inevitable that his death seems to have cut into the natural order of things.

Years later, Jack would say that Joe had challenged him to set high standards in everything he did. He so appreciated his encouragement that he did the same with his younger brother, Bobby.

In 1945, *As We Remember Joe* was printed and sent to about five hundred people as a private testament to Joe. Jack sent a copy to a teacher that both he and Joe had admired at Choate, with the following note:

> The war makes less sense to me now than it ever made and that was little enough—and I should really like—as my life's goal, in some way and at some time to do something to help prevent another.

As president, he would do exactly that.

CHAPTER SEVEN

A DEATH SENTENCE

That young American friend of yours, he hasn't got a year to live.
— Dr. Sir Daniel Davis after examining
Jack Kennedy in 1947.

IN JUNE 1860, an elderly man broke away from his caretakers and climbed atop a nine-foot-high stone fence in front of his home in London. Without hesitation, he hurled himself headfirst toward the ground, fracturing his skull. His wish was granted—he died within hours.

Today this man, Dr. Thomas Addison, is considered the father of modern endocrinology. In the 1850s, working at Guy's Hospital in London, Addison became curious about people who had come to him suffering from severe nausea and diarrhea, constant fevers, pain in the joints and muscles, and fatigue. Something had made their skin turn yellow or bronze. Many of them died after minor illnesses or a tooth extraction. They were often sick, weak, and emaciated.

At autopsy, Addison found that each of these people had atrophied adrenal glands. This common link allowed him to discover what later became known as Addison's disease. A century later, his pioneering research would prolong Jack Kennedy's life and the lives of thousands of others who suffered from this devastating illness.

The adrenals sit atop each kidney, small, orange-colored glands that produce hormones that play a role in vital bodily functions. The adrenals of those suffering from Addison's disease do not produce adequate levels of steroidal hormones, without which the human body cannot defend itself against even the most moderate infections and illnesses.

FINALLY, A DIAGNOSIS

IN AUGUST, 1947, Jack traveled to Ireland to visit Kathleen at her home. The trip would afford him the chance to meet former British Foreign Secretary Anthony Eden and discuss world affairs. Kathleen wrote to a friend that, "by the end of the week he and Jack will have fixed up the state of the world."

Kathleen had Jack's intelligence, self-deprecating wit, insatiable curiosity about the world, and innate kindness. Her participation in the war had paralleled some of Jack's experiences. Turned down when she tried to join the Red Cross, like Jack, she turned to Joe Kennedy for help. One of his friends happened to be the head of the Red Cross, and with a little pressure from Joe, Kathleen was given a choice posting in London, working in a rest and recreation club. She greeted American servicemen on leave, and, while playing games or chatting, she encouraged them to speak about their fears of being killed or wounded.

Kathleen felt it was her responsibility to do her job well and was soon widely admired for her diligence. A Kennedy family friend who followed her progress wrote to Joe, "She is really a delight and a real Kennedy, straight and true, in every sense of the word, and I can assure you that any little thing I can do for her is amply repaid by gaining her friendship."

In London, Kathleen was reunited with William "Billy" Cavendish, a member of one of England's most wealthy, influential families. They had met four years earlier at a garden party given by the king and queen.

Writing in *The Fitzgeralds and the Kennedys*, historian Doris Kearns Goodwin said Billy Cavendish:

> had a well-bred air, a quiet ease that covered his handsome face and lent a certain grace to his tall, lanky frame. For nearly an hour the two stood talking amid a constant swirl of activity, and when the conversation was over they both knew, Kathleen later said, that something special was going to happen.

But for something special to happen, Billy and Kathleen would have to overcome the twin obstacles of geography and religious bigotry. The war diverted them to different corners of the world; Billy joined the Cold Stream Guards, an elite unit of the British army, and Joe sent Kathleen and the rest of his family back to the States when the Nazis began their terror bombing of London.

Religion, however, was a more formidable obstacle, as Billy came from a wealthy Protestant family. They had been a powerful force in Great Britain since the mid-1800s, while the Kennedys, of course, were Catholic.

The couple at first announced that they would never take the relationship as far as marriage. Kathleen wrote her parents that Billy's ancestors "would jump out of their graves" if he married a Catholic.

But when Kathleen came back to London to work for the Red Cross, the two continued their courtship and it became apparent that nothing would keep them apart. When they announced their engagement, Rose cabled Kathleen that she was "horrified" and warned her daughter that a Catholic woman who marries outside of her faith would not be granted eternal life in Heaven.

To Kathleen's great relief, Jack, Joe Kennedy, and Joe Jr. stood up to Rose and supported Kathleen.

AGAIN, DEATH

ON MAY 6, 1944, Billy and Kathleen were married in a civil ceremony. Kathleen and Joe Jr. had grown close during the previous months; he was the only member of the Kennedy family to attend the wedding. Jack was much too ill to attend.

Joe Kennedy wired his congratulations, saying, "Remember that you still are and always will be tops with me." Rose feigned an illness and entered a hospital to avoid reporters seeking comment about the wedding.

Within four months, both Billy and Joe Jr. were dead. Joe perished in July and Billy died on September 9. He had been serving in Belgium; the company he commanded was trying to capture the town of Happen, held by German SS troops. On September 8, his unit was badly mauled by the Germans and many were killed.

The following morning, Billy tried to inspire his weary, despondent troops by walking conspicuously ahead of them and urging them forward. A sniper shot him through the heart, and he died as he fell. Kathleen was in New York, trying on dresses at Bonwit Teller when she was told to hurry back to her hotel.

Joe Kennedy stood at the door of her room when she arrived. He wrapped his arms around her and delivered the brutal news.

Billy's family adored Kathleen and allowed her to stay as long as she wished at Lismore Castle, their ancestral home. Situated in County Waterford in southern Ireland, the magnificent castle was acquired by the Cavendish family in 1753, purchased from the famous adventurer Richard Boyle, who had bought it from Sir Walter Raleigh in 1602.

When Jack visited in 1947, Kathleen introduced him to Pamela Churchill, the ex-wife of Winston Churchill's son, Randolph. Jack and Pamela became friends immediately, and in late September, they took a side trip to London. In his hotel room, Jack suddenly became seriously ill. He fell to the floor, suffering from severe nausea and violent stomach cramps, barely able to move. He phoned Pamela's room for help.

Alarmed, Pamela summoned a renowned physician, Dr. Sir Daniel Davis, and Jack was rushed from his hotel to the London Clinic. The mystery of Jack's unremitting illness would finally come to an end. The doctor's at the hospital told Jack without equivocation that he suffered from Addison's disease, a lethal condition with no known cure.

"That young American friend of yours," Dr. Davis told Pamela Churchill, "he hasn't got a year to live."

Jack Kennedy had exhibited the symptoms of Addison's disease for years. When his body was stressed, his skin turned yellow or bronze. He suffered continually from fatigue, nausea, vomiting, and violent colitis, and he endured severe joint and muscle pain. That he had not been diagnosed earlier was testimony to the incompetence of the medical profession.

The many doctors who treated Jack had assumed that the source of his illness was malaria, colitis, or an ulcer; they had not considered Addison's disease a possibility. Jack himself may have unwittingly made his disease worse; for several years, he had sporadically taken a drug to treat his colitis. It was discovered years later that the compound he took actually hastened the atrophy of his adrenal glands.

Addison's disease is relatively rare. Accurate statistics on the incidence of the disease are hard to come by. A 1960 British study found

39 cases per 1 million people. The major cause is thought to be an unusual chemical reaction that causes antibodies to attack the adrenal cortex. There may also be a hereditary component; Jack's sister Eunice also suffered from the disease.

Doctors today believe that Jack suffered from "a slow atrophy of the adrenals," a condition likely worsened during the six days he spent exhausting his body in the Pacific, and by the drug that he took off and on for years.

Without the pioneering work of Thomas Addison, Jack likely would have died before he reached middle age. Addison discovered not only the disease that bears his name, but also other major diseases of the endocrine system. He could not find a cure, however, for his own clinical depression, which led to his suicide in 1860.

After leaving the hospital, Jack was taken by ambulance to the ocean liner, the *Queen Mary*, for the trip home. During the crossing, he remained in the ship's hospital, deathly ill. On his arrival, he slipped into a coma and was given the last rites.

Kennedy's family hid the seriousness of his condition. They said he had suffered a recurrence of malaria, a disease he had contracted during his service in the South Pacific.

Somehow, as he had in the Pacific, and had so many other times, Jack summoned the will to return from near death.

That Jack survived long enough to be accurately diagnosed is a minor miracle. Until the late 1930s, just 10 percent of those with the disease lived more than five years after diagnosis. A synthetic hormone replacement was developed in 1939 that, to a limited extent, improved a patient's ability to withstand infection. Today, more sophisticated artificial hormones are available and Addison's disease is no longer a death sentence.

Jack arrived home from his visit with Kathleen believing that his life would be cut short by his body's inability to fight off an infection. An incision was made in his thigh, and pellets containing a synthetic hormone were implanted inside, with a new pellet reinserted every three months. His doctors said the hormone would keep him alive, but that a severe infection or illness would likely kill him. Jack told friends that within ten years he would suffer from an illness powerful enough to overwhelm his weakened defenses and kill him.

He was advised to take life easy, to avoid stress, and certainly to think twice before subjecting his body to the rigors of major surgery.

Jack had already survived an appendectomy and two major surgeries on his back. One of them so badly weakened his immune system that he nearly died after the surgery. Then his lower spine was crushed when the violent collision with the *Amagiri* threw him against the bulkhead of PT 109.

Constant, agonizing back pain became a part of his life. Robert Kennedy said his brother was in severe pain "at least one-half of the days he spent on this earth. Those who knew him well would know he was suffering only because his face was a little whiter, the lines around his eyes were a little deeper, his words a little sharper. Those who did not know him well detected nothing."

In 1954, when x-rays revealed that his fifth lumbar vertebra had collapsed from spinal degenerative disease, Jack, unable to walk without crutches, was forced to choose between life in a wheelchair or a risky operation that would allow him to walk, but almost certainly would kill him.

Explaining that his back pain was now so severe that he would rather die than endure it any longer, he chose the operation. After surgery, he fell into a coma as his immune system struggled to fight off a massive post-operative infection. The Kennedy family gathered around Jack's bedside after a team of doctors predicted that he would die. Once again, he was given the last rites. And once again, he gave death the back of his hand and went on living.

Today, Jack's medical history is prominent in medical literature about Addison's disease. Before the development of modern hormone replacement drugs, Addison's patients did not survive one major surgery. Jack Kennedy may have been the only person in history to survive several major surgeries while suffering from Addison's disease. One of the doctors who performed his autopsy on November 22, 1963, said he could not find either of Jack's adrenal glands...because they had withered away.

TRAGEDY IN FRANCE

THE RAVAGES OF ILLNESS AND GRIEF had not yet finished making their mark on Jack Kennedy.

Kathleen did not return to the States with Jack when he became ill in London. Four years later, she had fallen in love with

Lord Peter Fitzwilliam, a wealthy, married Protestant. Fitzwilliam announced his intention to divorce his wife and marry Kathleen. Rose again protested the intended marriage with righteous fury, threatening to disown her eldest daughter if she dared marry a divorced man.

Joe Kennedy, however, agreed to meet with Kathleen and Fitzwilliam in Paris to discuss the matter. On May 13, 1948, the couple boarded a small plane in London for a flight to Cannes, the first leg of the trip to Paris. The pilot warned the couple that a thunderstorm was due to strike Cannes just as their plane would be approaching the airport. Commercial flights in the area had already been grounded.

Fitzwilliam insisted that they proceed. As the pilot feared, they ran into the thunderstorm, which produced strong winds and heavy rain. The light plane was driven off its course. Visibility was near zero as the pilot, trying to find his position, brought the plane down through the cloud cover. As they broke into the clear, the pilot saw a mountain ridge that was too close to avoid. The plane hit it nose first, killing all on board.

A devastated Joe Kennedy flew to a small French town near the crash site and was taken to a makeshift morgue to identify Kathleen's body.

A truly remarkable brother and sister relationship was over. Michael O'Brien wrote that:

> Kathleen adored Jack, but she could express her love only by teasing and joking with him. To her father, she confided her intense feelings for her brother. "She really thinks you are a great fellow," Joe wrote to Jack in February 1935. "She has a love and devotion to you that you should be very proud to have deserved. It probably does not become apparent to you, but it does to both Mother and me. She thinks you are quite the grandest fellow that ever lived and your letters furnish her most of her laughs."

Just eight months after being told that he suffered from a disease that would cut his life short, Jack lost Kathleen because she had taken an unnecessary risk to plead for the right to marry a man she loved.

The effect on Jack was intense. For weeks, he was unable to sleep. He shut himself off from the world. Any little reminder of Kathleen, a friend recalled, would cause Jack to convulse in tears.

Lem Billings said years later that Jack:

> told me that he couldn't get through the days without thinking of
> Kathleen at the most inappropriate times. He'd find his mind drift-
> ing uncontrollably back to all the things he and Kathleen had done
> together and all the friends they had in common. He thought of her
> now as his best friend, the one person in the family with whom he
> could confide his deepest thoughts, his complex feelings about Joe,
> and his questions about God and his doubts about the future. And
> now she was dead.

The depressed young man told friends that he did not have long
to live; there was little reason to go on with life. When a friend questioned his intention to take a flight in a small plane in stormy weather, Jack replied, "It really doesn't matter with me; I don't have that
long to go, anyway."

Kennedy listens to coal miners in West Virginia during the 1960 presidential campaign. He considered it his responsibility to research the important issues facing the country. He once read dozens of books on labor law in one sitting, because he considered his knowledge of that subject deficient. Photo by Hank Walker

PART TWO

THE BIRTH OF A PUBLIC SERVANT

CHAPTER EIGHT

USING POLITICS TO EXPRESS HIS IDEALS

He spoke about a career, not in politics, but rather, in what he called "public service." He had positively and absolutely made up his mind to devote it to public service. I could not get him to say the word "politics."
—Patrick J. Landan.

AFTER THE WAR, Jack Kennedy, like thousands of other young men, faced the task of finding or rebuilding a career. Jack was constantly ill and still reeling from Kathleen's death. He had no formal work history, having spent his 20s at Harvard, traveling around the world, and then fighting in the Pacific.

The career that most closely matched his fascination with government and history was journalism. He also considered going to law school. But these professions, he said, "were too passive." He wanted to be a man who made history, not one who sat passively in an ivory tower and wrote about it.

Jack was an idealist. Implanted deep in his psyche was the concept of altruism that his father had stressed repeatedly over the years. Joe

Kennedy put no limits on the methods he used to acquire wealth; he would do anything necessary to turn a profit. But he would not allow his children to succumb to his mercenary ways.

Historian David Nasaw said that Joe:

> told [his children] over and over again, "I'm making all this money so you don't have to make money, so that you can go into public service." He impressed on them that those who are privileged with money, with education, with good looks, have to give something back to those who don't have those privileges, and he truly believed that. And all of these kids grew up knowing they were not going to go into business. They didn't want to go into business. They were going to do some sort of public service and, in the end, they did.

The political world, more than journalism or law, offered Jack the opportunity to serve a cause greater than himself. His poor health, however, was still a problem. The cortisone pellets implanted in his thigh every few months had not slowed the ravages of Addison's disease. Doctors insisted that he avoid any activity that would compromise his immune system.

As he approached his 30th birthday, when he was healthy, Jack was a handsome man. He had blue eyes and wavy, sun-streaked hair. He glowed with intelligence and humor. But when his body became stressed, he lost so much weight that he looked sunken and bony, like a patient in the last stages of a wasting disease. Sitting atop his skeletal body, his full head of hair made him appear top heavy, like a golf club with legs. Friends described him as looking "yellow as saffron and thin as a rake."

WHY HE ENTERED POLITICS

IT HAS BEEN ARGUED that Jack entered politics because his father demanded that he do so. Joe had the ability to see important economic and political trends developing long before others. Before the Great Depression, businessmen—the captains of industry—had a strong influence on the nation's economy and politics. But in 1929, their collective greed caused the economy to collapse. In the wake of the misery that followed, the government took on a greater role in policing the business community.

Joe Kennedy believed this would create a major change in the

United States. Big business would lose its iron grip on the country and government would become more powerful than ever. In 1930, he predicted that, "the people who run the government will become the biggest people in America."

Jack was fully aware that his father expected him to enter politics. In the summer of 1945, he told a friend, "I can feel pappy's eyes on the back of my neck…it's my head on the chopping block next," meaning that he knew that Joe would push and push until Jack committed to a life in the political arena.

To some minor degree, Jack may have run for Congress to please his father, but he had no desire to be "one of the biggest people in America." His wanted instead to use the knowledge and sophistication he had acquired to serve his country.

Patrick J. Landan, a wealthy Chicago businessman who became Jack's lifelong friend, was uniquely situated to observe Jack's decision to run for office.

When he was discharged in late 1944, navy doctors, unable to find a cause for his poor health, had advised Jack to rest for a long period, "in a secluded, outdoor environment." In January 1945, he went to Arizona, where he stayed at a hotel in Castle Hot Springs. He told his father that the clean air was "wonderful" and the hot springs "amazing," and that he was getting stronger. But this enthusiasm was meant to lessen his father's worry. A doctor who examined Jack in Phoenix wrote Joe Kennedy that he "didn't think he was getting along well at all."

Landan and Jack shared a room at the hotel. Years later, Landan said that:

> Jack was completely and absolutely concerned about his future. He talked a great deal about finding something meaningful to do with his life. He spoke about a career, not in politics, but rather, in what he called "public service." He had positively and absolutely made up his mind to devote it to public service. I could not get him to say the word "politics."

The thought that Jack would have become anything but a politician is preposterous. Lem Billings said that, "nothing would have kept Jack out of politics; I think this is what he had in him, and it just would have come out, no matter what."

Ted Sorensen echoed Billing's assertion, saying that Jack entered politics, "not to take Joe's place, as is often alleged, not to compete subconsciously with him, but as an expression of his own ideals and interests."

Robert Dallek expressed the same sentiment:

> For someone who prided himself on his independence—whose sense
> of self rested partly on questioning authority, on making up his own
> mind about public issues and private standards—taking on his older
> brother's identity was not Jack's idea of coming into his own.

A PARTNERSHIP THAT CHANGED THE COUNTRY

LANDAN ALSO PROVIDED INSIGHT into the complex relationship between Jack and his father. During one of their late night discussions in Arizona, after Jack had made it clear that he was thinking of running for Congress, Landan told him that, "labor law was going to be a very important force in the country." He admonished him for neglecting this important topic, joking that he did not know "the difference between an automatic screw machine and a lathe and a punch press."

Jack wrote to his father, asking him to send books on labor-related topics. A crate full of books soon arrived, and Jack "sat up to one or two in the morning reading those books until he finished the whole crate," according to Landan.

Jack's decision to enter politics was his own, but he would have accomplished little without his father. The two formed a partnership. Jack's contributions to the partnership were his prodigious hunger for knowledge that would make him an effective public servant, his remarkable intellectual capabilities, and his idealism and charisma. Joe provided the money Jack would need to acquire knowledge and to run for office. Equally as important, he gave him his love.

After Jack was murdered, he would be lauded for, among other things, his remarkable self-confidence. Much of this confidence came from his father. According to Landan, he phoned every day at five o'clock in the evening to check up on Jack. He sent packages of food to help him gain weight, and he kept a sharp eye on Jack's health issues. Anything Jack needed was a phone call away, including confidence-building, emotional support, and love. Again and again he told Jack, "You are tops with me."

GETTING STARTED

I N 1946, JOE KENNEDY used his friendship with William Randolph Hearst to get Jack freelance reporting assignments for Hearst's chain of newspapers. This would push Jack into the spotlight, making his name known to as many future voters as possible, as his byline would appear in newspapers across the country.

Jack's first assignment was to cover the founding of the United Nations in San Francisco in April 1945. Appalled by the carnage of World War II, Jack, like many other Americans, hoped the U.N., unlike its predecessor, the League of Nations, could offer the nations of the world a way to work out their differences before war became unavoidable.

Jack's job was to cover the conference that would give birth to the peacekeeping organization. At first, as Michael O'Brien observed, Jack's articles from San Francisco were sophomoric, "cliché-ridden, inconsequential, and boring," as he spent more time pursuing women than researching the factors that were shaping the structure of the U.N.

But gradually, as the events he witnessed became more compelling, Jack's writing became insightful. He correctly described the U.N. as a body doomed to become ineffective, unable to fulfill its mandate of preventing future wars. "Its powers will be limited," he wrote. "It will reflect the fact that there are deep disagreements among its members."

Angry that the U.N. promised to be an impotent organization, incapable of preventing war, Jack wrote the following to a friend who had served with him in the Pacific:

> When I think of how much this war has cost us, of the deaths of Cy and Peter and Orv and Gil and Demi and Joe and Billy and all those thousands and millions who have died with them—when I think of all those gallant acts that I have seen—it would be a very easy thing for me to feel disappointed and somewhat betrayed...You have seen battlefields where sacrifice was the order of the day and to compare that sacrifice to the timidity and selfishness of the nations gathered in San Francisco must inevitably be disillusioning.

PREDICTING CHURCHILL'S DOWNFALL

Jack's next assignment took him to Great Britain, where Winston Churchill had called for a general election in early July. Jack covered the political campaign leading up to the election. Churchill, by telling the truth about Hitler, had rallied the people around him. He was the most beloved British prime minister of all time, with a public approval rating in 1945 of 83 percent.

After spending a short time in Great Britain, Jack was one of the few journalists who predicted that Churchill would lose to his opponent, Clement Atlee. During his travels through Europe with Lem Billings in 1937, Jack had relentlessly questioned anyone who would speak with him about the role of government in their lives.

In London, he continued his practice of constant inquiry, inviting British political leaders to his room at the Grosvenor House at five o'clock each evening to discuss political events. A British politician who knew him during this time said, "He always asked an enormous number of questions. For every one I asked he asked two, at least. He always wanted to know why things were and how things worked, the root cause of things. He had an inquisitive mind."

Based on what he learned by talking to both sides in the campaign, Jack concluded in a newspaper article two weeks before the election that the British people would reject the revered Churchill. He argued that Churchill during the war had repeatedly asked the people to sacrifice for the sake of the country. They had complied, sending their sons to war and enduring deprivation and economic hardship at home. More than 450,000 British citizens now lay dead, including 383,000 military deaths. The nation was tired of sacrifice.

As the election drew close, Jack lost his nerve and backed off his prediction, saying in articles that the election would likely be very close. The election was far from close; Churchill lost in a landslide and Jack summed up the loss as follows:

> The Socialists promised that things will be better for the working man, and to the Socialist Party just about everyone is a working man. Churchill, on the other hand, took the same line in this campaign that had been so successful in 1940. He offered them nothing but "toil and sweat" and said that the Conservative party would make no

glib promises that it could not keep.

> Unfortunately for the Conservatives, the people of this island have been on a diet of toil and sweat for the past five years. The British people will take that diet in an emergency, but they feel that the emergency has passed.

Churchill's loss reinforced Jack's belief that world leaders must offer the people hope that their future will be better than their past. Atlee had offered the British people this hope, Churchill had not...and that is why he lost.

Jack was becoming an astute observer of the relationship between the people and their government.

He was also refining his writing skills. During a tour of post-war Germany after his assignment in Great Britain, Jack wrote the following about Berlin, a city controlled by the Russians, British, French, and the United States after the war:

> Berlin today is a gutted ruin. Its destruction far surpassed anything that I had ever imagined. The buildings which still stand are merely shells, and where the three million people who still remain in Berlin live, is a mystery. The streets are filled with them—their faces colorless, their lips a pale tan, their expressions lifeless and dead, as though they were suffering from shock. Occasionally, and it appears incongruous, you see a dog. They won't last through this winter.

Joe's efforts paid off, as Jack's reporting was noticed in political circles and by the general public. In 1946, he could have run for lieutenant-governor of Massachusetts or Congress, but Joe argued that a seat in Congress would give Jack more public recognition than any other office. He believed the 11th district, with its hefty share of Irish Catholic voters, would be the best place to launch Jack's career in politics.

This seat was already held by James Michael Curley, the corrupt Irishman so popular among the working class in Boston that he won reelection as mayor while serving time in prison. Joe made him an offer that he could not refuse. Curley would resign from Congress and run again for mayor. In return, Joe would give him $140,000 to pay legal fees and finance his bid for mayor.

Into this void would step Jack Kennedy. There were headwinds that made victory seem improbable at first. To mask his poor health, the Kennedy campaign staff told the press that Jack was thin because he had contracted malaria in the Pacific.

Jack's shyness was also a problem at the start of his career. At election time, Boston politicians would stop at homes where wakes were being held for departed loved ones. A few handshakes and effusive but fake expressions of sympathy could result in enough votes to determine an election.

This was not for Jack, who was uncomfortable and introverted among people he did not know. If a conversation had no point, he was lost. During the brief and inane exchanges he had while shaking hands with voters, he had little to say and found it difficult to make eye contact. He was uncomfortable projecting fake kinship and stubbornly refused to indulge in phony displays of concern at wakes or anywhere else.

Political leaders in the Democratic Party resented Jack. The seat in the 11th district was supposed to go to someone who had waited his turn, not a newcomer. An influential Democrat, the owner of a funeral home, told Jack, "You can't win this seat. You're a carpetbagger. We don't want you here."

Jack's response was, "I don't think I'll have him handle my funeral arrangements."

Jack worked long hours, greeting workers in front of factories and dockyards, and climbing, one step at a time because of his bad back, the stairways of the many three-decker apartments in the 11th district.

As a speaker, he was shy and awkward before an audience, unable to talk effectively without a prepared text. He raced through his speeches at breakneck speed. When he lost his place, his sister Eunice, sitting in the first row, would mouth the words of his speech and get him back on track.

"Many a night," she said years later, Jack would:

> come over to see Daddy after a speech; he'd be feeling rather down admitting that the speech hadn't really gone very well....I can still see the two of them sitting together, analyzing the entire speech and talking about the pace of delivery to see where it had worked and where it had gone wrong.

In his campaign speeches, Jack spoke about idealism as a necessary part of life in America, saying that:

> a nation's character, like that of an individual, is elusive. It is the result of physical factors, intellectual factors, spiritual factors. It is well for us to consider our American character, for in peace, as in war, we will survive or fail according to its measure. Idealism, this fixed regard for principle, has been an element of the American character from the birth of this nation to the present day.

The day before the primary election, while walking in a parade in Boston, in a state of exhaustion, Jack collapsed and briefly lost consciousness. His aides at first thought he had suffered a heart attack. As his doctors had predicted, his body was rebelling against the rigors of campaigning. Within a few minutes, however, Jack was back on his feet and hard at work.

VICTORY

JACK KENNEDY WAS ELECTED to represent the 11th Congressional District in Massachusetts in May 1946, little more than a year after he returned from the Pacific. Despite his illness, he easily defeated eight other men in a primary election for the seat and then won the general election by a wide margin.

He won the election because he was a war hero and had an Irish name. He won because his father had spent without restraint on the campaign. He won because his mother and his sisters and brothers had fanned out across the district, charming voters at teas and rallies.

And he won because voters, despite his shyness, saw his intelligence and sensed that his concern for their future and the future of the country was genuine, not contrived for political purposes.

CHAPTER NINE

GREEDY MEN HIDING
BEHIND IDEOLOGY

*Little mattered to him more during his term in the House than
making clear that he operated primarily in the service of national
rather than more limited group interest.*

—Robert Dallek

I F YOU WERE AMONG THE THOUSANDS of Americans who toured
the U.S. Capitol in 1947, you may have noticed a thin, attractive
young man on the floor of the House of Representatives. Instead
of a business suit, he wore khaki slacks and loafers, a breach of eti-
quette in this chamber.

The thought that he was a congressman would never cross your
mind. He looked more like the son of a congressman, dutifully visiting
his father but counting the minutes until he could flee and head to a
party in Georgetown, or hop into his convertible and pick up one of
the countless young women who waited for his call.

But Jack Kennedy was indeed a congressman, and the rumpled
clothing he wore was an improvement over the days when he wore
socks of different colors or forgot to tuck in his shirt.

Jack's appearance was a reflection of his boredom. He thrived on
constant intellectual stimulation. When there was no book to read, no

great issue to ponder, he would become restless and his concentration would ebb.

Congress did not provide him with these challenges. It was his job to learn the rules and wait his turn. If he showed the proper respect for senior House members, if he blindly supported his party's political and legislative efforts, he could in the decades to come gain the seniority to get things done in the House.

This passivity was not in his character. Jack generally supported President Truman and the Democrat's agenda, but his sense of intellectual honesty compelled him to turn against Truman when he disagreed with his policies.

Robert Dallek later described Jack's time in the House as follows:

> He wished to be known as a public servant whose judgment rested not on narrow ideological or personal prejudices, and little mattered to him more during his term in the House than making clear that he operated primarily in the service of national rather than more limited group interest.

There was another drawback for Jack. Objective debate, unbiased give-and-take between political leaders, was an aspect of public service that Jack deeply valued. But most of the senior members in the House were in their late 60s or early 70s and their views were cemented in place. There was little room for a free exchange of ideas or the consideration of both sides of an issue among these political ideologues.

Lem Billings said that Jack:

> Found most of his fellow congressmen boring, preoccupied as they all seemed to be with their narrow political concerns. And then, too, he had terrible problems with all the arcane rules and customs which prevented you from moving legislation quickly and forced you to jump a thousand hurdles before you could accomplish anything. All his life he had had troubles with rules externally imposed and now here he was, back once again in an institutional setting.

Years later, Jack would summarize his feeling about his time in the House by saying, "You are one of 435 members. You have to be there many, many years before you get to the hub of influence, or have an opportunity to play any role on substantive matters." Freshmen congressmen, he said, were "worms" who were expected to stay below the surface.

There were times when Jack retreated into his life as a bachelor and ignored his responsibilities in the House. There were also times when he exhibited early signs of his profound contempt for the destruction caused by ideologues.

THE HOUSING SHORTAGE

ONE EXAMPLE involved his handling of the severe nationwide housing shortage that was making life difficult for many Americans. The problem reached crisis proportions when thousands of young men came back from the war in 1945.

New construction had come to a halt during the war. When the fighting ended, 30 percent of the population lived in substandard housing, some of them in boxcars and abandoned buildings. It was estimated that at least five million new housing units nationwide would have to be built to lessen the problem.

As a congressman, Jack threw himself into this issue. First, he studied the facts, learning, for example, that in Boston alone 40 percent of married veterans were living in substandard rental housing or packed into small apartments or homes with several other families.

Convinced that his constituents badly needed housing, in April 1947, Jack urged his fellow congressmen to pass the Taft-Wagner-Ellender bill, a measure that called for the construction of 12.5 million new housing units over the next ten years, along with government low-interest loans and subsidies to stimulate housing development.

The bipartisan bill had been approved by the Senate and needed House approval. A group of conservative Republicans on the House Banking Committee, however, refused to hold hearings on the bill before Congress adjourned for the year, saying they needed more time to study the legislation. Their delay effectively killed the bill.

The Republicans said they opposed the bill because they did not believe that government should interfere with the free market or private industry. Jack viewed them as political hacks rather than as politicians who represented the will of the people. He also discovered that their ideology was a smoke screen for greed.

On the floor of the House, Jack delivered a fierce attack on the Republicans, charging that, instead of the people, they represented the interests of lobbyists who worked for the real estate industry.

In Jack's mind, the Republicans were not, as James Madison called for, elected officials whose "patriotism and love of justice" impelled them to serve the common good. Instead, they were something both Madison and Jack Kennedy detested, greedy men hiding behind an ideology.

Barely able to contain his rage when the bill was delayed, Jack said:

> I was sent to this Congress by the people of my district to help solve the most pressing problem facing this country—the housing crisis. I am going to have to go back to my district on Saturday, a district that probably sent more boys per family into this last war than any in the country, and when they ask me if I was able to get them any homes, I will have to answer, "not a single one...not a single one."

Jack lashed out at the American Legion, the veterans group, as one of the forces that opposed the bill on behalf of real estate concerns. "The leadership of the American Legion," he said, "has not had a constructive thought for the benefit of the country since 1918." Jack knew that this comment could damage his political career, as the Legion was an incredibly powerful lobbying group.

When a housing bill was finally passed in 1949, Jack mocked his Republican colleagues for allowing people to suffer while they conducted an unneeded study. "For over four years now the Congress has been studying and investigating the housing shortage in the country. The facts are plain."

THE RIGHTS OF UNIONS

JACK VOICED A SIMILAR VIEW when Republicans charged that trade unions had become too powerful, and introduced legislation that would dramatically curtail their power.

Kennedy agreed that unions held unnecessary power and that reform was needed, but he said the draconian Republican solution to the problem was not based on an intelligent analysis of the issue. To Republicans, the debate was not about the proper role of unions, but rather their belief that unions put a crimp in corporate profit-making.

In a statement opposing the bill, Jack said:

> This bill would in its present form strike down in one devastating blow the union shop, industry-wide bargaining, and so strangle collective bargaining with restraints and limitations as to make it ineffectual. In seeking to destroy what is bad, they [Republicans] are also destroying what is good.

John Kennedy had displayed his opposition to using ideology to justify greed, a practice that today rules our government. Eventually, the Senate passed a modified version of the Republican bill, a compromise that today is known as the Taft-Hartley law.

THE TYRANNY OF TIME

AS THE SON OF A RICH MAN, Jack had everything he could ever want, except time. With his health not improving, to make a contribution to his country, he would have to leapfrog ahead of his peers by working harder than everyone else and planning his career years in advance.

Most congressmen focus their efforts on becoming members of important committees so they may eventually gain power and influence. Jack took a different path. Almost from the day he entered the House, he had his eye on higher office, either the governor's office or the Senate, which offered a larger platform for his commitment to public service and brought him closer to the White House.

His health and his impatience stood in his way. In the House, he set a record for absenteeism that still stands, as he spent long periods of time in hospitals. A staffer said that, "during staff meetings, Jack would collapse on a couch in his office and go to sleep. His back was so bad that sometimes we had to pick him up and carry him across the street to the House for a vote."

Jack's fellow congressman, Tip O'Neill, said that Jack "didn't get along with the leadership, and they resented his frequent absences and his political independence. He was a fish out of water."

In 1951, after spending six years in the House, Jack Kennedy told his staff that he would rather run for governor or the Senate and fail "than go back and serve another term as a Congressman."

Many saw Jack's naked ambition as arrogance. The truth was that he was an honest and principled politician whose understanding of both foreign affairs and American democracy was light years ahead of his peers. He had unique skills to offer the people of Massachusetts... but his health was bad, the clock was ticking. So why wait?

CHAPTER TEN

THE SICKLY FELLOW WINS

I don't look forward to sitting over there in the governor's office dispensing sewer contracts.
—Jack Kennedy

J ACK KENNEDY LEANED BACK IN HIS SEAT and closed his eyes. The speech had gone well. He had learned to slow his delivery and lower his speaking voice, and to add emphasis he was now chopping the air with his right hand as he spoke. He tried to relax; the next stop was miles away and he had time to review what he would say in his next speech.

But then the car would hit a bump or a pothole and a sharp pain in his lower back would cause him to nearly faint, a reminder that he had ruptured the spinal disc between his fifth lumbar vertebra and his sacrum when a Japanese destroyer slammed into PT 109 in 1943.

Jack said nothing about the debilitating pain, not to the driver nor to the aides who sat in the backseat. He had asked for this life; he badly wanted to leave the House for a higher office, so he bit his lip and took the pain in silence.

From his first race for Congress in 1946, Kennedy's campaign strategy had been to meet people on a one-to-one basis. He wanted to shake their hands and discuss their concerns and his proposals for addressing those concerns. Now, as he campaigned for the Senate, travelling across the back roads of Massachusetts had become part of his life. Over the last four years, on weekends, at his own expense, he had gone on the road. He stayed in dingy motels, living on cheeseburgers and milkshakes that he gulped down between stops, taking hot baths at night, and sleeping with a board under his mattress to ease his back pain.

He visited each of the 39 cities and 312 towns in the state of Massachusetts, something no other Massachusetts politician had ever done.

The purpose of this exhausting travel was twofold: His speeches would give him statewide exposure in anticipation of a run for either the governor's office or the Senate. And it would allow him to build a staff of citizen volunteers rather than professional campaign aides.

As he traveled, Jack engaged the people he met, particularly community leaders, in discussions about political issues. When people seemed particularly well-informed, he would jot down their names so they could be contacted later and asked to join the Kennedy campaign. He was assembling a network of citizens who were willing to embrace their civic responsibility to participate in government.

In 1951, when Paul Diver, the incumbent Democratic governor, decided to run again, Jack set his sights on the Senate. He had preferred the Senate all along, telling an aide that he did not "look forward to sitting over there in the governor's office dispensing sewer contracts."

Jack's opponent was Henry Cabot Lodge, the son of noted poet George Cabot Lodge and a prominent member of the Boston aristocracy of wealthy WASP families. After he made his millions, Joe Kennedy had sought acceptance from this upper class, but he was viewed as a crude Irishman, a Catholic who had made his fortune running whiskey and making movies. Joe, a tough, independent soul, was wounded by this rejection.

AN UNBEATABLE OPPONENT

LODGE HAD BEEN IN THE SENATE since 1936 and was considered unbeatable. He was a tall, attractive man, 15 years older than Jack, an honors student at Harvard, and his war record made Jack's efforts in the Pacific seem tame.

Jack had been a second lieutenant, decorated with a relatively insignificant medal for getting his men out of danger after his boat went down. Lodge had resigned from the Senate to join the army and had seen combat in Italy and France. In 1944, he single-handedly captured a German patrol and came home a lieutenant colonel, decorated with the French Legion of Honor, a Bronze Star, and other medals. The voters sent him back to the Senate.

Some of Jack's political advisers told him to wait for a lesser opponent, pointing out that losing in his first attempt to leave the House could end his career. The Lodge family had maintained a tight grip on the state's political infrastructure for decades. And in all of Massachusetts history, only two Democrats had been elected to the Senate.

It also appeared that a major political shift was about to occur in the United States. Twenty years earlier, Franklin Roosevelt had calmed a terrified nation by proclaiming, "The only thing we have to fear is... fear itself." Then he initiated New Deal programs that lifted the country ever so slowly out of the worst depression it had ever experienced. He held the presidency for 12 years, winning an unprecedented fourth term during the war. Harry Truman assumed the presidency after Roosevelt's death and was reelected in 1948.

By 1952, however, it appeared inevitable that the nation would remove Democrats from office. The Cold War with the Soviet Union was causing panic across the country. The public was also disturbed by reports of corruption in the federal government and disappointed by President Truman's failure to end the war in Korea.

When Truman decided not to run again, Democrats turned to Adlai Stevenson, a brilliant man but a hopelessly bland politician. His opponent was Dwight Eisenhower, the five-star general who had commanded the Allied Forces during World War II. Campaigning against "Korea, Communism, and Corruption," Eisenhower was expected to take the White House, sweeping Republicans into office with him. If Jack could beat Lodge in a Republican year, his victory would be noticed across the nation. Joe Kennedy told his son, "When you've beaten him, you've beaten the best. Why try for something less."

As he had during Jack's run for the House, Joe pumped money into his son's Senate campaign. Most of the major daily newspapers in Massachusetts endorsed Lodge, but the *Boston Post*, a conservative publication, endorsed Jack. It was later discovered that Joe had given the publisher a "loan" to help bail the paper out of its financial woes.

Lodge badly underestimated Jack, believing that he was a playboy and much too sick to withstand the rigors of campaigning. It was well known in Washington that in the House Jack had been seriously ill and at times could not even walk more than a few feet without help.

Democratic Florida Congressman George Smathers, Jack's best friend in the House, said, "In those days he was a rather sickly fellow. In addition to his bad back he was constantly plagued with colds and one thing after another, constantly laid up." No one, least of all Lodge, expected Jack to put up much of a fight.

Lodge had convinced Eisenhower to run for the White House. He managed the general's presidential campaign, spending long periods away from his own Senate campaign. He had built a stronghold in the Senate and did not believe the rich man's son, the tomcat who spent more time chasing women than he did in the House, could bring him down.

Jack took full advantage of his opponent's lapse in judgment, putting together a campaign effort that got off to a slow start but became one of the most effective Senate campaigns in Massachusetts history. He had learned to live with pain and sickness and was working long, hard hours. Only Jack and his family knew that he had Addison's disease and this secret would be safe until long after his death. As Jack had learned in the Pacific, he could will himself to succeed, despite his illness.

His family rallied to support his campaign effort. His mother and sisters again held teas, where women stood in line to shake hands with Jack and other members of the Kennedy family. There was something about this family approach, and something about Jack himself, that the voters found endearing.

It was during this campaign that Robert Kennedy, just 26-years-old and with little political experience, became Jack's right arm, the one man he trusted above all others and who worked as hard as the candidate himself. John T. Shaw, in his book, *JFK in the Senate*, said that Bobby and campaign strategist Lawrence O'Brien:

> built a formidable political operation. Drawing on John Kennedy's years of contacts, the campaign developed extensive files of community leaders who would become the organizational foundation of the campaign. The Kennedy team built its operation city by city, town by town, appointing nearly 300 people to serve as campaign secretaries to organize and monitor the campaign effort in their communities.

By the time Lodge realized that he faced an unusually effective political machine, it was too late. In an eerie foreshadowing of the presidential race of 1960, the winner of the 1952 senatorial race was not known until the morning after the election, when it became clear that Jack had won by just 70,000 of the 2.4 million votes that had been cast. As expected, Eisenhower carried both Massachusetts and the nation in a landslide.

But Jack had done it, he had beaten "an unbeatable" candidate and he was front-page news across the nation. Larry O'Brien would later describe the Kennedy juggernaut in 1952 as "the most nearly perfect political campaign I've ever seen. It was a model campaign because it had to be. Jack Kennedy was the only man in Massachusetts who had the remotest chance of beating Henry Cabot Lodge that year and Kennedy couldn't have won without an exceptional political effort."

CHAPTER ELEVEN

AN OLD-FASHIONED PATRIOT

*Jack Kennedy…set a pattern for the rest of us, showing how
we can discuss the problems which we face and relate them to
the total problem of the United States.*
—Hubert Humphrey.

ONE DAY IN FEBRUARY 1953, as his congressional office
was being dismantled for the move to the Senate Office
Building, Jack Kennedy took a few minutes to interview
Ted Sorensen, a young man from Nebraska who wanted to
work for a senator as a legislative aide. Amid the bustle and hubbub,
the two men sat and talked for a few minutes in a cramped space near
the doorway. The meeting may have been brief, but the partnership
they formed would last until Jack's death.

Eighteen months earlier, after graduating from law school at the
University of Nebraska, Sorensen had moved to Washington. According to the *New York Times:*

> He knew no one. He had no appointments, phone numbers or contacts. Except for a hitchhiking trip to Texas, he had never left the
> Midwest. He had never had a cup of coffee or written a check…after
> short stints as a junior government lawyer, he was hired by John F.

Kennedy, the new Democratic senator from Massachusetts.

Jack Kennedy was an intellectual whose process was to learn everything he could about a given topic. He needed an aide who understood and shared this approach to government. He had no interest in experts who would help him "spin" issues in the media or seek the favor of more powerful senators.

He found that man in Sorensen. Ted admired Jack's intellect and shared his hatred of war. His mother was a pacifist and he had registered with his draft board as a conscientious objector. Jack, a combat veteran, saw this as a sign of Sorensen's enlightened instincts, not as a weakness. Years later, Jack would say, "War will exist until that distant day when the conscientious objector enjoys the same reputation and prestige that the warrior does today."

Sorensen shared Jack's disdain for politicians who were little more than ideologues. From his days at Harvard to his last day in the White House, Jack believed that governing in this manner was counterproductive because it served the needs of partisan politics, not the people.

Sorensen's first assignment was to help Jack develop an economic redevelopment plan for the state. The two men studied the problem with an intellectual tenacity that would typify their long association. As always, Jack asked endless questions and picked the brains of experts. In Sorensen, he had an aide who could not only get the answers to Jack's many questions, but would also write summaries of his research in precise and informative terms.

The result was a highly sophisticated economic redevelopment plan for not only Massachusetts, but all of New England. Jack unveiled his program in three separate speeches in the Senate in May, 1953.

Each speech, said John T. Shaw, "lasted for more than two hours and was dense with details on how to ignite the region's economic revitalization."

Kennedy emphasized that he wanted to help New England in a way that was also good for the nation, as follows:

As a senator's responsibility is not only to his state but to his Nation. I think that it's proper to point out that even though many of the recommendations I have made are of special importance to New England, nevertheless, none is contrary to the national interest, but rather would, if enacted, be of benefit to all of the people no matter where they may live.

Jack concluded that the region's economic woes were caused by outmoded thinking by management in major industries. "Too often," he said, "government, management, and labor have resisted new ideas and local initiatives." The solution, he said, was not massive infusions of money by the federal government, but rather local efforts to build more modern plants and equipment.

Hubert Humphrey, a Democrat from Minnesota, said that because Jack dealt with the problem through study and factual analysis rather than political ideology he had, "set a pattern for the rest of us, showing how we can discuss the problems which we face and relate them to the total problem of the United States."

COMING TO GRIPS WITH COMMUNISM

ONE OF THE INTELLECTUAL CHALLENGES Jack set for himself in the Senate was to understand Communism from the perspective of those who had come under its influence. He traveled to nations in which Communists were seeking to influence internal affairs. These trips, said Shaw, "were not elaborately staged photo opportunities, but lengthy and grueling fact-finding missions by a man who wanted to understand the world and be respected as a foreign policy expert."

As a congressman, he had traveled to Europe several times, as well as Hong Kong, India, Indochina, Iran, Israel, Japan, Korea, Malaya, Pakistan, Thailand, and Yugoslavia.

The Asian part of this trip alone lasted for two months as Jack and his brother, Robert, traveled more than 25,000 miles. Based on these travels, he came to believe the American people and their political leaders were ignoring the importance of foreign affairs. He believed they should be encouraged to understand how events abroad could ultimately determine the quality of life at home. In a speech after his return, Jack warned that, "any Congressman, any Senator today, to be worthy of his salt must lift his vision from the immediate problems of his constituency to reach for an understanding of the role that America will play in this world."

This pattern of exhausting, intensive travel, and inquiry continued in the Senate. Returning from a trip to Poland, Jack would give speeches and write articles about what he had learned. Written with Sorensen, these articles were, "well-informed, confident and sometimes controversial," said John T. Shaw. "He placed issues in their historical content and sharpened his argument with historical analogies. Possessing a broad view, he could also dive into details."

As a voracious reader, Jack appreciated skilled writing. He had little formal training in the craft of composition, but he understood that brevity is the soul of articulate speech and prose. With Sorensen's help, he worked hard to master the art of clear expression.

Sorensen said the following about Jack's efforts to make language an effective weapon in his communication with the people:

- Words were regarded as tools of precision, to be chosen with a craftsman's care to whatever the situation required. He liked to be exact. But if the situation called for a vagueness, he would deliberately choose a word of varying interpretations rather than bury his imprecision in ponderous prose.

- He disliked verbosity and pomposity in his own remarks as much as he disliked them in others. He wanted both his message and his language to be plain and unpretentious, never patronizing. He wanted his major policy statements to be positive, specific, and definite, avoiding the use of "suggest," "perhaps" and "possible alternatives for consideration."

- He used little or no slang, dialect, legalistic terms, contractions, clichés, elaborate metaphors or ornate figures of speech. He refused to be folksy or to include any phrase or image he considered corny, tasteless, or trite.

Among the most important of Sorensen's observations of Jack were the following:

- Kennedy in 1953 was shy and unpretentious. "He did not," Sorensen wrote, "try to impress me, as office holders so often do on first meetings, with the strength of his handshake or the importance of his office, or with the sound of his voice." Kennedy, Sorensen said, "never put on an act, feigning anger or joy when he did not feel it."

▪ Kennedy did not wear his emotions on his sleeve, which masked the intensity of his feelings and concern for issues. He was, Sorensen said, much like a character in *Pilgrim's Way* by John Buchan, Jack's favorite book, who "disliked emotion, not because he felt lightly but because he felt deeply."

Referring to the sadness Kennedy had experienced, Sorensen said he possessed "an acute awareness of the most sobering kinds of tragedy. Add to this a history of illness, pain, and injury since childhood, and the fact that another sister was confined to a home for the mentally retarded, and one understands his human sensibility."

Politically, in Sorensen's view, Kennedy was:

an old-fashioned patriot, not in the narrow nationalistic sense but in his deep devotion to the national interest. He shared Buchan's belief that democracy was primarily an attitude of mind, a spiritual testament, and that politics is still the greatest and most honorable adventure.

THE PRESIDENCY AT ALL COSTS

JACK WAS ALSO A PRAGMATIC POLITICIAN who badly wanted to become president. In the Senate, he avoided taking stands on highly charged issues such as civil rights. In the White House, he would come to believe that confronting racism was a moral imperative for this nation. But as a Senator he had no such conviction. He supported bills that advanced civil rights, but he did so without passion or great commitment. Jack reasoned that if he positioned himself as a crusading liberal on civil rights, or any other controversial issue, he would, as a mere Senator, accomplish nothing, but might jeopardize his ability to work with the Southern Democrats who controlled the Senate. Above all else, he wanted a clear path to the presidency.

This obsession with becoming president also led Jack to remain silent about Joseph McCarthy, an act of political cowardice. The Republican Senator from Wisconsin terrorized the nation from 1950 to 1954, charging without cause that the U.S. government was rife with

Communists. He elevated the fear of Communism to a level that all but paralyzed the nation. It was a time when the country should have been looking for ways to co-exist with communist nations, but Mc-Carthy instead fueled our suspicion and paranoia, and we turned on each other.

In time, after McCarthyism had run its course, after the nation realized that it had been cowed into submission by a monster, the few political leaders who had spoken out against McCarthy would be hailed for their courage. Jack Kennedy was not among them. As he campaigned for the Senate in 1951, Jack kept silent about McCarthy's deplorable tactics. In an editorial, the *Boston Post* said, "Attacking him [McCarthy] in this state is regarded as a certain method of committing suicide." Jack would let nothing keep him from taking the next step on his march to the White House.

On December 2, 1954, the Senate voted to censure McCarthy. Jack Kennedy had a legitimate excuse for missing the vote; he was in serious condition in a New York hospital after doctors fused sections of his spinal vertebrae.

Later, Jack said he would have voted for censure, but he never actually condemned McCarthy. His silence amounted to tacit approval of McCarthy and his tactics. Some argued that Jack remained silent because his father and McCarthy were friends. Jack, however, had gone against his father many times on many issues. He was a principled man who honored and promoted political courage throughout his life. He believed political leaders should protect the people by warning them about threats to their welfare...yet he said nothing about Joe McCarthy.

CHAPTER TWELVE

THE MIRACLE OF 1960

*By any historical test, even apart from his unprecedented religion
and youth, Kennedy seemed likely to be defeated.*
—Ted Sorensen

MANY AMERICANS today assume that John Kennedy became president in 1960 because the voters knew that he had traveled the world and studied the art of government like few other candidates before him.

This is not the case. The nation was not sure exactly who Kennedy was or where he would take us. As he campaigned, he had not spoken in detail about his youth. He did not disclose the precarious nature of his health, fearing that this information would end his chance of becoming president. We had no idea of the suffering that he had endured, that he had nearly died several times, or that he had Addison's disease. The most important aspects of Jack's life, the events and experiences that made him the man he was, would be unknown to the public until many years after his death.

It was readily apparent that Jack was physically unlike other presidents. Harry Truman was five-feet nine-inches tall with thinning hair and a plain demeanor that could never quicken the nation's pulse. Dwight Eisenhower was admired for his lifetime of service to the nation, but he looked like everyone's favorite uncle and he had a dry persona that made him seem ordinary.

Kennedy shattered that mold. He was tall and new and sleek and bold. He was also putting on weight, filling out as he approached middle age. Inga Arvad had said of him, "He had the charm that makes the birds come out of their trees…thick mop of hair, blue eyes, natural, engaging, warm and when he walked into a room you knew he was there, not pushing, not dominating but exuding animal magnetism."

Still, in the 1960 presidential election, there were actually more reasons to vote against Kennedy than to vote for him. Newspapers warned that as the first Catholic president, he would allow his religious beliefs to influence his stewardship of the nation. One editorial suggested he might take orders "from the Pope of Rome."

There were also whispers that Joe Kennedy, by now one of the richest men in the country, was desperate to obtain the political power that had eluded him for so long and would make policy decisions from behind the scenes.

Newspaper and magazine editors and publishers across the nation endorsed his opponent, Richard Nixon, by a six to one margin, warning that the nation would pay a price for electing an untested man, rather than the more seasoned Nixon. The influential *New York Times* gave Kennedy a mild endorsement.

There was simply no good reason for the nation to put Kennedy in the White House in 1960. The average age of the 34 presidents before him was 55. At 43, he was a dozen years younger than this average; he would be the youngest man ever elected president.

His Republican predecessor, Dwight Eisenhower, had left office on a sour note. The Paris Peace Talks of 1960 were supposed to lessen the growing tensions of the Cold War, but a few weeks before the talks were to begin, a U.S. spy plane was shot down 1,300 miles inside Soviet territory.

The pilot was captured and put on trial in Moscow. The talks went ahead, but Soviet leader Nikita Khrushchev publicly berated Eisenhower and then stormed out of the talks, leaving the five-star general embarrassed and helpless.

Eisenhower had paid scant attention to economic issues, resulting in seven periods of recession during his eight years in office. Now the economy was weakening once again at the end of his term.

Despite these failures, Ike retained his popularity; the people liked him and did not eagerly welcome the end of his administration. If the law had not limited the president to two terms, he likely would have beaten anyone who ran against him in 1960, including John Kennedy.

Nixon was the beneficiary of Eisenhower's popularity. He represented the logical extension of Ike's style of government, and he had been in the public eye since he became vice-president in 1953.

Nixon had more experience in domestic and world affairs than Kennedy, and he had established himself as a fierce opponent of Communism. Americans felt no sense of urgency to elect a Democrat like Kennedy to restore economic growth or confront the Soviets.

Ted Sorensen said, "By any historical test, even apart from his unprecedented religion and youth, Kennedy seemed likely to be defeated" in 1960.

How then did this untested 43-year-old man manage to become president?

Was it because there were 17 million more registered Democrats than Republicans in the United States in 1960? This was certainly an advantage, but many Democrats believed that Kennedy was either too liberal or not liberal enough, and this divisiveness muted his party's numerical advantage.

Was it because he had publicly confronted the subject of his Catholicism? During the campaign, he had said, "I believe in an America where the separation of church and state is absolute, where no Catholic prelate would tell the president how to act, and no Protestant minister would tell his parishioners for whom to vote."

This helped his cause somewhat, but religious intolerance remained a major obstacle to his presidency, as Protestants in the United States vastly outnumbered Catholics.

Kennedy's wealth was also an advantage, but in fact, Nixon had received larger campaign donations from business leaders and the wealthy.

Kennedy's choice of Lyndon Johnson as his running mate helped him carry Texas, a major boost to his electoral vote tally. Liberal Democrats, however, disliked Johnson, judging him a man of crude sensibilities and no friend of liberal thought. He was also lesser known than Nixon's running mate, Henry Cabot Lodge.

There was also a segment of the population, it is impossible to say how large, that felt Kennedy was more cerebral than Nixon. Kennedy talked about "the people's responsibilities in America" and said he would not coddle us, but rather challenge us to meet these responsibilities.

Nixon, in contrast, spoke in platitudes and offered party slogans rather than progressive ideas. Kennedy once commented that Nixon found inspiration for his speeches in *Poor Richard's Almanac*, a collection of seasonal weather forecasts, practical household hints, puzzles, and other amusements.

Did Kennedy's vow to ask Americans to meet their responsibilities as citizens put him in the White House? That is unlikely. "The people were not sure about a candidate who asked them to make sacrifices," said historian Arthur Schlesinger Jr. "They were going back and forth; the lead changed every day. If the campaign had lasted another few days, Kennedy might have lost."

Just weeks before the election, Kennedy's candidacy received a surprise boost when Martin Luther King Jr. was arrested in Atlanta as he led a rally against segregation in a department store restaurant. King now sat in handcuffs and leg irons in a state prison.

King's wife feared that her husband would be murdered in prison. She called Harris Wofford, Kennedy's civil rights aide, and asked for Kennedy's help. Wofford suggested that Kennedy call Mrs. King and express concern for her husband's safety, and Kennedy agreed.

Word of the call spread through the black community. Robert Kennedy, at first angry that his brother had risked losing votes in the South, became distressed by the injustice of King's imprisonment. He, too, made a call on King's behalf.

King went free shortly after these calls, prompting his father, who had supported Nixon, to switch to Kennedy. Kennedy captured 70 percent of the black vote, which contributed to his razor thin victory in the popular vote.

Still, this was not enough to put him over the top.

THE MAGIC OF TELEVISION

I F A MAN NAMED Philo Taylor Farnsworth had not been born in a log cabin in the wilderness of Utah in 1906, it is unlikely that John Kennedy would have defeated Richard Nixon in 1960.

The American people largely ignored the issues in 1960 and voted for either the man they liked more as a person, or the man they saw as the more attractive. The campaign was, if not a beauty contest, a clash of personalities and physical appeal that tilted heavily in favor of Kennedy.

Farnsworth made this possible. He was a genius, a self-educated farm boy. While still in high school, he had devised a way to electronically scan images and transmit them to a new medium called "television."

This miraculous invention allowed voters to see and hear presidential candidates in a live format. In this medium, Kennedy found the edge he needed to defeat Nixon. He had been blessed with a handsome face, charm, and eloquence. In contrast, Nixon appeared uncomfortable in his own skin, frozen in formality. Norman Mailer once described him as looking like a stern deacon of a midwestern church who would eject an unruly boy from a service...and twist his ear once outside.

Both men were young, but Nixon, as historian Richard Reeves later observed, came across as "an old man's idea of a young man, eager to please his elders."

The two men had engaged in four live, televised debates. In the first debate, in his opening remarks, Kennedy made it clear that he rejected the Republican contention that big government would ruin the nation, an ideological belief later made dominant by Ronald Reagan.

Instead of railing against government, Kennedy stressed his belief in the importance of civic responsibility. He said:

> I know that there are those who say that we want to turn everything over to the government. I don't at all. I want the individuals to meet their responsibilities and I want the States to meet their responsibilities. But I think there is also a national responsibility.

> The argument [against government] has been used against every piece of social legislation in the last 25 years...I don't believe in big government, but I believe in effective governmental action, and I think that's the only way that the United States is going to maintain its freedom; it's the only way that we're going to move ahead.

Still, this wisdom was not the reason for Kennedy's victory. It was the difference in their physical appearance in the first debate, rather than the issues they discussed, that determined the outcome of the election.

When Jack arrived at the set for the debate, he noticed its light gray background. He sent an aide back to his hotel to fetch a suit that did not clash with this color.

122 · All His Bright Light Gone

Even on the black and white televisions of the era, Jack appeared healthy and vigorous. Nixon had jammed his knee into a car door during the campaign, and his wound had become infected. His knee bothered him during the debate. The camera at one point caught him wiping sweat from his upper lip. His shirt collar was too big and he seemed to be swimming in his suit.

In contrast, Kennedy was tanned and refused to use makeup. Simply because Kennedy had declined, Nixon also turned away the make-up man. We would learn years later that throughout his life, Nixon had avoided looking at himself in a mirror.

Perhaps because he had a self-destructive streak, Nixon failed to comprehend what other politicians had already learned: television was the most effective way to reach the people. He was still attached to the idea of whistle-stop campaigning. By 1960, the vast majority of American families owned televisions. Nixon, however, believed "the novelty" of this new political tool had worn off.

More than 70 million Americans watched the debate. The attendance at all previous presidential debates in history added together would still be a fraction of this number. The viewers were already familiar with Nixon; they watched in such record numbers because they were curious about the handsome young man from Massachusetts.

Thus, it was television that allowed Kennedy to prevail in a heart-stopping race. The term "cliffhanger" hardly does justice to the excitement and tension of that long night. At first, Nixon was in the lead because the vote in the big cities, where Kennedy had an advantage, was light, while the vote among Southern Protestants was heavy. Then Kennedy pulled ahead by an eyelash and held the margin until 10:00 a.m., when Nixon again pulled ahead.

Finally, victories in Minnesota, Pennsylvania, Illinois, Missouri, and Michigan gave Kennedy 303 electoral votes to Nixon's 219 votes. He also had 119,000 more popular votes than Nixon. John Kennedy became president, as the *New York Times* said the morning after the election, "by the astonishing margin of less than two votes per voting precinct." If just two voters in each of the nation's 165,826 voting precincts had voted for Richard Nixon, Kennedy would have been defeated.

Kennedy had gone to bed at 4:00 a.m., before the final result was known, and did not learn that he had won until his wife and daughter, Caroline, awoke him the next morning with, "Good morning, Mr. President!"

When asked to explain his improbable victory, Jack called it "a miracle."

FAMILY MATTERS

TELEVISION ALSO ALLOWED the Kennedy family to fill an emotional need for some Americans. Jack's mother was devoted to the needs of her nine children, and the media constantly reminded voters of her maternal vigilance. When the children went swimming off Cape Cod, for example, Rose Kennedy made them wear distinctive bathing caps so she could see where they were at all times. She recorded their medical histories on index cards, making them available to doctors when medical attention became necessary.

At the head of this seemingly perfect family was Joe Kennedy, the millionaire with a checkered past who ferociously protected his brood. Jack's sisters helped him perfect his speaking style, straightened his tie, and nagged him to tuck in his shirt. Bobby Kennedy became his campaign manager; he would march into hell for his brother. Ted Kennedy worked tirelessly on his brother's behalf.

If we could not ourselves have a family like this, we could at least elevate to high office a handsome, charming member of a family that clearly loved and supported each other. Letting the public vicariously bask in the warmth of such a loving family was a political strategy that helped Kennedy move effortlessly from Congress to the Senate to the White House. He offered Americans family values we could observe for ourselves, not merely an abstract slogan.

CHAPTER THIRTEEN

THE WORLD THAT AWAITED HIM

When we hang the capitalists, they will sell us the rope we use.
—Joseph Stalin.

AS INAUGURATION DAY APPROACHED, as he contemplated the issues he would face as the nation's 35th president, John Kennedy would not have been blamed if he feigned an illness and retired to a tropical beach.

Just 15 years earlier, the United States, war-weary and unwilling to send 100,000 young men to their deaths during an invasion of Japan, had dropped atom bombs on Hiroshima and Nagasaki and ended the bloody war in the Pacific in a matter of days.

Now, in 1960, both the United States and the Soviet Union possessed stockpiles of weapons even more powerful than those dropped on Japan. With the push of a button, missiles could be sent across continents or launched from submarines. A humorist of the era said it was like two men standing in a basement knee-deep in gasoline, each holding a box of matches.

THE RED MENACE

THE SEEDS OF THIS CONFLICT had been planted centuries earlier. From 1513 to 1917, tsars and wealthy landowners had maintained an iron grip on Russia, controlling the land and natural resources that generated the nation's wealth. The working class and peasants, however, endured endless cycles of poverty, isolation, and famine.

Then in 1848, two German philosophers living in England, Karl Marx and Friedrich Engels, offered the Russian masses a way out of their misery. In *The Communist Manifesto*, they urged workers to overthrow the ruling class and allow the state to own and control property and the creation of wealth. If people broke the chains that kept them in poverty, Marx said, they could live in an egalitarian society with no distinct social classes, no poverty, no haves and have nots.

In 1917, festering contempt for the imperious rule of Tsar Nicholas II finally exploded into revolution. Food shortages had brought the population close to starvation, prompting dissidents to demand a relaxation of tsarist rule.

But Nicholas clung to his belief that he had a God-given right to rule and that the masses must bend to his will.

On February 23, protesters in St. Petersburg shut down the city's factories and shops. Workers went on strike. The police and military units ordered by Nicholas to put down the protests instead joined the mutiny. Enraged by the appalling conditions in their land and the tsar's inept handling of Russia's involvement in World War I, revolutionary army units took control of the city. Nicholas was arrested as he rushed back from the front lines of the war. In July of the following year, Nicholas and his family were murdered, bringing to an end the rule of the Romanovs after more than three hundred years.

What followed was total political and social chaos, as different factions, with differing views of what Russia should become, struggled for dominance. Into this turmoil, from exile in Switzerland, stepped Vladimir Lenin, a dedicated Communist.

On October 24, Lenin and his supporters seized control of St. Petersburg. The following day, with barely a shot fired, they took over the seat of Russian government, the Winter Palace.

More than 15 million people lost their lives during the next four years as the Bolsheviks, or Communists, struggled with anti-Communists for power. In the end, Lenin prevailed. The Soviet Union, a Communist state, was established in 1922. Two years later, Russia was renamed the Union of Soviet Socialist Republics. Lenin died that same year and his ruthless colleague, Joseph Stalin, took control of the ruling Communist Party.

For the next 17 years, Stalin struggled to implement the Communist system in the vast country he ruled, but his efforts were futile. State ownership of the economy failed to produce the economic utopia its architects had promised, because Communism lacks a mechanism for producing the investment capital that is generated efficiently by capitalism.

LEGITIMIZED BY WAR

LIKE ADOLF HITLER, Stalin was profoundly disturbed, possessing a paranoid personality and a sociopath's inability to comprehend the suffering he caused. For 30 years, he stifled dissents with mass murder, torture, show trials, and purges. He committed his crimes in a closed society; they were largely unknown to the rest of the world until after his death. If not for World War II, he would have been just another in a long list of loathsome killers of his own people. Most likely, in time, he would have been murdered in the dead of night when his cruelty finally became intolerable.

He was, however, an effective military strategist. In 1941, Hitler sent three million soldiers into the Soviet Union. Initially, the Nazis were unstoppable, advancing to within a few miles of Moscow. While the brutal Russian winter halted the fighting, Stalin built the Soviet war machine and brutally hardened his generals and his ground troops. Commanders who lost decisive battles were executed; soldiers who deserted were shot. With this "win or die" imperative driving them, the Soviets encircled the Germans at Stalingrad in 1942, winning the bloodiest battle in the history of warfare and shattering Hitler's dreams of conquest.

In 1944–1945, as his forces pursued the broken German army across Eastern Europe, Stalin gained control of Poland, Romania, Bulgaria, Austria, Hungary, Czechoslovakia, and Finland. After the war, it became apparent that he intended to remain in these countries and impose Communism upon them.

In America, apprehension about the spread of Communism began to replace the joy felt after the surrender of Germany and Japan. Our Founding Fathers had created a country in which individual rights were cherished. Its economy was based on private ownership, not state ownership, of the means of production, and we transferred political power in free elections.

But in the Soviet Union, the individual had no rights, and its dictators ruled as long as they could hold on to power. America was held together by the glue of its morality, while the Soviet Union was held together by terror and enforced conformity. Communism had promised social equality, but it had produced only bloodshed, fear, and death.

At first, America's reaction to Soviet aggression was optimistic. Franklin Roosevelt, physically and mentally exhausted after more than two decades of powerful leadership, had become a weakened man as the war ended. He believed the Soviets would honor the promise they had made at the Yalta Conference in 1945, when they agreed to create parliamentary governments in the eastern European nations they occupied.

Roosevelt died on April 12, 1945, and his successor, Harry Truman, had no such illusions about the Soviets. He correctly believed that they would never relinquish power in their satellites and would aggressively seek to expand their influence to Western Europe and beyond.

In 1946, Winston Churchill, now a private citizen, traveled to the United States to deliver a speech in a small town in Missouri. Two words in his speech captured the attention of the entire world:

> From Stettin in the Baltic to Trieste in the Adriatic, an iron curtain has descended across the Continent. Behind that line lie all the capitals of the ancient states of Central and Eastern Europe. Warsaw, Berlin, Prague, Vienna, Budapest, Belgrade, Bucharest and Sofia, all these famous cities and the populations around them lie in what I must call the Soviet sphere, and all are subject in one form or another, not only to Soviet influence but to a very high and, in many cases, increasing measure of control from Moscow.

The image of a powerful enemy holding entire nations captive behind an "iron curtain" alarmed the people and policy makers in the United States The nation became preoccupied with a single question: Will Soviet tyrants attempt to take over the world?

In 1947, U.S. foreign policy became openly defiant toward the Soviets. President Truman pledged support to "free peoples who are resisting attempted subjugation by armed minorities or by outside pressure." He sent massive amounts of military and economic aid to

Greece and Turkey, where the Communists were using guerrilla warfare to try to topple existing governments.

That same year, Secretary of State George Marshall formulated a plan to make American aid available to all European nations to keep them from the clutches of the Communists. "It is logical," Marshall said, "that the United States should do whatever it is able to do to assist in the return of normal economic health in the world, without which there can be no political stability and no assured peace."

Stalin countered by also sending money and materials to Soviet satellite nations. This began a contest between the two nations to win the allegiance of recovering nations in Europe by giving them economic aid.

THE COLD WAR

IN 1947, INFLUENTIAL NEWSPAPER columnist Walter Lippmann wrote a book called *The Cold War.* The title was soon used to describe the ideological struggle between the United States and the Soviet Union. Americans believed the Soviets would try to dominate the world by taking over many small countries around the globe.

For a few years after the fighting in Europe ended, the United States was the most powerful nation on earth. It possessed the lion's share of the world's natural resources, the most enlightened form of government ever devised by man, the most efficient economic system ever devised by man, and the most powerful weapon ever devised by man, the atom bomb.

By comparison, the Soviet Union possessed vast natural resources but lacked the industrial capacity to develop them. Its agrarian economy had been ruined by the cost of fighting the war; it possessed a powerful army, but its people were captives of a morally repugnant system of government.

This changed on August 29, 1949, when the Soviets exploded their own implosion-type nuclear bomb. The Soviet people had suffered famine and harsh repression and were governed by monsters. But suddenly, they were citizens of the second most powerful nation in the world.

In March 1953, Joseph Stalin suffered a stroke and died. After a bloody power struggle, Nikita Khrushchev became first secretary of the Communist Party and in 1958 the head of the Soviet government as well. The bomb gave him the leverage to step up Soviet expansion beyond Europe to emerging nations around the world.

Many of these nations were struggling to survive. If they accepted Soviet money and materials, they would have to accept a Soviet presence in their countries. Communists could then work their way into positions of power so they could later exploit the country's resources and economy.

There was nothing altruistic about the Soviet offers to help impoverished nations; it was a way to strengthen its own failing economy. Satellite nations could become pawns used in the ideological struggle with the United States.

In 1956, Khrushchev said about America, "We will dig you in," which was loosely translated as "We will bury you." He was referring to a statement in the Communist Manifesto that read, "What the bourgeoisie therefore produces, above all, are its own grave-diggers. Its fall and the victory of the proletariat are equally inevitable."

In America, politicians began launching their careers by pandering to the "us versus them" sentiment generated by Khrushchev's comment. They solemnly warned that if Soviet aggression around the world went unchecked, Americans would one day wake up and find the occupying forces of "Godless Communism" marching through their towns.

At a news conference in April, 1954, speaking about Soviet aggression in Indochina, President Eisenhower intentionally inflamed America's fear that Communism was spreading around the world like a cancer when he said:

> Finally, you have broader considerations that might follow what you would call the "falling domino" principle. You have a row of dominoes set up, you knock over the first one, and what will happen to the last one is the certainty that it will go over very quickly. So you could have a beginning of a disintegration that would have the most profound influences.

The notion that if the Soviets managed to convert one foreign nation to Communism, surrounding nations would soon do the same became known as the domino theory. Objective political leaders who studied the issue understood that the concept had some merit, but they also knew that Communism was not as monolithic as many feared. Foreign countries usually accepted aide from the Soviets because they were desperate, not because they admired or even understood the concepts of Communism. Rice farmers in Vietnam worried about feeding their families, not geopolitics.

But intelligent politicians kept their views to themselves, fearing they would be called "soft on Communism."

In this atmosphere, rational discussion of the actual threat posed by Communism became impossible. During the 1950s, Communism was viewed as an unstoppable force of evil that would spread without opposition through any third world country in which it was introduced. Little allowance was made for the notion that some nations might reject Soviet advances for moral or economic reasons, or that they sought independence, not domination. Any emerging nation that embraced Communism soon became our "enemy."

As the 1960s approached, there were a few political groups around the world who feared Communism would eventually dominate the entire human race. Rather than die in a nuclear holocaust that preceded this takeover, they believed the major powers should capitulate to Communism. They adopted the slogan "better red than dead." Those who opposed this "cowardly" surrender countered by reversing the slogan to "better dead than red."

Guiding the United States through the minefields of the Cold War would be John Kennedy's major responsibility. It would prove be a difficult task. The Soviets had taken control of Eastern Europe; Mao Tsetung, a Communist revolutionary, ruled China; and in 1950, North Korea, with close ties to Communist China, invaded South Korea. The "Red Menace" was spreading to Cuba, Laos, some emerging African nations, and Vietnam.

JIM CROW AMERICA

WHILE THE COLD WAR was the most potentially dangerous issue Kennedy faced, racism was also an urgent concern, silently eating away at the nation's sense of morality. "Jim Crow," the term used to describe laws designed to enforce segregation, was an ugly stain on the nation.

In the years after World War II, the nation had gone through sweeping social and demographic changes. Couples were getting married in much greater numbers than ever before, and they were having more children at an earlier age than their grandparents did. After four years of death and destruction around the world, there was an urgency attached to creating new life and new families, unlike anything the nation had ever experienced.

Black couples were part of this "baby boom." Many of them had fled the discrimination and violence they faced in the South to start families in Northern cities. But these cities practiced segregation, forcing blacks into menial jobs.

Soon, white families began an exodus from large cities and moved into the suburbs, where jobs were abundant, housing was affordable, and blacks were easily excluded. This "white flight" was a symptom of the fears and racism that infected the nation.

The black race began to fight back. On December 1, 1955, a 43-year-old woman name Rosa Parks boarded a bus in Montgomery, Alabama. She took the last available seat in the "colored" section of the bus. When a white passenger entered the bus, the driver ordered Parks to give up her seat. She refused and was arrested and charged with civil disobedience.

Parks was not the first black person to defy segregation on a city bus, but she possessed the courage to take the matter to court, attracting the attention of Martin Luther King Jr., who had recently become a minister in Montgomery. With his involvement, the civil rights movement was born.

Few people in 1960 possessed the insight to understand the cruel environment in which black Americans were forced to live and the toll these conditions took on them. Living in ghettos, black men and women earned far less than whites did. They had little opportunity to receive the training needed for skilled jobs. The medical care available to them was substandard, as was the level of education, nutrition, sanitation, and crime prevention.

White Americans living in the suburbs had jobs that allowed them to buy cars and appliances. Employment also provided health insurance and pensions. Whites were able to give their children the means to achieve prosperity and pride in themselves. Their children were well-nourished, educated, and secure.

This was the world that awaited President Kennedy in 1960. A nuclear war in which the survivors would envy the dead was getting closer, and black Americans were still living in bondage a century after the writing of the Emancipation Proclamation. To complicate matters, the economy was faltering, with a painful downturn on the horizon.

What the nation needed desperately was a leader capable of defusing rather than exacerbating tensions that could lead to a nuclear war. He would also have to understand that, as the writer James Baldwin said, "…Ignorance allied with power is the most ferocious enemy justice can have."

134

President Kennedy informs the nation about the growing problems in Laos and Vietnam. He believed the president should give the people information free of what he called "doctrinaire beliefs." To that end, in less than three years he held more than 60 press conferences. Photo by Abbie Rowe

PART THREE

THE NATION KENNEDY WAS BUILDING

CHAPTER FOURTEEN

AN IDEALIST WITHOUT ILLUSIONS

With a good conscience our only sure reward, with history
the final judge of our deeds, let us go forth to lead the land we
love, asking His blessing and His help, but knowing that
here on earth God's work must truly be our own.
—John F. Kennedy, Inaugural Address

WHAT SHOULD WE MAKE OF JOHN KENNEDY at this point in our journey through his life and times, as he prepared to assume the burdens of the presidency?

He was the product of his fragile health, the unique nature of his family, his wartime experiences, his extensive travel, his physical and emotional suffering, and his innate intelligence.

As a young boy, his heroes were characters in *Ivanhoe* and the *Knights of the Round Table,* who introduced him to the concept of chivalry. As he lay in bed daydreaming, he merged chivalry into government. Political leaders became knights who protected the people, not with a sword or lance, but rather with their heroic defense of the common good.

Kennedy grew into a young man determined to become a public servant. Despite his precarious health, he forced his way into combat. He was a PT boat skipper who urged his crew "to get involved in the process" of democracy. He became a man who would stay up all night reading a crate full of books on labor law because he wanted to master the issues that determine the quality of life in the United States.

As he went out into the world, however, Kennedy began to see cracks in his idealistic view of government. Leaders in France and Great Britain did not have the courage to warn the people about the looming danger of Nazi Germany. Kennedy vowed not to let a similar lack of courage cause harm to the United States.

Then, during his years in Congress, Kennedy learned that political leaders are capable of making decisions, not according to the merits of a particular issue, but rather according to their ideological beliefs. And to his horror, during his fight to obtain adequate housing for his constituents, he realized that some of his peers were capable of putting self-enrichment above the needs of the people, using ideology to conceal their greed.

Slowly, he realized that our government will never operate exactly as it was originally designed. Still, he reasoned, it must be preserved; we must come as close as possible to the principles that gave us birth, because they insulate the American people from economic and political slavery.

When his wife asked him to define his political philosophy, he said that he was "an idealist without illusions."

Kennedy's fierce determination to govern with rational idealism is what drove him to travel the back roads of Massachusetts in pain. It is what compelled him to read and research issues in depth and learn to write and speak with precision. It is what made him refuse to hide behind pre-determined beliefs and instead use his intellect to understand the issues that determine the quality of our lives. It is what made him consider the needs of both his state and his nation when he made decisions in the House and Senate. It is what made him pursue the presidency with such urgency, before death caught up with him.

THE SPEECH THAT DEFINED AMERICA

AND RATIONAL IDEALISM was also behind what Kennedy devotees today refer to simply as "the speech."

A nor'easter swept through Washington the night before Kennedy's inauguration, leaving eight inches of snow on the ground. Flame throwers were brought out of storage to melt the snow on Pennsylvania Avenue so the new president could make his way to the Capitol and take the oath of office.

By noon, the sky was clear and bright. Dressed in formal cutaway tails, but without a coat or hat to ward off the cold, Kennedy gave the nation a brief but elegant address, a product of the years he had spent studying the nature of our government and the hours he had spent with Sorensen perfecting a writing style that mobilized the power of brevity.

The speech sent chills down the spines of those who understood what he was trying to accomplish. Its 29 paragraphs reflected his belief that a president must govern as if the nation faced constant threats, and that an alert, informed nation, ready to embrace its civic responsibilities, was the key to meeting these threats. That is what the famous phrase, "Ask not what your country can do for you, ask what you can do for your country," was all about. He was introducing us to his vision of idealism, which involved making civic responsibility a vital component of patriotism.

This became clear when he said:

> In your hands, my fellow citizens, more than mine, will rest the final success or failure of our course. Since this country was founded, each generation of Americans has been summoned to give testimony to its national loyalty. The graves of young Americans who answered the call to service surround the globe.
>
> Now the trumpet summons us again—not as a call to bear arms, though arms we need—not as a call to battle, though embattled we are—but a call to bear the burden of a long twilight struggle, year in and year out, rejoicing in hope, patient in tribulation—a struggle against the common enemies of man: tyranny, poverty, disease and war itself.

As Kennedy intended, the speech awakened the idealism that lies deep within the psyche of the American people. A *New York Times* editorial said, "The evangelical and transcendental spirit of America has not been better expressed since Woodrow Wilson and maybe not since Ralph Waldo Emerson. For, like all true expressions of the American ideal, this was a revolutionary document."

Eleanor Roosevelt, who had publicly doubted Kennedy's ability to govern, told the new president, "I think gratitude best describes the kind of liberation and lift to the listener to which you gave. I have re-read your words several times and I have been filled with thankfulness."

The *Albany Times Union* said, "The Inaugural will be recalled and quoted as long as there are Americans to heed its summons."

All of this was testimony to the fact that John Kennedy's life had been a perfect training ground for the presidency. The little boy who studied government in his sickbed had discovered that when we take pride in our government, we become proud of our country and ourselves.

Kennedy had reached his goal: he had captured the White House before death caught up with him. He possessed uncommon intelligence, a sophisticated knowledge of government, and an unbreakable desire to serve.

Now the real work would begin. He had to build a nation that would rise above the lunacy of the Cold War, make its economy productive, and honor the rights of all its citizens. In a remarkably short time, in each of these areas, he pointed this nation in the right direction.

CHAPTER FIFTEEN

A BEACON TO THE WORLD

What your government believes is its own business; what it does in the world is the world's business.
—John F. Kennedy in a letter to Nikita Khrushchev in 1961

THE UNITED STATES AND MUCH OF THE WORLD did not disappear in a nuclear holocaust during the Cold War because President Kennedy suppressed the ancient impulse to use war to resolve the differences between nations.

He did this with an elegantly conceived foreign policy. It was based on his belief that war with the Soviets must be avoided at all costs, and that the United States should be held aloft as a beacon of freedom and prosperity for other nations to follow.

He did not always possess this enlightened view. During the 1950s, Kennedy made his share of pedestrian, hawkish, politically motivated speeches about Communism. He was the quintessential cold warrior. In 1957, he charged that the nation's defense budget had been "slashed away at, hacked, clipped, stretched out, cut back and frozen," by Eisenhower and his fellow Republicans who were ignoring "the star and the moons…the Red Star on Soviet moons."

He may have been influenced by his Catholicism, which utterly rejected Communism. In 1937, Pope Pius XI said that it "aims at upsetting the social order and at undermining the very foundations of Christian civilization."

Gradually, however, particularly during his second term in the Senate, Kennedy developed a more sophisticated worldview. Sorensen said that he observed a change in his attitudes, "as he learned by experience, grew in wisdom and mastered those complexities he had previously oversimplified."

As he matured, Sorensen said that Kennedy:

> Dealt with the factual, the rational, and the realistic. He insisted on making careful distinctions—between different kinds of Communist countries, for example, or between differing stages of development in various Latin-American countries—instead of lumping superficial similarities under one label.

> Above all, he believed in retaining a choice—not a choice between "Red or dead," or holocaust and humiliation, but a variety of military options in the event of aggression, an opportunity for time and maneuver in the instruments of diplomacy, and a balanced approach to every crisis which combined both defense and diplomacy.

Reflecting this view was a speech Senator Kennedy gave at Washington University in 1958. He said:

> We must face the fact that the United States is neither omnipotent nor omniscient...that we cannot impose our will upon the other 94 percent of mankind—that we cannot right every wrong or reverse each adversity—and that therefore there cannot be an American solution to every world problem.

This was a major departure from the rigid posture of the Truman and Eisenhower administrations. Many intelligent, highly educated men who had served these presidents as foreign policy advisers viewed Communism as a monolithic system that must be eliminated.

Allen Dulles, head of the Central Intelligence Agency (CIA), for example, believed the Soviets would not stop until they had taken over the world. He often ranted about "Godless Communism." If it took a full-scale nuclear war to remove this malignancy, so be it. He believed that any country that accepted Soviet aid was part of a global conspiracy directed by the Kremlin.

PERFECTING AMERICA

KENNEDY, HOWEVER, ROSE ABOVE THIS HYSTERIA. In their book, *John F. Kennedy: A Sense of Purpose,* Charles Markmann and Mark Sherwin said:

> Kennedy views the Presidency as a mission. His own task, as he conceives it...is the extension of the American concept of freedom and opportunity to the entire world. The American example, in Kennedy's thinking, must be purged of flaws if it is to be held up to other nations as a goal; as it is brought closer to the ideal it must by its own merit ultimately become the goal of all who have the freedom to choose.

> Therefore, he considers it part of his mission to do everything possible to make that freedom available to those to whom it is denied. He counts on the good sense of self-preservation of the American people to help him carry forward his social planning; he counts on the traditional idealism of the American people to help him overcome poverty and bondage in other countries.

Kennedy's idealism and sophisticated social planning was put to the test immediately. He did not have a "honeymoon" period in which he could ease into the presidency. Instead, a series of momentous Cold War events rushed toward him at lightning speed the minute he walked into the Oval Office. A magazine writer said that while the new president was "still trying to move in the furniture...he found the roof falling in and the doors blowing off."

The architect of this drama was Nikita Khrushchev. After World War II, the city of Berlin had been divided into two sectors, with the Allied powers controlling West Berlin and the Soviets controlling East Berlin.

The economy in the Soviet sector had stagnated after the war while economic growth in the Western sector had been strong. Thousands of East Berliners, desperate to improve their lives and escape harassment by Soviet secret police, were fleeing across the open border to West Berlin.

In 1958, Khrushchev, embarrassed by this public repudiation of Communism, fearing the loss of skilled workers and professionals would make the economy in East Berlin even weaker, declared that if the Allied powers did not withdraw from West Berlin within six months, he would cut off access to East Berlin.

President Eisenhower had ignored his ultimatum, but it was still an open threat as Kennedy took office. The situation in Berlin was dangerous, the most likely flash point for war, because both superpowers had troops stationed within yards of each other at the border between the two sectors.

Communication between Khrushchev and Eisenhower came to an end after the U-2 incident in May, 1960. In his inaugural speech, Kennedy opened the door to renewed talks with Moscow, suggesting that both sides "explore what problems unite us instead of belaboring those problems which divide us."

In January, 1961, Khrushchev rebuffed Kennedy's overture with a stunning announcement. In a bellicose speech, he said the Soviets intended to wage wars of "national liberation" in emerging nations around the world.

The meaning was clear: he would step up his efforts to spread Communism in Europe, Southeast Asia, Africa, and the Caribbean.

Alarmed, Kennedy met with officials from the Pentagon and State Department to address Khrushchev's threat. He was, according to Sorensen, "stunned by what he heard" from the experts, who assured him that Khrushchev was not bluffing. The Communists were already on the move. Nations in Africa and Latin America were taking aid from both the United States and the Soviet Union, playing both sides against each other, and Communism was taking hold in Laos, Vietnam, and Cuba.

Khrushchev's Berlin ultimatum, coupled with his pledge to fight wars of national liberation, inflamed Cold War fears that the Soviets were building a global empire that would eventually dominate the United States. Khrushchev was reaffirming his earlier pledge to "bury" the United States under an avalanche of Communism.

Kennedy sent copies of Khrushchev's speech to his top White House and military aides with an order to "read, mark, learn and inwardly digest" the Soviet leader's words. He told them to form study groups and provide him with their best strategies for a response to Khrushchev.

When he received the advice of his advisers, Kennedy was horrified. For years, the military had been perfecting a strategy of "massive retaliation" by B-29 bombers and intercontinental ballistic missiles if a war ever began.

But now, whipped into hysteria by Khrushchev's acts of aggression, the Joint Chiefs of Staff wanted Kennedy to make the first move. They exhorted him not to think about retaliation, but rather to launch a preemptive nuclear strike that would destroy the Soviet Union. Repeatedly, they told Kennedy, "You can't let Khrushchev get away with this."

The eagerness of the Joint Chiefs to fight a nuclear war disturbed Kennedy. "The military," he told his aide Dave Powers, "should want to make peace as urgently as it wants to make war." He refused to consider a sneak attack on the Soviet Union.

Ted Sorensen said Kennedy believed that:

> a policy of preemptive first strike or "preventive war" was no longer open to either side, inasmuch as even a surprise missile attack would trigger, before those missiles reached their targets, a devastating retaliation that neither country could risk or accept. Nor had either country developed a reliable missile defense against missiles or even the prospect of acquiring one, despite claims on both sides to the contrary.

"No matter who fired first or was annihilated last, there will be no winners," Kennedy said.

In his speeches and public comments, Kennedy turned the avoidance of war into a drumbeat. Repeatedly, he expressed the following sentiment in differing ways:

> Because of the ingenuity of science and man's own inability to control his relationships with one another, we happen to live in the most dangerous time in the human race. The world has long since passed the time when armed conflict can be the solution to international problems.

Kennedy toured a Strategic Air Command base and was shown a massive 20-megaton bomb. He asked incredulously, "Why do we need one of these?"

After a meeting in which his generals had exhorted him to vaporize an estimated three hundred million people, Kennedy turned to Secretary of State Dean Rusk and said, "And we call ourselves members of the human race." Later, speaking of his military advisers, he told an aide, "Keep those people away from me. They are crazy."

Kennedy stood alone against the entrenched, mindless fear of Communism. Economist Murray N. Rothbard, in a magazine article called *The Myth of Monolithic Communism,* described the ideological view held by so many political leaders as follows:

> For decades it was an axiom of conservative faith that international Communism was and must be a monolith, that Communism in all its aspects and manifestations was simply pure evil (because it was "atheistic" and/or totalitarian by definition), and that therefore all Communism was necessarily the same...This meant that all Communist parties everywhere were of necessity simply "agents of Moscow," which was true only during the 1930s and most of the 1940s.

> There are...vast differences among the various Communist regimes throughout the globe, divergences that literally spell the difference between life and death for a large part of their subject populations. If we want to find out about the world we live in, therefore, it is no longer enough...to simply equate Communism with badness, and let it go at that.

Rothbard believed the key to understanding Communism was finding out about the world we live in. This was an undertaking that Kennedy truly loved. He had visited many of the nations the Soviets wanted to dominate, not to seek publicity, but rather to see firsthand how they responded to Soviet aggression. He refused to lump the nations that accepted Soviet aide into the category of rogue nations who opposed the interests of the United States.

In 1954, Kennedy said, "The existence of inherently good, bad, or backward nations" was one of the "myths" of foreign policy that should be considered outmoded and unproductive. He realized that the spread of Communism must be dealt with on a country-by-country basis, not according to the simplistic, uncompromising belief that it must be destroyed.

This wisdom made Kennedy's initial response to Khrushchev's wars of liberation speech a pivotal moment in the Cold War. In a private letter, Kennedy made it clear to Khrushchev that his objective was not to, as Sorensen described it:

> drive the partisans of Communist ideology from the face of the earth. He sought to halt the external expansion of Communism, not its internal philosophy and development. He regarded Communist aggression and subversion as intolerable, not Communism itself. "What your government believes," he wrote to Khrushchev in 1961, "is its own business; what it does in the world is the world's business."

This was an elegant form of conflict resolution. Kennedy was saying that he was not a crazed ideologue so blinded by contempt for the Soviet Union that he would abandon reason and start a war.

Kennedy and Khrushchev were leaders of vastly different social and economic systems. But Kennedy believed their responsibility was to find a way for both nations to live in peace. In the nuclear age, war was no longer an option.

Fortunately, this non-confrontational approach worked. The Soviet leader responded with a letter to Kennedy that suggested a "step-by-step" approach toward lowering Cold War tensions. In turn, Kennedy told Khrushchev that he was "ready and anxious to cooperate in any move for peace."

Khrushchev began this process when he summoned Llewellyn Thompson, the U.S. Ambassador to Russia, to talk with him about the issues that divided the two nations. Then, on January 17, 1961, the Soviet leader released two American pilots held in a Soviet prison since being shot down over the Barents Sea on July 1, 1960.

Kennedy began his first press conference as president by announcing the release and saying that it, "removes a serious obstacle to improvement of Soviet-American relations."

Khrushchev had earlier broached the subject of a meeting between the two leaders. Kennedy later accepted his proposal, and a summit was scheduled for June 3–6 in neutral Vienna, Austria.

The world turned its attention to the upcoming summit, hoping the two superpowers could find a way to avoid the impending crisis in Berlin and other hot spots around the world.

In just a few months, Kennedy had reversed the hostility caused by the U-2 incident and opened the door for the discussion of a pause in the Cold War,

But it would be Kennedy, the sophisticated young peacemaker, not Khrushchev, the primitive dictator, who brought this progress to a halt. He had skillfully lowered the tension between the two superpowers...and it was at this point that he made a serious mistake.

CHAPTER SIXTEEN

A STEP BACKWARD

How could I have been so stupid?
— John Kennedy, reflecting on the Bay of Pigs fiasco

D URING THE EISENHOWER ADMINISTRATION, the Central Intelligence Agency had devised a plan for an amphibious invasion of Cuba. It called for Cuban exiles to rush ashore, take Castro's forces by surprise, and incite an uprising against the dictator. The agency had been training brigades of exiles in guerrilla fighting techniques in Guatemala.

Allen Dulles, head of the CIA, briefed Kennedy on the plan shortly before he took office and urged him to give it the green light. He described the action as too small in scale to be called an "invasion."

The exiles would land at the coastal city of Trinidad, not far from Havana, which had a large anti-Castro population. The people would be encouraged to rise up against Castro. Afterward, a provisional, non-Communist government friendly to the United States would take control of the country.

Prominent government leaders opposed the invasion. Senator J. William Fulbright and Under Secretary of State Chester Bowles warned Kennedy that it was wrong on both moral and legal grounds.

The Cubans themselves in the U.N. warned that Kennedy was

about to attempt an overthrow of Castro. In response, on April 12, 1961, Kennedy at a press conference said flatly that the United States did not intend to intervene in Cuban affairs.

Kennedy had lied; the invasion began five days later.

He approved the mission for a variety of military and political reasons. Castro had overthrown the oppressive Batista regime, but he, too, was a tyrant who was executing dissidents. He was already accepting Soviet aide and training revolutionaries to spread Communism in Latin America.

A few Cuban pilots were learning to fly MIG jets in the Soviet Union. It was important to take action now, the CIA said, before they could fly combat missions. Now was the best time for action.

If Kennedy canceled the invasion, Republicans would charge that he lacked a quality he spoke of frequently: courage.

The chief planner of the invasion was Richard Bissell, the CIA's legendary deputy director of operations, the father of the U-2 spy plane program, who many considered as "the most brilliant man in Washington."

EVERYTHING WENT WRONG

KENNEDY MADE CHANGES to Bissell's invasion plan that doomed it to failure. The success of the assault depended on a popular uprising against Castro, the reason Trinidad had been selected as the landing site.

Kennedy, however, believed that invading near such a large city would make the operation appear "massive and spectacular," clearly indicating American involvement. Somehow, he naively believed the CIA's role in the invasion could be hidden. He ordered that another site be found.

Bissell chose the Bay of Pigs, a small peninsula known as the Zapata Swamp on the south coast of Cuba, fairly close to Havana. It was a steaming, impenetrable wilderness. Before storming the beach, the exiles would have to cross sharp coral ridges. The area was remote and sparsely populated; there would be no mass insurrection there.

Bissell told Kennedy that a new site had been found, but he withheld the vital information that the Bay of Pigs was a terrible choice for the new landing site.

Kennedy also began chipping away at other aspects of the plan. Before the invasion began, 16 CIA-owned B-26 bombers, flown by Cuban pilots, were supposed to cripple Castro's air force in two separate air strikes.

Kennedy decided to cut the number of bombers to eight and ordered them repainted to look like aircraft flown by the Cuban air force. The eight bombers attacked Castro's airfields, but they missed their targets and did little damage.

On Monday, April 17, 1961, 1,200 Cuban exiles landed at the Bay of Pigs. So much went wrong so quickly that it defies brief description. The outnumbered exiles were surrounded and their morale broken by the end of the first day of action.

In a panicked midnight meeting at the White House, the CIA and the military pressed Kennedy to allow American bombers to attack Castro's forces the next morning. This action, as Kennedy knew, would constitute a full-scale attack on Cuba by the United States. He refused the request.

Instead, Kennedy ordered aircraft flown by Cuban pilots to provide air cover for the ground troops in the morning. He also allowed navy jet fighters to fly with them.

The Cuban-piloted planes, however, arrived at the wrong time, ahead of the navy jets that were supposed to escort them, and chaos ensued. Faced with disaster, the CIA insisted that Kennedy decimate Castro's forces with a stronger attack from the air. He refused. They insisted that he send in Marines stationed on a warship offshore. He again refused. After three days of fighting, the exiles surrendered.

President Kennedy had made a mistake that cost the lives of 114 Cuban exiles and four American airmen. More than a thousand of the exiles were captured and imprisoned, and some were tortured and executed. At trial, some were convicted of treason and sentenced to 30 years in prison.

Badly shaken by the deaths he had caused, Kennedy warned Castro to end the executions and eventually negotiated the release of captured exiles in exchange for $53 million in food and medicine.

Kennedy had botched the invasion. He should have pressed Bissell for details about the strategic value of the Bay of Pigs as a landing site. A second lieutenant fresh out of West Point could have done a better job of assessing the dangers of the invasion.

Richard Nixon called Kennedy "spineless" for refusing the second request for air cover, and ever so briefly, there was talk of impeachment.

It is possible that the CIA purposely provided Kennedy with a flawed battle plan. Anti-Communist ideologues in the agency may have hoped that, faced with the tragic end of a heroic mission, Kennedy would agree to a last minute, massive attack by U.S. forces to rescue the exiles and take down Castro. To admit defeat, they believed, would be a blow to his masculinity.

Kennedy's rage was monumental when he considered this possibility. He fired both Dulles and Bissell, believing they may have manipulated his actions because they hoped for total war with the Soviet Union, with Cuba as the flash point.

It was later determined that Castro knew the exiles were training in Guatemala and that the Soviets had even given him advance warning that the attack was coming.

Still, Kennedy's policies toward Cuba would continue to be driven by his blind opposition to Castro. He did nothing to stop covert operations against the Cuban leader hatched by the CIA and his brother, Attorney General Robert Kennedy.

One of these actions, called Operation Mongoose, was conceived and supervised by the attorney general. He wrote in his diary:

> My idea is to stir things up on the island with espionage, sabotage, general disorder, run and operated by Cubans themselves with every group but Batistaites and Communists. Do not know if we will be successful in overthrowing Castro but we have nothing to lose in my estimate.

The operation, according to Arthur Schlesinger, was "poorly conceived and wretchedly executed. It deserved greatly to fail." Both the Bay of Pigs and Operation Mongoose made the Kennedy brothers seem immature and reckless. In later years, pundits would say that Kennedy's decision to permit the invasion had been guided by his adolescent sense of machismo. The testosterone-driven Kennedy brothers wanted to begin the Kennedy years by appearing to be tough and masculine.

Kennedy's preoccupation with eliminating Castro was amateurish and counterproductive. Operation Mongoose included absurd CIA attempts to assassinate or neutralize Castro with exploding cigars, poisoned toothpaste, and creams that would cause the hair of his beard to fall out.

Before he became president, Kennedy had said political leaders should be "men of judgment of our own mistakes as well as the mistakes of others, with enough wisdom to know what we did not know, and enough candor to admit it."

After the Bay of Pigs fiasco, in a press conference, Kennedy admitted his mistake, saying that he alone had been responsible for the failure. The American people admired his candor, rallying behind their president, and his approval rating soared to 90 percent.

In private, Kennedy berated himself, continually asking his aides, "How could I have been so stupid and let them go ahead?"

During the last months of his presidency, Kennedy would begin to doubt his uncompromising approach to Castro. On June 10, 1963, he gave a landmark Cold War speech at American University. He used it to outline his vision for world peace in the nuclear age. He said:

> So let us not be blind to our differences, but let us also direct attention to our common interests and the means by which those differences can be resolved. And if we cannot end now our differences, at least we can help make the world safe for diversity. For in the final analysis, our most basic common link is that we all inhabit this small planet. We all breathe the same air. We all cherish our children's futures. And we are all mortal.

Listening in Havana, Fidel Castro was impressed by Kennedy's assertion that nations can resolve their differences peacefully. He invited William Attwood, an American working for the U.N., to visit Havana secretly for talks on improving relations with the United States.

President Kennedy approved the meeting. Seventeen days later, he went to Dallas.

CHAPTER SEVENTEEN

FACE TO FACE WITH THE DEVIL

It's going to be a cold winter....
—John Kennedy's reply to Khrushchev's warning
that he would go to war over Berlin

I T WAS IN THE VOLATILE ATMOSPHERE created by the failed Bay
of Pigs invasion that President Kennedy and Premier Khrushchev
met in Vienna in 1961. Historians have said that Kennedy was
"bullied" during the summit, that he allowed Khrushchev to lec-
ture him about the superiority of Communism without offering a passionate defense of capitalism.

A review of the meeting, however, shows that this assessment is
flawed.

Kennedy and Khrushchev were different men from different worlds.
Kennedy was the idealistic, Harvard-educated son of a millionaire. He
lived in the clouds of idealism; his goal was to make this country an
advanced civilization.

Khrushchev grew up in poverty, illiterate until his 20s. He had men
arrested and murdered as part of Stalin's purges. He served as a political officer during the battle of Stalingrad and feared that Stalin would
have him executed if the Germans took the city.

The two-day summit took place in early June. Kennedy had two objectives, to determine whether Khrushchev would follow through on his threats of war, and to impress upon the Soviet leader his fear that a "miscalculation" of some sort would cause the two nations to unleash their nuclear arsenals.

FEAR OF LETHAL MISTAKES

A S A STUDENT OF HISTORY, Kennedy was aware of the role mistakes had played in starting past wars. He urged his staff to read *The Guns of August,* Barbara Tuchman's Pulitzer Prize–winning account of the way unforeseen events had sparked the slaughter of World War I.

An account of the conversations held by the two men, culled from the notes of those who were present and later reported by Sorensen, provides a fascinating look at Kennedy's attempts to reason with Khrushchev.

The two held their first talk about substantial matters on June 1, when they debated the merits of their respective systems of government. In a quick-take format, the following is a summary of a segment of one of their conversations:

- Khrushchev told Kennedy that just as feudalism was replaced by capitalism, Communism would replace capitalism.
- Kennedy replied that spreading Communism by coercion would inevitably lead to a war that neither country would survive. At a time when a miscalculation could lead to war, the competition between the two superpowers must be conducted peacefully.
- Khrushchev seemed confused about Kennedy's use of the word "miscalculation." Kennedy said it meant that he feared a mistake could lead to war, adding that his mistake at the Bay of Pigs could have escalated into a shooting war.
- Khrushchev said Cuba had become anti-American because it had supported the repressive dictator Fulgencio Batista, who had been ousted by Castro. He said the United States treated Cuba as its colony.
- Kennedy said he had long objected to colonialism, citing his early support for Algerian independence. If Castro had come to power through free elections, he said, the United States might have supported him.

Khrushchev told Kennedy they should talk about Berlin during their next meeting. He added, offhandedly, that if the United States refused to withdraw from West Berlin, the Soviet Union still planned to end Western access to East Berlin. This was close to a declaration of war.

Kennedy's response, again in a quick-take form, was the following:

- He told Khrushchev that he would not allow the United States to lose its access to East Berlin, because the rest of the world would lose confidence in U.S. commitments.
- The Soviet leader said that no force on earth would keep him from following through on his threat. If the Western powers intervened or tried to stop him, it would mean war.
- Kennedy asked Khrushchev to clarify his position; did he really mean that he would fight a war over Berlin? Would he like to reconsider his stand?
- Khrushchev responded that his position was firm. When the conversation ended, Kennedy told Khrushchev, "It's going to be a cold winter."

Later, when Kennedy mentioned that millions of people would die in a nuclear war, Khrushchev shrugged his shoulders. The young president appeared shaken by this madness, and in response, the media reported that he had "lost" the summit. Kennedy, however, did not view the meeting as a contest. There was no winner or loser.

Kennedy's triumph in Vienna was that he drummed into the head of a primitive dictator the idea that killing millions of people would solve nothing.

CHAPTER EIGHTEEN

MAKING WAR INSANE

Without having a nuclear war, we want to permit what
Thomas Jefferson called "the disease of liberty" to be caught
in areas which are now held by Communists.
—John Kennedy

WHEN HE RETURNED FROM THE SUMMIT, President Kennedy resumed his effort to make America, with its enlightened form of government and respect for freedom, a beacon for other nations to follow.

He had no desire to impose democracy on other countries. He believed emerging nations should be allowed to choose between the American system and the Soviet system without coercion or violence.

"Without having a nuclear war," he said, "we want to permit what Thomas Jefferson called 'the disease of liberty' to be caught in areas which are now held by Communists."

To make this policy work, Kennedy had to lessen the possibility of a war between the superpowers. The constant fear of war, he believed, kept much of the world numb to the wonders of peace. He declared that the United States would never be the first to launch a nuclear strike. This meant he had discarded the "first strike" concept. The U.S. military would be confined to retaliation if the Soviets struck first.

Kennedy then stepped up production of weapons used to respond to a first strike by the Soviets. Because they would be at sea and thus survive a Soviet sneak attack, he called for the number of submarines capable of carrying Polaris missiles increased from 19 to 29 by 1963. He directed that the range of these missiles be increased from 1,500 miles to 2,500 miles so that submarine commanders could hit their targets without going close to shore.

He decided to build 1,700 nuclear missiles, a 66 percent increase over the number when he came into office. He also asked for an additional 150 long-range Minuteman missiles, and the quickening of the research and development of more deadly missiles.

Simultaneously, Kennedy ordered a buildup of non-nuclear weapons and ground forces used to fight conventional land battles. He created the Green Berets and increased the number of more conventional forces. This strategy pushed the use of nuclear weapons into the background and shifted the focus of the conflict with the Soviet Union to ground battles rather than full-scale war.

General Maxwell Taylor, Chairman of the Joint Chiefs of Staff, called this approach a "flexible response" strategy with the "capability to react across the entire spectrum of possible challenge, for coping with anything from general atomic war to infiltrations and aggressions."

Kennedy was making war so potentially lethal that sane men would never allow it to happen. But if somehow a mistake occurred or the warhawks prevailed, the United States. would be prepared to fight.

THE WALL

ON AUGUST 13, 1961, Khrushchev started construction of a concrete wall, complete with guard towers and anti-vehicle trenches that sealed off East Berlin from West Berlin, and the rest of the free world.

Kennedy's advisers urged him to retaliate with military force. He refused, however, to start a war because Khrushchev had erected a wall. His focus remained on preventing war from starting due to a tragic mistake.

This almost occurred when a U.S. general in Berlin ordered his tanks to assume nose-to-nose positions with Soviet tanks. Kennedy immediately defused the situation, ordering the wayward general to back off, and the tension dissipated.

The Berlin Wall became a symbol of the suffering that Communism imposes on civilization. On June 26, 1961, Kennedy decided to exploit this symbol. He visited West Berlin to show support for the courage of its citizens and to illustrate the differences between the two systems.

It was here that he said:

> Two thousand years ago, the proudest boast was "civis Romanus sum." Today, in the world of freedom, the proudest boast is "Ich bin ein Berliner."
>
> There are many people in the world who really don't understand, or say they don't, what is the great issue between the free world and the Communist world.
>
> Let them come to Berlin.
>
> There are some who say that communism is the wave of the future. Let them come to Berlin.
>
> And there are some who say, in Europe and elsewhere, we can work with the Communists.
>
> Let them come to Berlin.
>
> And there are even a few who say that it is true that communism is an evil system, but it permits us to make economic progress.
>
> Lass' sie nach Berlin kommen.
>
> Let them come to Berlin.

Kennedy's words gave dignity to a city of frightened people. He eloquently exposed to the world a system designed to reduce human beings to slaves. Without firing a shot, he offered emerging nations around the world an incentive to catch "the disease of liberty."

Almost unnoticed in the media was the following: Kennedy had circumvented Khrushchev's earlier promise to go to war over Berlin.

He also had changed the world's focus from war to peace, thus muting the ancient tendency to resolve issues through warfare.

If he had lived, his policy of holding America aloft as a beacon of freedom and prosperity may well have changed the world.

KENNEDY'S THREE PRINCIPLES

NO MATTER HOW CHAOTIC and dangerous the Cold War became, President Kennedy never lost sight of the three principles he brought to the White House. He assessed the danger posed by Communism, encouraged the people to learn about these dangers, and gave them unbiased information about the threats they faced.

Alarmed by Khrushchev's wars of national liberation speech and the extent of Soviet expansion, for example, Kennedy candidly informed the people of his concerns.

In his first State of the Union address on January 30, 1961, he said:

> Each day the crises multiply. Each day their solution grows more difficult. Each day we draw nearer the hour of maximum danger....I feel I must inform the Congress that our analysis over the past ten days makes it clear that in each of the principal areas of crisis, the tide of events has been running out and time has not been on our side. There will be further setbacks before the tide is turned.

Kennedy was preparing the people for a time when he would need them to shed their complacency and embrace the need for change. The media and his Republican opponents called the address "alarmist" and accused Kennedy of hysteria and war mongering. In reality, he was acting according to his belief that the United States cannot successfully compete with other nations unless its leaders tell the truth.

He was equally candid about his Vienna meeting with Khrushchev. When he arrived home, he reported the substance of the talks directly to the people. His message was truthful and purposely grim. In a televised address, he said:

> I will tell you now that it was a very sober two days. There was no discourtesy, no loss of tempers, no threats, no ultimatums by either side; no advantage or concession was either granted or given; no major decision was either planned or taken; no spectacular progress was

either achieved or pretended...neither of us tried merely to please the other, to agree merely to be agreeable, to say what the other wanted to hear....At least the channels of communication were opened more fully....and the men on whose decision the peace in part depends have agreed to remain in contact.

Kennedy's remarks were clear and direct, free of ideological fervor. Interested citizens who listened to the address did not turn away, unable to stomach a clearly partisan point of view. Instead, intrigued by hearing facts rather than self-serving statements, they became interested in learning more about the summit and the nation's progress in the Cold War.

This, of course, was Kennedy's objective.

Before television, presidents communicated with the people through newspapers and magazines and with speeches and public statements. Press briefings were recorded on newsreels, and excerpts were shown in theaters. Only a few newspapers, such as *The New York Times,* carried full transcripts of the president's remarks.

Kennedy was the first president to hold live, televised press conferences. He selected a fresh setting for his meetings, a bright and spacious auditorium at the State Department, rather than the stuffy, smoke-filled White House office used by his predecessor.

He used these meetings to educate the people about affairs of state. Their major responsibility, he said, was to "participate in the affairs of liberty" by learning about important events and developing the "courage and perseverance" to understand that with "calm determination and steady nerves....peace and freedom will be sustained."

Kennedy redefined the presidency by making the nation feel it had the right to expect transparency from its president. The White House was no longer a place where government was practiced behind closed doors by a president who spoke to the people only when it was necessary.

A citizen of the United States today can view all 64 of Kennedy's press conferences in one or two sittings and receive a college-level class in conflict resolution, domestic affairs, and diplomacy.

CHAPTER NINETEEN

GETTING OUT OF VIETNAM

The last thing he wanted was to put in ground forces.
I don't recall anyone who was strongly against this except
one man, and that was the president.
— General Maxwell Taylor on Kennedy's Vietnam policy.

I N A RATIONAL WORLD, historians and media pundits would have long ago acknowledged the following: In November 1963, President Kennedy was in the process of ending this country's involvement in Vietnam. He believed the United States was slipping into the quicksand of an unwinnable, unnecessary war. His decision was ignored after his death, leading to the longest war in U.S. history.

This assertion is not a matter of opinion. It is, as we will see, a matter of fact.

FALLING DOMINOS

During the Kennedy era, foreign policy experts in the Pentagon and State Department viewed Communism as an evil system run by tyrants who were determined to destroy everything that was good in the world.

They clung without reservation to President Eisenhower's falling domino theory, which, as noted earlier, held that if one foreign nation fell to Communism, it would spread like wildfire to its neighbors. Vietnam, because it was geographically a perfect staging point for Communist aggression in Southeast Asia, became a lightning rod for their paranoia. They aggressively urged President Kennedy to draw a line in the sand, to take whatever action necessary to prevent communist forces from overrunning Vietnam.

In reality, this doctrine was irrational, based on fear rather than fact. It had grown over the years to become a political religion whose followers were reactionaries who made little or no effort to test its validity.

In a 1968 article in *The Atlantic*, James Thompson, an East Asia specialist who worked in the State Department and the White House from 1961 to 1965, said the domino theory came from:

> profound ignorance of Asian history and hence ignorance of the radical differences among Asian nations and societies. It resulted from a blindness to the power and resilience of Asian nationalism. It may also have resulted from a subconscious sense that, since "all Asians look alike," all Asian nations will act alike. As a theory, the domino fallacy was not merely inaccurate but also insulting to Asian nations; yet it has continued to this day to beguile men who should know better.

Thompson blamed our involvement in Vietnam on:

> the rise of a new breed of American ideologues who see Vietnam as the ultimate test of their doctrine....those men in Washington who have given a new life to the missionary impulse in American foreign relations: who believe that this nation, in this era, has received a threefold endowment that can transform the world. As they see it, that endowment is composed of, first, our unsurpassed military might; second, our clear technological supremacy; and third, our allegedly invincible benevolence.

Throughout his career, John Kennedy fought against this type of ignorance. He insisted on researching important issues in detail, rather than relying on a narrow set of beliefs. Thus, he considered it his responsibility as a public servant to visit countries in which the spread of Communism was considered a threat to America to see whether the threat was real.

In 1954, when sentiment for American involvement in Vietnam was growing, he traveled to Indochina (Vietnam), Cambodia, and

Laos. He spent a good deal of time in Vietnam, learning about its history, culture, military capabilities, and politics. He was there when the French lost the battle of Dien Bien Phu, which forced them to withdraw as occupiers of that country.

When he arrived home, Kennedy made a speech in the Senate that outraged the "hawks" in the Eisenhower administration, the military, and the State Department. He said:

> Mr. President, the time has come for the American people to be told the blunt truth about Indochina.
>
> I am reluctant to make any statement which may be misinterpreted as unappreciative of the gallant French struggle at Dien Bien Phu and elsewhere; or as partisan criticism of our Secretary of State just prior to his participation in the delicate deliberations in Geneva. Nor, as one who is not a member of those committees of the Congress which have been briefed—if not consulted—on this matter, do I wish to appear impetuous or alarmist in my evaluation of the situation.
>
> But to pour money, material, and men into the jungles of Indochina without at least a remote prospect of victory would be dangerously futile and self-destructive. Of course, all discussion of "united action" assumes the inevitability of such victory; but such assumptions are not unlike similar predictions of confidence which have lulled the American people for many years and which, if continued, would present an improper basis for determining the extent of American participation.
>
> I am frankly of the belief that no amount of American military assistance in Indochina can conquer an enemy, which is everywhere and at the same time nowhere, "an enemy of the people" which has the sympathy and covert support of the people.

MISTAKES

DESPITE HIS RATIONAL UNDERSTANDING of communism, Kennedy made mistakes in Vietnam, some of them disturbing. His initial strategy was to protect the South Vietnamese people from communism by sending military advisers to train South Vietnamese soldiers to fight against communist insurgents. Sorensen said:

His desire was to halt a communist-sponsored guerrilla war and to permit the local population to peacefully choose its own future. He sought neither a cold war pawn nor a hot war battleground.

This approach was well intentioned, but ineffective. In a country as culturally and politically complex as Vietnam, it was doomed to fail. The Vietnamese had a long history of repelling even passive interference in their affairs. Their country had been occupied several times over the centuries, but one by one its occupiers cut their losses and fled after realizing that the cost of defending themselves against the fierce will of the people was far too great.

Kennedy, a student of history, a scholar, should have realized from the start that any sort of intervention in Vietnam would be problematic. He possessed the intelligence to understand that sending advisers to Vietnam could be the start of a deadly cycle of involvement in a nation of determined warriors. President Truman had sent advisers and aides to Vietnam in 1950, with little results. Nonetheless, Kennedy believed that he could blunt communist aggression with a nonviolent approach.

NOTHING WORKED

IN 1961, WHEN KENNEDY TOOK OFFICE, Ngo Dinh Diem, the prime minister of South Vietnam, was struggling to keep the country from being overrun by Communist forces, led in the north by Ho Chi Minh.

Diem, a strutting, corrupt autocrat, had appointed friends and family to important posts in his government. A Catholic in a predominately Buddhist country, he seized farmland from Buddhist peasants and gave it to his Catholic supporters. He refused to enact social and land reforms to improve the lives of South Vietnamese peasants, instead instituting a policy of torturing and executing suspected Communist supporters without a trial.

In late 1961, Kennedy sent Diem 3,200 U.S. military personnel as advisers, assigned to train members of the Army of the Republic of Vietnam (ARVN) to use American-made weapons to fight the North Vietnamese.

Diem recommended a strategy, which Kennedy approved, called the Strategic Hamlet Program. It forced villagers to move into fenced-in hamlets guarded by ARVN forces. The goal was to prevent contact between the villagers and Communist insurgents, who were using villages as safe havens to recruit new troops and as staging points for guerrilla attacks on the ARVN.

The program was massive in scale, calling for the construction of more than 10,000 hamlets. It was, however, an utter failure. ARVN fighters were no match for the insurgents, who repeatedly attacked the hamlets. More than 8,000 hamlets were established, but only 1,000 were adequately defended.

Kennedy also approved the secret use of chemicals to destroy rice crops and thus force peasants and villagers to move into the protected hamlets. This program continued after Kennedy's death. Between 1961 and 1967, the U.S. Air Force sprayed 20 million gallons of concentrated and toxic herbicides over six million acres of crops and trees.

None of these strategies worked; nothing Kennedy tried produced positive results. He sent Diem more advisers, a total of 16,500 by 1963, including Green Berets who were officially non-combatants but who had authorization to fight if they were fired on.

Still, the South Vietnamese could not make headway. Diem and his brother and chief adviser, Ngo Dinh Nhu, were brutally repressive. In May 1963, Buddhist priests held a peaceful protest against the religious oppression inspired by the Diem brothers, who responded by ordering troops to fire on them, killing nine. A month later, newspapers around the world carried the shocking photo of a priest who doused himself in gasoline and died in flames to protest Diem's persecution of Buddhists.

The situation in Vietnam was becoming ugly, uncontrollable. Kennedy believed that Diem was an obstacle to progress. Told that ARVN generals were planning to depose the tyrant, expecting him to be forced out of the country, Kennedy stood aside.

On November 2, 1963, Diem and Nhu fled Saigon as the coup began. The two men surrendered after securing an offer of safe passage out of the country. On route to an air force base, however, as they cowered in the back of an armored personnel carrier, they were shot and stabbed multiple times by ARVN forces. Henry Cabot Lodge, Kennedy's ambassador to Vietnam, had learned that the coup might turn violent, but he took no action to stop it. When the killing was over, he congratulated the ARVN generals, tacitly celebrating the murder of the Diem brothers.

Kennedy went to Dallas 21 days later, where he, too, was assassinated.

A WRITTEN ORDER TO WITHDRAW

It would take nearly 30 years before the public would learn that Kennedy had decided to withdraw from Vietnam. In 1992, U.S. Army Major John Newman, who had spent a decade researching President Kennedy's policies in Vietnam, made the startling announcement that shortly before his death Kennedy had issued an order calling for the complete withdrawal of all military personnel from Vietnam by the end of 1965.

If true, Newman's claim meant that Kennedy had realized that he was doing more harm than good in Vietnam and dragging the United States into a quagmire in the process. It meant that more than 58,000 young Americans, and more than one million Vietnamese soldiers and two million Vietnamese civilians, would not have died in an unnecessary war.

And it meant the United States would not have suffered through a decade of nation-changing self-destructive social and political upheaval caused by the war.

Newman's claim, published in his book, *JFK and Vietnam: Deception, Intrigue, and the Struggle for Power,* did not get the media attention it deserved. The nation was angry, seeking political leaders to blame for the lives and money wasted in Vietnam. We did not want a hero; we wanted villains. Newman was attacked as a Kennedy apologist and doubt was cast on his research.

Newman's claim, however, was based on solid, unimpeachable evidence. Working his way through a mountain of recently declassified documents, he discovered National Security Action Memorandum (NSAM) 263, signed by Kennedy on October 5, 1963, which called for the withdrawal from Vietnam of a thousand advisers by the end of 1963, to be followed by the complete withdrawal of all advisers by the end of 1965.

Because he was a political pragmatist, Kennedy delayed informing the public about his intention to get out of Vietnam. In 1963, he could not have failed to notice that Barry Goldwater, a hawkish conservative, could be his opponent in 1964. If he announced his plans to get out of Vietnam, Goldwater would charge that he was "soft on communism" and would undoubtedly start a war in Vietnam if he became president.

With this in mind, Kennedy made conflicting statements about the presence of U.S. advisers in Vietnam. In 1963, he said:

> We want to see a stable government there, carrying on a struggle to maintain its national independence. We believe strongly in that. We are not going to withdraw from that effort. In my opinion, for us to withdraw from that effort would mean a collapse not only of South Vietnam, but Southeast Asia. So we are going to stay there.

Also in 1963, during an interview with Walter Cronkite, Kennedy said:

> I don't think that unless a greater effort is made by the Government to win popular support that the war can be won out there. In the final analysis, it is their war. They are the ones who have to win it or lose it. We can help them, we can give them equipment, we can send our men out there as advisers, but they have to win it, the people of Vietnam, against the Communists.

Despite the confusing nature of his comments, Kennedy had never wanted a land war in Vietnam. At no time during his stewardship of events in Southeast Asia had he seriously considered escalating the war by sending combat troops to fight there. He often repeated to his staff the warning given to him by General Douglas MacArthur: "Anyone wanting to commit American ground forces to the mainland of Asia should have his head examined."

He also repeatedly rejected requests from his staff and military advisers to send combat troops to Vietnam. At a meeting with his staff in 1963, when he again was urged to send troops, Kennedy said, "No... now what else do you have." General Maxwell Taylor said, "The last thing he wanted was to put in ground forces. I don't recall anyone who was strongly against this except one man, and that was the president."

Kennedy's ambiguity made the question of his withdrawal a partisan political issue. His critics said the complete withdrawal of American advisers called for in NSAM 263 would take effect only if the Vietcong insurgency had been significantly reduced by 1965.

Defense Secretary Robert McNamara, however, denied that this was the case. In a White House tape recording made on October 2, 1963, he said, "I am sure that if we don't meet these [withdrawal] dates in the sense of ending the major military campaigns, we nonetheless can withdraw the bulk of our US forces according to the schedule we've laid out." This policy was still in effect 50 days later when Kennedy was assassinated.

As a student of American history, Kennedy likely knew the Founders feared that when given too much power, the military would create endless, unnecessary wars. And surrounding the military would grow a group of profiteers that lobbied for constant aggression to keep their coffers full. The Founders feared that these two factions, when joined together, would eventually become more powerful than the government.

Kennedy undoubtedly had read James Madison's remarks before the Constitutional Convention in Philadelphia in 1787. He said:

> A standing military force will not long be safe companions to liberty. The means of defense against foreign danger have been always the instruments of tyranny at home. Among the Romans it was a standing maxim to excite a war, whenever a revolt was apprehended. Throughout all Europe, the armies kept up under the pretext of defending, have enslaved the people.

He also must have listened intently when President Eisenhower, in his farewell address to the nation in 1961, warned that "the military industrial complex" was becoming the most powerful force in America.

Eisenhower, in effect, warned that the two factions were plotting to loot the public treasury. The military was pushing for endless wars, while contractors were waiting to turn these wars into tens of billions of dollars in profits.

John Kennedy was getting out of Vietnam because it was becoming a threat to the nation's welfare. The political courage he displayed by beating back the beasts of war has remained underappreciated and underreported in the media.

Kennedy's decision to withdraw from Vietnam was also entirely consistent with his overall foreign policy, which was based on purging the United States of its flaws, thus allowing it to become a beacon for other nations to follow. He wanted foreign nations to choose peacefully between the U.S. system and the Soviet system.

A continuation of the U.S. presence in Vietnam was also at odds with Kennedy's contempt for predetermined views, such as the domino theory. He refused to commit this country to a shooting war in a country six thousand miles away to satisfy those who believed that communism must be eliminated at any cost.

Aside from his early naivety, Kennedy's handling of Vietnam was free of destructive ideological fervor. It should have been a model for future presidents to follow when making decisions about war and peace, but as we will see in coming chapters, they did not possess his intelligence, sense of history, or respect for the wisdom of the Founders.

CHAPTER TWENTY

KENNEDYNOMICS

Let us not seek the Republican answer or the Democratic
answer, but the right answer. Let us not seek to fix the blame
for the past. Let us accept our own responsibility for the future.
—John F. Kennedy

APRIL 10, 1962, was sunny and mild in Washington, D.C. The Yoshino cherry blossoms, which cast a pleasing pink glow across the city, had almost reached their peak bloom. In the White House, President Kennedy had just finished a phone call, when his secretary told him that Roger Blough, the chairman of U.S. Steel, was in her office and wanted to speak with him.

Kennedy was confused; he thought his business with the industrialist had been concluded. Nearly a year before, steel workers across the country had asked for wage increases. The steel companies had closed ranks and refused the request, claiming the industry was operating at just 65 percent of its capacity and would have to increase steel prices to pay for higher wages.

For months, Kennedy and Arthur Goldberg, his Secretary of Labor, had negotiated with the workers' unions and steel executives to resolve the issue. Their hard work had seemingly paid off, as U.S. Steel and Bethlehem Steel had signed contracts that did not give workers a pay raise but did provide a 2.5 percent increase in their pension benefits. Thus, a crippling strike that would have forced a half million workers to walk off their jobs had been averted, as was the threat of a rise in steel prices. As Kennedy recalled, both sides seemed happy.

Then Blough walked into the Oval Office and dropped a bomb. He handed Kennedy a memo that declared that U.S. Steel was raising its prices to $176 per ton, a $6 per ton increase over the current price. As he read the memo, Kennedy could barely contain his rage.

Blough calmly said that as soon as U.S. Steel announced its price increase to the media, the five other major steel companies would likely do the same. Then he turned on his heel and walked out the door.

U.S. Steel was the nation's first billion-dollar corporation. Its board of directors included some of the most powerful industrialists in the country. They had obviously listened during the 1960 presidential campaign when Kennedy warned that if big business threatened the interests of the nation, he would fight back.

The price hike was an attempt to weaken Kennedy's credibility as a president who demanded responsible behavior from big business. If they could force him to accept the price increase, Kennedy would be their puppet.

Instead, without hesitation, Kennedy fought back. As he well knew, steel was one of the most important commodities in the world. If he stood by and allowed a $6 per ton price increase, the negative effects could reverberate across the economy, driving up the prices of many steel-related products Americans worked hard to purchase.

For years, the price of steel had been rising more rapidly than the prices of other commodities. Adding yet another price increase could cause the economy to enter a period of inflation.

The day after Blough's visit to the White House, at the start of his 30th news conference, Kennedy tore into the steel industry, his righteous fury a revelation to those who had thought their young president might be vulnerable to pressure from corporate interests.

The heart of his remarks came when he said,

> In this serious hour in our nation's history when we are confronted with grave crises in Berlin and Southeast Asia, when we are devoting our energies to economic recovery and stability...and asking union members to hold down their wage requests at a time when restraint

and sacrifice are being asked of every citizen, the American people will find it hard, as I do, to accept a situation in which a tiny handful of steel executives whose pursuit of private power and profit exceeds their sense of public responsibility can show such utter contempt for the interests of 185 million Americans.

Some time ago I asked each American to consider what he would do for his country and I asked the steel companies. In the last 24 hours we had their answer.

AN ASSAULT ON THE COMMON GOOD

KENNEDY'S PASSIONATE REMARKS sent a message to Americans that corporate greed was "un-American," an assault on the common good that he would not tolerate.

When steel executives failed to respond to Kennedy's reprimand, he ordered a federal grand jury investigation of U.S. Steel under the Sherman Antitrust Act. Attorney General Robert Kennedy charged that the increase was based on greed, not on the company's professed need to compensate for declining profits.

The attorney general also said that he would investigate allegations of collusion and price fixing by the steel giant. The Defense Department, one of U.S. Steel's biggest clients, announced that it would buy the steel it needed elsewhere.

Faced with the possibility of falling profits and made to appear greedy by President Kennedy and the attorney general, the steel executives withdrew their demands; it was all over in three days.

After the crisis ended, the conservative media charged that Kennedy had used "quasi-fascist" tactics to make the steel companies yield on the price hike. The administration's tactics were indeed forceful. Robert Kennedy, seeking evidence of illegal price fixing, sent FBI agents to interview steel executives at their homes. Overzealous agents, however, against Kennedy's orders, arrived at the home of an executive late at night, leading to charges of "Gestapo tactics" by the Kennedy brothers.

Stunned conservatives called Kennedy "an enemy of freedom." John W. Bricker, the former Republican governor of Ohio, said, "The recent display of dictatorial power by President Kennedy has made us realize that freedom in its largest sense is at stake. The Republican

Party is the last and only remaining bulwark."

Bricker was not speaking of "freedom" in the generally accepted meaning of the word. He believed that government should never interfere with big business. And he feared that Kennedy would use the steel dispute as an excuse to hamper U.S. Steel's ability to earn a profit, or worse, call for greater government regulation of business.

Kennedy, to the conservatives who opposed him, was just another naive liberal who did not understand that the free market system will fall apart if government regulates big business. "Freedom" in the ideological view held by conservatives, meant the freedom of a corporation to make a profit while blindly ignoring the needs of the people.

Kennedy had used the power of the presidency to prevent a corporation from indulging in greed. From then on, he was detested in corporate boardrooms across the country. A few months after the steel crisis, a poll found that an astounding 88 percent of the businessmen queried believed that Kennedy was "anti-business."

These fears were absurd. At no time during his negotiations with U.S. Steel did Kennedy show an inclination to hurt the steel giant as a company or to tighten government's regulation of business. In fact, he put most of his effort into negotiating a settlement that would help the company increase its profits. He became an opponent of big business only when it went too far, when it placed its interests above those of the people.

A year after U.S. Steel withdrew its demand it again sought a price increase, but this time the company asked for an increase of just $4.85 a ton. Kennedy said the increase was "not incompatible with a framework of general stability and steel price stability" and he did not oppose the increase.

Kennedy was actually a defender of the free market system. During his presidency, he proposed a series of sophisticated measures to make it more efficient, such as tax credits for research and development and the modernization of plants and equipment. He consistently defended and encouraged corporate attempts to increase profits, as long as they did not harm the national interest.

Kennedy's handling of the steel crisis has faded into history with little notice. A comment he made during his televised address, however, made this brief skirmish an important moment in our economic history. Because American corporations are granted the right to conduct business, Kennedy said, they also have a responsibility to contain their greed. He explained this concept as follows:

> Price and wage decisions in this country, except for a very limited restriction in the case of monopolies and national emergency strikes, are and ought to be freely and privately made. But the American people have a right to expect in return for that freedom, a higher sense of business responsibility for the welfare of their country than has been shown in the last two days.

With these words, Kennedy reminded the people that the United States asks its citizens to put the common good above self-interest. He defended our right to demand that corporations control their greed.

When he took on the steel industry, Kennedy employed all three of the principles he brought to the White House. First, he assessed the threat to the nation posed by an increase in the price of steel. Then, he communicated his concerns to the people, elevating them to the status of involved, alert citizens. Finally, his decision to fight the price increase was based on his analysis of the facts, not on an overarching ideology that was either for or against big business.

SEE THINGS AS THEY ARE

IN MAY 1962, concerned that a slowing economy could undermine the quality of life in America, Kennedy convened a meeting of his Council of Economic Advisers at the White House. He asked them to determine why the economy had become sluggish, and to suggest ways to make it grow faster.

Before they went to work, Kennedy gave his economists some advice, a pep talk of sorts. He asked them to avoid basing their conclusions about the economy on predetermined beliefs:

> Most of us are conditioned for many years to have a political viewpoint...but the fact of the matter is that most of the [economic] problems we now face are technical problems, administrative problems, [requiring] very sophisticated judgments that do not lend themselves to the great passionate movements that have stirred this country so often in the past. They [our economic problems] deal with questions that are beyond the comprehension of most men, most governmen-

tal administrators, over which experts may differ, yet we [continue] to operate through our traditional political systems.

Note that Kennedy did not tell his advisers to find a way to blame the slowdown on Republicans. He did not tell them to base their conclusions on economic policies favored by Democrats in Congress. Instead, he asked them to "look at things as they are, not through party labels or through position labels, but as they are, and figure out how we can maintain this economy so that it moves ahead."

It is hard to imagine a president today taking this eminently sane position, refusing to use ideology to reach a conclusion. Perhaps, this is because we have gone mad with ideological fervor, no longer able to distinguish between reason and ideological beliefs.

As noted earlier, Kennedy warned business executives and the nation that economic policy should not be determined through:

> some grand warfare of rival ideologies which will sweep the country with passion…but with the practical management of a modern economy. What we need are not labels and clichés but more basic discussion of the sophisticated and technical questions involved in keeping a great economic machinery moving ahead.

After the steel crisis ended, as Republicans charged that Kennedy was a "socialist" determined to stamp out the free enterprise system, he told an aide, "If I had failed to get a rescission, [of the steel increase demand], that would have been an awful setback to the office of the presidency." The aide replied that U.S. Steel had "picked the wrong president to double-cross."

The term "Kennedynomics" does not roll easily off the tongue. It should be used, however, to describe an economic policy conceived with reason and objective analysis rather than rigidly held ideological beliefs. And it should be used to honor the last president with the courage to face down a huge corporation in the name of the common good.

Perhaps because he did not pretend to be a profound economic thinker, historians have given little weight to Kennedy's approach to economics. Regrettably, this undervalues his contribution to economic policy. When he urged his economic team to fashion economic policy from reason, rather than ideology, Kennedy established a precedent for subsequent presidents, but sadly, it has not been followed.

Nearly 45 years after the steel crisis ended, President George W. Bush faced a similar situation. Multi-billion-dollar oil companies were driving the price of gasoline to unheard of levels, inflicting financial distress on U.S. citizens. In response, Bush said, "I wish I could simply wave a magic wand and lower gas prices tomorrow. I'd do that."

Bush did not go on television to dress down oil executives. Nor did he ask why a tiny handful of oil executives should allow their desire for power and profit to override the welfare of millions of Americans.

Unlike John Kennedy, he lacked objectivity; he was trapped by the dictates of his belief that government should never interfere with business. Thus, he could not make economic decisions on a case-by-case basis and relieve American citizens of their suffering, even though the situation demanded intervention.

Kennedy's economic policies were based on flexibility. When he asked his Council of Economic Advisers for a list of methods to stimulate growth, they suggested lowering the tax rate. The president agreed and asked Congress to lower the income-tax rate for wealthy individuals from 91 percent to 70 percent, and the rate on corporations from 52 percent to 48 percent.

Conservatives have argued that because he lowered taxes, Kennedy was an early advocate of the rigid tax policies later offered by Reagan. This assertion is self-serving and ignores the truth.

Kennedy would have *raised* taxes if needed to stimulate growth. "If I ever believed that taxes should be raised to help the economy, I would do that," he once said. This all-important flexibility came to an end under Reagan, as raising taxes became unacceptable under any circumstances. This destructive policy is still a sacred mantra among conservatives.

Kennedy's wisdom concerning economic policy was surprising because he was so young and he never completed a formal study of economics. When he assumed the presidency in 1960, he freely admitted this shortcoming, confessing to his economic advisers that he had difficulty remembering the difference between fiscal and monetary policy. He considered himself a blank slate, a pupil with the responsibility to learn economic theory quickly and without bias.

Tutored by Walter Heller, chairman of the Council of Economic Advisers, Kennedy, in a remarkably short time, acquired a comprehensive knowledge of economic theory. In 1987, Heller said, "Economic advisers always claim their President is savvy, but Kennedy really was."

Heller, along with James Tobin, a brilliant member of Kennedy's Council of Economic Advisers, and economist Kermit Gordon, found the president to be an eager pupil. They sent him more than three hundred lengthy reports on economic theory, which he actually read, cover to cover.

Kennedy, Tobin said, was:

> remarkably free of preconceived doctrines and deeply committed to more rapid growth as an instrument of the common good and eager to put the power of modern economics to work.

There is a long history in the United States of battles between presidents who opposed the encroachment of corporations and the Republican leaders who represented their interests. In 1936, as he campaigned for re-election, Franklin Roosevelt spoke of the need to control greedy businessmen:

> We [his administration] had to struggle with the old enemies of business and financial monopoly, speculation, reckless banking, class antagonism, sectionalism, war profiteering. They had begun to consider the government of the United States as a mere appendage to their own affairs. We know now that government by organized money is just as dangerous as government by organized mob. Never before in all our history have these forces been so united against one candidate as they stand today. They are unanimous in their hate for me...and I welcome their hatred.

While Kennedy was not the first president to beat back the beasts of corporate America, tragically, he was the last to do so. In his book, *Battling Wall Street: The Kennedy Presidency,* Donald Gibson wrote:

> President Kennedy was the kind of national leader who actually promotes the general welfare and the kind a country needs most when that welfare is threatened by powerful groups. For three years, Kennedy fought against certain tendencies within those groups, and immediately after his death, some of those tendencies were reasserted. Within ten years of Kennedy's death the progress he had

fought for was disappearing as those tendencies became expressed in a most flagrant and destructive way.

When they assess his presidency, historians give little weight to Kennedy's non-ideological approach to the economy and to government in general. Considering what happened to the economy after his death, however, "Kennedynomics" may have been his most important contribution to the welfare of the nation.

CHAPTER TWENTY-ONE

THE FIGHT AGAINST GREED

He felt the control of the national economy should not be allowed
to continue in the hands of the few, but should be enlarged to
include millions of citizens or be taken over by the government,
which in a democracy is responsible to the people.
—James Hepburn describing Kennedy's economic policy

THE FOLLOWING MAY COME AS A SURPRISE: The Founding Fathers feared that political leaders would one day turn corporations loose on America. They knew that without restraints, driven by obsessive greed, they would eventually corrupt the economy and with it the government. They purposely limited corporations to activities that benefited society, such as the construction of roads, canals, bridges, and highways. They strictly forbid them from influencing the political process or elections.

Doing business on a large scale in the United States was viewed as a privilege that comes with its own set of civic responsibilities.

This view prevailed for more than a century after the U.S. Constitution was signed. Corporations were not permitted to contribute to political candidates or participate in campaigns, elections, or any other aspect of public policy. Businessmen who wanted to start a corporation were required to obtain charters, which were limited to a given period of time, and could be revoked at any time.

The terms of these charters were determined by the states, most of which stipulated that corporations could pursue only the activities specified in their charter. They could not hold property owned by other corporations or shares of stock in other corporations. It was the owners of a corporation who were responsible for illegal acts or harm caused by their companies.

In the 1800s, citizens held debates before corporate licenses were granted to decide whether a corporation would enhance or harm the community in which it operated. Corporations could not expand their businesses if these citizens thought expansion was unnecessary. Even the amount of profit a corporation could earn was controlled. If corruption was suspected, state legislatures could seize a corporation's financial statements.

This era established the concept that citizens had the responsibility to oversee corporations.

Sadly, it did not last. Over the decades, profit-obsessed industrialists found ways around the restrictions that held them in check. In the mid-1800s, they attacked first the concept of the corporate charter. When the Supreme Court rejected their challenges, they simply ignored their rulings by creating monopolies and trusts without charters.

The enormous amount of wealth these companies accumulated during the Civil War allowed them to bribe state and federal officials, and gradually the corporation became more powerful than the government itself.

Eventually, the perception of corporations underwent a profound change. The public, desperate for jobs during periodic downturns and particularly during the Great Depression, began to view corporations as benign businesses that offered them, no matter the low wages, a way to feed their families.

The notion that owning a business in the United States was a privilege began to fade away.

John Kennedy tried to bring this concept back to life. By the time he took office, corporations based in the United States had begun the process of establishing profit centers in foreign countries. Tax law allowed them to park income overseas to avoid paying taxes at home.

Kennedy, like the Founders, believed the right to conduct business was a privilege. He saw the evasion of taxes, which robbed the Treasury of billions of dollars, as a violation of this privilege.

In tax reform legislation and other proposals he sent to Congress between 1960 and 1963, Kennedy took aim at the loopholes corporations were using to evade their taxes. He proposed a tax on profits made by corporations doing business in tax havens such as Switzerland and other low-tax countries. This measure, Kennedy said, would address "the inequity that arises when this powerful segment of our society asks for more than it is entitled to receive."

Kennedy was an astute economic thinker, capable of invigorating economic growth in both the long and short term. In an effort to stimulate the economies of undeveloped nations, for example, he proposed that multi-national corporations doing business in poor countries be exempt from the profit tax. This exemption, he hoped, would lead to economic growth in depressed countries, which decades later would enable them to trade and do business with the United States.

Further, he offered a 15 percent tax credit to large companies when they built new plants and equipment, with the provision that the construction take place in the United States. Smaller firms would receive a 30 percent tax credit. Kennedy was stimulating growth in the present, but linking it as well to mechanisms that would benefit the economy in the future.

In his message to Congress in 1961, Kennedy said,

> The tax system must be adequate to meet our public needs. It must meet them fairly, calling on each of us to contribute his proper share to the cost of government. It must encourage efficient use of our resources. It must promote economic stability and stimulate economic growth. Economic expansion in turn creates a growing tax base, thus increasing revenue and thereby enabling us to meet more readily our public needs, as well as our needs as private individuals.

TAKING ON THE OILMEN

KENNEDY AGAIN TRIED to enforce these ideals when he went head to head with wealthy Texas oilmen over the oil depletion allowance, a system of special privileges and loopholes they used to avoid paying taxes.

The measure gave oil producers the right to exempt 27.5 percent of their income from federal income tax, to compensate for the depletion of their reserves of oil. In reality, the allowance was designed to put millions of dollars into the pockets of Texas oilmen such as H. L. Hunt, Sid Richardson, and Clint Murchison.

Journalist Robert Bryce said the oilmen "were getting a tax break that was unprecedented in American business. While other business-men had to pay taxes on their income regardless of what they sold, the oilmen got special treatment."

Lobbyists and politicians in Congress protected the oilmen. Lyn-don Johnson used his position as majority leader of the Senate to head off legislation that threatened the exemption. President Eisenhower, who had received campaign contributions from the oil industry be-fore the presidential election in 1952, blocked a grand jury investiga-tion of the oil industry.

On January 24, 1963, Kennedy presented a bill to Congress that called for an end to the oil depletion allowance. He said laws that give special tax breaks to oil companies, and all other companies that re-ceived such consideration, were wrong, a violation of the privilege of doing business in this country. The bill was under consideration when Kennedy was murdered. President Johnson withdrew the legislation.

Kennedy's message, however, was clear. He was not a glassy-eyed anti-capitalist. He understood that both large corporations and the cigar store on the corner provide the jobs and income that fuel the nation's economic growth. What he could not tolerate was corporate greed, because it eventually destroys the ability of political leaders to make the welfare of the people the sole objective of government.

What Kennedy was trying to accomplish with the oil depletion bill, said James Hepburn in *Farewell America,* was a:

> re-examination of the principles of profit-making and free enterprise from the moral, social or even national point of view. He felt the control of the national economy should not be allowed to continue in the hands of the few, but should be enlarged to include millions of citizens or be taken over by the government, which in a democracy is responsible to the people.

There is little on record to indicate that Kennedy believed, as Hep-burn asserts, that the U.S. government should take over the economy if it were used to serve only a small segment of the population.

Still, the assessment may be correct. Kennedy's objective was to turn the corporate mandate to generate ever-increasing profits into a mechanism that boosted the nation's productivity in a way that benefited all Americans.

Donald Gibson said Kennedy felt:

> that wealth should be acquired through productive and generally beneficial investments. He took a dim view of profits accruing from speculation, purely financial transactions, and inheritance. He never opposed in any general way the right to own property, earn profits, or expand wealth. What he did try to do with everything from global investment patterns to tax breaks for individuals was to reshape laws and policies so that the power of property and the search for wealth would not end up destroying rather than creating economic prosperity for the country. In this, he was very clear, consistent, and coherent.

In the name of saving the country from corporate greed, Kennedy indeed may have advocated a measure as radical as turning the economy over to the government. If he had made this recommendation, he would have been a radical of the sort this country badly needs today.

After Kennedy, the nation fell into the hands of presidents who viewed corporations as cash cows for a select few. Kennedy's view that the nation's tax burden should be shared equally disappeared, as did his view that profits derived from speculation and purely financial transactions made some rich but did nothing to improve the nation's general welfare.

His attempt to force a reexamination of the "principles of profit-making and free enterprise from the moral, social or even national point of view" died with him.

Kennedy has not been given due credit for his ability to foresee what would happen to the economy if the nation lost sight of its founding values and greed became a way of life. He gave us a warning, but we did not listen.

CHAPTER TWENTY-TWO

CONFRONTING RACISM

*We preach freedom around the world, and we mean it, and we
cherish our freedom here at home, but are we to say to the world,
and much more importantly, to each other that this is the land
of the free except for the Negroes; that we have no second-class
citizens except Negroes; that we have no class or caste system, no
ghettos, no master race except with respect to Negroes?*
—John Kennedy in a 1963 televised address.

JOHN KENNEDY PICKED HIS BATTLES CAREFULLY. He did not
seek social or political change until he felt he had a good chance
of achieving his objective.

This pragmatism made him appear slow to join the fight for
civil rights, disappointing black leaders who complained that he did
not vigorously pursue remedial legislation nor do enough to bring the
issue of racism before the public.

There was some truth to these charges. Kennedy moved cautiously
on civil rights during the first two years of his presidency. He said
things that made him seem more concerned with his image than with
the plight of blacks. In May 1961, for example, a group called "The
Freedom Riders" was trying to force states to follow a recent Supreme

Court ruling that outlawed segregation in interstate transportation terminals. A bus carrying the activists was burned at a rest stop in Alabama and the activists were beaten.

Kennedy, fearing ugly headlines just as he prepared to meet Khrushchev in Vienna, asked Harris Wofford, his civil rights adviser, "Can't you get your god-damned friends off those buses?"

When viewed from his perspective, however, Kennedy's caution may have been justified. He worried that if he pressed the volatile race issue prematurely, the South would turn against him, he would lose the 1964 election to a Republican opponent, and the civil rights movement, which he was genuinely committed to supporting, would be dealt a serious blow.

Kennedy knew that Congress would never pass a civil rights bill because Southern Senators, including some Democrats, would block his attempts. Trying to force a doomed bill through Congress would backfire, becoming a setback for the cause of civil rights.

"When I feel that we can usefully move ahead in the field of legislation," Kennedy said at a press conference, "when I feel that there is a necessity for Congressional action, with a chance of getting that Congressional action, then I will recommend it."

Apart from legislation, the efforts that Kennedy did make on behalf of civil rights were impressive. He used executive orders to enforce the landmark 1954 Supreme Court decision, *Brown v. Board of Education*, which struck down state laws allowing separate public schools for black and white students.

Robert Kennedy's Justice Department also made inroads against segregation by issuing rules barring discrimination in interstate travel and in hotels and restaurants.

President Kennedy also tried to force top federal officials to confront racism in the departments they ran. During the 1961 Inaugural Parade, he noticed that there were no blacks (then called Negroes) in the Coast Guard honor guard.

He ordered his Treasury Secretary to give blacks the opportunity to join the Coast Guard, and the first black man entered the Coast Guard Academy the following year.

Over the next two years, more blacks were appointed to federal positions, including strategically important judgeships in the South, than at any time in the past.

VIOLENCE FORCES THE ISSUE

TERRIBLE EVENTS, however, ultimately forced Kennedy to decide that the time had come for a civil rights bill. In January 1963, George Wallace, on becoming governor of Alabama, declared "segregation now, segregation tomorrow, segregation forever." Civil rights demonstrators were beaten and jailed in Birmingham and elsewhere as they staged lunch counter sit-ins and protest marches. The police used high-pressure fire hoses and snarling dogs to turn them back. Wallace defiantly blocked the path of black students attempting to register for classes at the University of Alabama, relenting only when federal marshals forced him to step aside. Kennedy then called in the National Guard to protect the students and a night of violence and confrontation followed.

Once he joined the battle for a civil rights bill, in a haunting televised address on the evening of June 11, 1963, Kennedy accomplished something no other president had even attempted—he made the American people feel the ugliness of racism by daring them to walk in the shoes of its victims.

This address was Kennedy's attempt to govern according to the three principles noted earlier. He perceived that racism was a threat to the nation, and he informed the public of this threat truthfully, without resorting to ideological beliefs.

He began his speech by listing the challenges faced daily by black Americans. They had, he said, one-half the chance of graduating from high school as whites and one-third the chance of completing college. When they could find work, they earned $10,000 a year less than whites. They lived shorter lives than whites. The opportunities to achieve the American Dream that whites took for granted were denied to those with dark skin.

With these grim statistics established, Kennedy said, "Who among us would be content to have the color of his skin changed and stand in [their] place?"

The question presented the American people with an image they could not ignore. Who indeed would be willing to trade places with a black man in the America of 1963?

Kennedy said:

I hope that every American, regardless of where he lives, will stop and examine his conscience... This nation was founded by men of many nations and backgrounds. It was founded on the principle that all men are created equal, and that the rights of every man are diminished when the rights of one man are threatened.

The fight for civil rights, Kennedy asserted, was not a regional issue—by now it had spread to every state in the union. Nor was it strictly a legal or legislative issue. "We are confronted primarily," he said, "with a moral issue. It is as old as the Scriptures and is as clear as the American Constitution."

This statement elevated the cause of civil rights above partisan politics and made it a test of the nation's willingness to embrace change when it was most needed.

The bill Kennedy proposed banned discrimination based on race, color, sex, or national origin. It also made racial segregation illegal in schools, places of employment, and public facilities such as restaurants and hotels. It ended unfair voter registration practices and gave the government the power to file suit against schools that discriminated against black students.

It did omit some measures sought by civil rights leaders, such as greater powers to prevent violence against civil rights protesters.

Meanwhile, the violence continued. The day after Kennedy's address, civil rights activist Medgar Evers was murdered in his driveway in Jackson, Mississippi. On September 15, 1963, four black girls preparing for a service in the basement of a church in Birmingham were killed by a bomb set off by a racist.

An expanded version of Kennedy's civil rights bill was approved eight months after his death. It was a significant contribution to the advancement of civil rights.

President Kennedy receives a warm welcome on a trip to South Dakota. Charismatic and eloquent, Kennedy made us proud of our history and government, creating a palpable sense of forward motion in the nation that today has been replaced by mindless ideological warfare. Photo by George Tames

PART FOUR

THE NATION WE BECAME
WITHOUT KENNEDY

CHAPTER TWENTY-THREE

WHAT KENNEDY GAVE US

How few of the human race have ever had an opportunity of
choosing a system of government for themselves and their children.
—John Adams

ALMOST FROM THE MOMENT OF HIS DEATH, the American people have been struggling to understand why John Kennedy meant so much to them. They know he was a unique leader, but he was not here long enough for them to define exactly why he so quickened the pulse of America.

The key to Kennedy's enduring popularity is that he made us proud of the values that make us a great people and a great nation. To understand this concept, we have to go back to the past, back to the way we began.

In many countries during the 1700s, the common man was used as a mule. He had not been allowed to crawl very far from the primordial swamp of feudalism. His purpose was to serve monarchs, the kings and queens and tsars who, it was believed, derived their dominion over man directly from God.

What was needed to wrench mankind out of this misery was a spark of compassion, a new way of thinking about the value of human life and the way man is governed.

That spark was ignited here, in America, when the citizens of this country created a new form of government and changed the course of Western civilization.

The more you learn about what happened in America during the colonial era, the more you are compelled to stand back in awe and appreciation. The story of what the colonists achieved should be told again and again, as a method of preserving not only their memory, but also the essence of the way we should live today. Everything we have today we owe to men and women who were the most courageous, intellectually gifted, spiritually enlightened, and politically astute people this nation ever produced.

How else do you explain the following: With little hope of victory, our ancestors went to war with the most powerful nation on earth to free themselves from economic slavery. To win this war, they needed men of raw courage to do the fighting and dying. Such men quickly stepped forward and started the most necessary war this nation has ever fought, the American Revolution.

MEN OF COURAGE

ON THE MORNING OF JUNE 17, 1775, preparing for battle on a hill overlooking Boston Harbor was a group of men you could literally smell from a distance. They were teenagers and young men from Massachusetts and Connecticut, a militia called the Army of New England. They had little military training and carried the same muskets and shotguns they had used to hunt and protect their homes.

They were laborers, clerks, farmers, and drifters. The officers who led these men derisively called them "country folk," because they wore rough, unfashionable clothing that was torn and caked with weeks of sweat and dirt. They slept in dank tents made of burlap and stained cloth. Lice and water polluted by raw sewage had spread cholera and typhus in their encampments. Many died before the fighting began and many suffered from fever, dehydration, and diarrhea. Some were homeless because smallpox, dysentery, or flu had wiped out their families. These were hardened men who rebelled against the rigors of military discipline with acts of defiant laziness and drunkenness, unnerving the officers who would lead them in battle.

Ironically, both the enemy they had come to fight that day and the aristocratic man who would become their leader, George Washington, despised these men. In Great Britain, the foppish Lord Sandwich, First Lord of the Admiralty, had called the rebels in America "raw, undisciplined, cowardly men."

Washington called them "exceedingly dirty and nasty men." He wrote to a friend that he had observed an "unaccountable kind of stupidity in the lower class of these people." Many observers said that when the fighting started, this "rabble" would turn and run from the enemy, bringing disgrace to the cause of rebellion.

The fighting began when British warships in Boston Harbor opened fire on the colonists. They inflicted little damage, so after a leisurely lunch, the confident British forces crossed the harbor on barges and massed for an attack. They were well-equipped, well-trained soldiers who had spent their lives in the British army. Their hardened discipline in battle was celebrated around the world.

From atop Breed's Hill, later incorrectly called "Bunker Hill," the amateur colonial fighters looked down on a sea of more than two thousand bright red uniforms and glistening bayonets, a sight that sent fear rippling through their ranks.

As the British advanced up the hill, the colonists were ordered to hold their fire until the enemy was nearly upon them. . . "until they could see the whites of their eyes." They obeyed, and the savage fighting that followed lasted for hours. Cannon fire tore off limbs, the fighting was toe-to-toe, and no quarter was asked or given.

One of the defenders was Dr. Joseph Warren, a handsome, articulate, beloved patriot and friend of future president John Adams. It was Warren who earlier had dispatched Paul Revere on his legendary ride to warn his fellow colonists that, "the British are coming!"

Although he held the rank of major general, Warren fought that day as a private. At about noon, a British soldier shot him in the face at close range and then joined his comrades in mutilating his body with their bayonets.

Twice the British tried to take the hill, and twice they were driven back by musket fire at close range. During the third assault, the colonists ran out of ammunition and retreated, leaving the hill to the British. About 30 of the colonists unable to retreat were executed. A British regular later wrote his wife that his unit "advanced in formation with bayonets lowered, but these men held fast, they fought with a wildness in the eyes that I had not seen before."

When the fog of war cleared, something remarkable became apparent. More than 220 British soldiers lay dead, and 828 had been wounded.

The defenders of Breed's Hill had lost just 141 men, with 271 wounded. The most skilled army in the world had been broken in combat by a foul-smelling, undisciplined group of men who abandoned the field of battle only when they ran out of ammunition.

The fighting on Breed's Hill is an enduring symbol of courage and the fierce, uniquely American desire for freedom. At the time, however, it was not a harbinger of things to come. The war dragged on for eight more bloody years after this initial triumph. Often, it appeared that the British would decimate the Continental Army, and keep the colonies under their control.

In the end, it was Washington's daring escapes and surprise attacks that kept the Revolution alive during its darkest hours, long enough for the fortunes of war to change when the French came to our aid. The combined strength of the Continental Army and the French naval and ground forces proved fatal for the British. They surrendered in 1781 after a long siege at Yorktown, Virginia. The war ended two years later with the signing of the Treaty of Paris in 1783.

This nation exists today because Washington and his officers were skilled and daring tacticians who, although badly outnumbered and without sufficient equipment, managed to hold together a force of men who fought with the "wildness in the eyes" that had so frightened the British regulars on Breed's Hill.

The cost of this victory was unimaginable suffering by both those who fought and those who stayed at home. A colonial wife wrote to her warrior husband, "Buried our son yesterday. Grace went last January. There is no food, the cattle taken by the army. Come home."

In its scope, the American Revolution was the equal of any great conflict the world has ever known. It was a world war, involving the United States, Great Britain, France, and Spain. The fighting went on for 80 months, 17 months longer than World War I and World War II combined. More than 4,000 men died in combat, and more than 6,000 were wounded. About 17,000 men died from disease or starvation.

When war-related deaths are added to these figures, such as the family members who starved to death because the man of the house was absent, the total number of fatalities swells to 50,000, which is more than one million people relative to the population today.

MEN OF VIRTUE

WHEN THE WAR ENDED, the colonists faced a seemingly impossible task: They had to create a new form of government from the ashes of the Revolution. An estimated 2.8 million people, roughly the population of Chicago today, lived in 13 states, each governed by legislatures and other forms of local government. Badly needed was a central government that would tie the states together and provide Americans with the right, as mandated by the Declaration of Independence, to life, liberty, and the pursuit of happiness.

Remarkably, without decades of experimentation to guide them, the system of government the colonists created, while not perfect, so precisely matched the needs and the psyche of the American people that it has lasted for more than 200 years.

This system was not, as many assume, a democracy, the form of self-rule that made Ancient Greece an advanced civilization. In a pure democracy, individual citizens themselves enact laws that govern the nation. They attend meetings and vote on proposed laws and referendums. Every citizen who meets eligibility requirements has one vote, and a majority vote is required to pass a law.

A democracy, however, as the Founding Fathers perceived, will inevitably fail the people. Man has always been and will always be corruptible. Those with the wealth to buy votes will eventually control a democracy.

Acutely aware of this weakness, the Founders instead based our government on the principles of a *republic*. Rather than allowing the people to vote on issues directly, a republic requires them to elect political leaders to represent them in a central, or federal, government. In the houses of this government, they will make decisions that reflect the will of their constituents.

THE PUBLIC GOOD

THIS SYSTEM IS SUPERIOR TO A DEMOCRACY, James Madison said, because the responsibility for making laws is delegated:

> to a small number of citizens elected by the rest [who would] refine and enlarge the public views by passing them through the medium of a chosen body of citizens whose wisdom may best discern the

true interest of their country and whose patriotism and love of justice will be least likely to sacrifice it to temporary or partial considerations.

Under such a regulation, it may well happen that the public voice, pronounced by the representatives of the people, will be more consonant to the public good than if pronounced by the people themselves, convened for the same purpose.

How did the colonists acquire the wisdom to create a republic for America?

These rough-hewn freedom fighters were also intellectuals who prized learning and critical thinking. About 40 percent of the colonial population, and certainly all of the Founding Fathers, had avidly read the works of the Ancient Greek philosophers who promoted the concept of democracy. George Washington is said to have kept two books on his night table, one the work of Cicero and the other the Bible.

THE ENLIGHTENMENT

THEY ALSO READ THE WORKS of the philosophers, novelists, playwrights, satirists, and humorists who had ignited the Enlightenment, often called the Age of Reason, an 18th-century social reform movement that changed the world.

During the Enlightenment, writers such as Francis Bacon, John Locke, and Jean Jacques Rousseau, challenged the medieval wisdom that men without wealth or title were incapable of rational thought and thus the property of the nobility and upper classes. They urged people to think for themselves, to question authority and religious dogma, to shed medieval thinking and embrace science and reason. They argued that man, simply because he exists, simply because he is a human being, has the right to govern himself.

Thus, the Founders used their knowledge of history, philosophy, science, religion, and the nature of man himself to create a new form of government. It was based on two concepts. The first was the Enlightenment notion that man has the right to govern himself. The second was the colonial obsession with "civic virtue," the belief that a government that values the public good more than the individual's ability to attain wealth or political power is the most productive and equitable form of government available to man.

This new form of government was a democracy based on the ideals of a republic, or more precisely, a "democratic republic."

This was a wonderful beginning for this country. We were glued together by the principles of republican government and the belief that we are our brother's keeper. The colonists so ardently believed in the concept of the public good that they called their state governments "Commonwealths."

There was, however, a problem. This type of government, as the Founders understood, is fragile; it would succeed only if the following conditions were met:

- The people and their political leaders must maintain their belief that a central government is necessary to give society a legal and legislative structure and to prevent chaos.

- The people must educate themselves about the issues that affect the quality of their lives. An informed public will tend to elect principled political leaders who, as Madison said, will "best discern the true interest of their country."

- Political leaders must devote themselves to serving the common good, not to gaining personal wealth or directing wealth to others. When this happens, the government will become corrupt and unable to promote the welfare of the nation. "The happiness of the people," John Adams said, "is the sole end of government."

The Founders stressed these prerequisites over and over, drumming them into the consciousness of American citizens. John Adams said, "Liberty cannot be preserved without knowledge among the people." James Madison said, "Knowledge will forever govern ignorance; and a people who mean to be their own governors must arm themselves with power which knowledge gives."

There was a beautiful logic, a near perfect symmetry, to the system created by the Founders. When the people value government and become well informed about important issues, they do indeed tend to elect political leaders who will honor their responsibility to serve the common good. And when both the people and the politicians they elect do nothing to dilute or exploit this remarkable system, they form a partnership that is the foundation of the political and social enlightenment that makes the United States a great country.

THE PRESIDENT WHO UNDERSTOOD AMERICA

JOHN KENNEDY IS THE MOST STUDIED president in history. Every aspect of his childhood, his wartime experiences, his political career, his presidency, his sex life, and the manner of his death, has been dissected, probed, and reviewed in thousands of books and countless magazine articles and documentaries.

Yet, not found anywhere in this mountain of material is the following assertion: It is astonishing how close he brought this country to the ideals established by the Founders. More completely than any president who followed him, and perhaps more completely than any president in history, he understood the beautiful logic of a republic. He possessed the insight, so rare in political leaders, to understand that the engine that runs a republic is the reciprocal relationship between the people and their government.

In 1960, as he campaigned for the presidency, Kennedy sat in front of a dictabelt, an early version of the tape recorder, and spoke about the role of government in America. Among his comments, as published in *Listening In: The Secret White House Recordings of John F. Kennedy,* was the following:

> But the fact remains that politics has become one of our most abused and neglected professions. . . . Yet it is this profession, it is these politicians who make the great decisions of war and peace, prosperity and recession, the decision whether we look to the future or the past. In a large sense everything now depends upon what the government decides.

> Therefore, if you are interested, if you want to participate, if you feel strongly about any public question, whether it's labor, what happens in India, the future of American agriculture, whatever it may be, it seems to me that governmental service is the way to translate this interest into action, that the natural place for the concerned citizen is to contribute part of his life to the national interest.

This was a soon-to-be president of the United States advocating participatory democracy, a vital component of our unique political system. Kennedy did not merely pay lip service to republican values; he believed in them, and understood that the Founders had devised a system that should never be tampered with or changed.

It is also astonishing how far the country has drifted from the form of government the Founders gave us and that Kennedy championed.

This drift was something the Founders feared. In Philadelphia on September 17, 1787, shortly before the final draft of the American Constitution was signed, Benjamin Franklin spoke before the Constitutional Convention to offer his unvarnished view of the four-page document that would in minutes become the supreme law of the land.

Franklin predicted that "for a course of years" the United States would be "well administered" by men who understood the values spelled out in the Constitution.

He warned, however, that when this course of years reached an end, when the nation ceased to follow the Founder's original design, the country would succumb to "Despotism, as other forms of government have done before it, when the people shall become so corrupted as to need despotic government, incapable of being any other."

Franklin was leaving Independence Hall, when a woman asked him the following question: "Well, Doctor, what have you given us, a republic or a monarchy?" After pausing for a moment, Franklin replied, "A republic, Madam, if you can keep it."

For 1,036 days, Kennedy pointed us in the right direction. Then he went to Texas and his inspired leadership disappeared. Traumatized by the horror of his murder, we could not follow his lead, and the "course of years" in which we honored the original intent of the Founders came to an end.

CHAPTER TWENTY-FOUR

SOMETHING GROTESQUE AND SENSELESS

Dallas is a very violent place. I wouldn't go there. Don't you go there.
— Senator J. William Fulbright to John Kennedy.

I N 1963, DALLAS WAS A MECCA for those who disdained anything soft or compassionate. Every year, more than a hundred people were murdered in the Big D, most of them by handguns or rifles. It was a city that admired men who settled their disputes with gunfire.

Writing about Dallas in *Death of a President,* William Manchester said the city exhibited a "stridency, a disease of the spirit, a shrill, hysterical note suggestive of a deeply troubled society."

Violence was just one symptom of the "disease of the spirit" in Dallas. Right-wing politicians and oil billionaires funded and encouraged the fanaticism of militant groups such as the John Birch Society and the Minutemen.

Those who joined these fringe groups saw enemies everywhere; they believed that liberals and Jews were bent on taking over the world by controlling banks or by secretly aiding and abetting the evil overlords of Communism. These citizens had armed themselves and stockpiled weapons. They stood ready to fight, and when the enemy finally arrived on their shores, they would rise with righteous fury and defend their God-fearing way of life.

John Kennedy became a lightning rod for their contempt. He asked Americans to view the Soviet Union not simply as a potential enemy, but also as a nation whose people cherished the future of their children and sought to enjoy life, just like us.

This manner of thought did not go down well in a city that valued blind toughness. Schoolchildren in certain areas of the city were encouraged to boo when his name was mentioned; racists and extremists openly wished for his death because he was a "communist and race mixer" who had no respect for decency or democracy.

Kennedy's decision to ride in an open limousine in this city, with his wife at his side, is perplexing. He had been warned by many people to avoid Dallas. Just months before, his trip, U.N. Ambassador Adlai Stevenson had been attacked in Dallas by frenzied right-wing demonstrators who chased him into his car and rocked it back and forth in an effort to turn it over.

During the 1960 campaign, Lyndon Johnson and his wife had been spit upon in a hotel lobby in Dallas. The perpetrators of this disgraceful incident were right-wing Dallas housewives, who believed that Johnson was too liberal. For the rest of her life, Lady Bird Johnson trembled when she entered the city and counted the minutes until she could depart.

In 1961, Kennedy invited a group of Texas newspaper publishers to a White House lunch. Among them was Ted Dealey, publisher of the *Dallas Morning News*. His contribution to the proceedings had been to launch an attack on his host that shocked those who heard his rants.

"We can annihilate Russia and should make that clear to the Soviet government," he shouted. Addressing Kennedy directly, he said, "You and your administration are weak sisters. We need a man on horseback to lead this nation, and many people in Texas and the Southwest think that you are riding Caroline's tricycle."

The most violent of these sentiments, of course, were not representative of the views of the majority of Dallas citizens, who likely viewed Kennedy as a Harvard-educated northern liberal, too effete to stand up to the march of Communism, as evidenced by his failure to engage the Soviet Union in a nuclear war during the Cuban missile crisis.

Kennedy was aware of the city's menace, and he expressed a vague sense of apprehension about the trip. Two days before his departure, he suddenly looked up from his paperwork and told an aide, "I wish I didn't have to go to Texas."

Not long after arriving in the city, he said to Jackie, "We are in nut country now." He had listened when Senator J. William Fulbright of Arkansas described Dallas as a city so poisoned by violence that he would not visit friends who lived there. "Dallas is a very violent place. I wouldn't go there. Don't you go there," he emphatically told the president. It is not known whether Kennedy received the message sent by evangelist Billy Graham, also warning him to stay out of Dallas.

One warning in particular would haunt Kennedy intimates for the rest of their lives. On November 4, Byron Skelton, a Democratic Party official in Texas, sent a letter to Attorney General Robert Kennedy begging him to call off the trip. Skelton believed the violence in Dallas was building to a crescendo. Billionaire H. L. Hunt had given a speech in Houston in which he said the Kennedy was the head of a "Communist government." At a dinner party, he said the only way to get the Kennedys out of government was "to shoot them out."

This type of insanity, Skelton feared, could inspire an unstable person to harm the president. His was the first warning to express the notion that Kennedy faced physical danger in Dallas rather than merely the shouted epithets of the deranged.

Bobby Kennedy knew and respected Skelton. Alarmed, he forwarded the letter to Ken O'Donnell, the president's aide and appointments director. Skelton sent a similar letter to Lyndon Johnson's top aide and spent hours pleading with party officials to cancel the trip. They decided that Skelton was miffed because he had not been invited to meet the president in Dallas and dismissed his pleas.

In his 80s, still filled with sorrow that his warnings had not evoked a reaction, Skelton in 1988 choked back his emotions when he told a newspaper that he could not believe that Kennedy had been allowed to "drive down the streets of Dallas."

President Kennedy went to Texas because two of the state's most powerful political leaders, Governor John Connally and Senator Ralph Yarborough, were embroiled in a political squabble over the dispensation of patronage. If their feud escalated, it could fracture the unity of the state's Democrats, a threat to Kennedy's chance of carrying the state in the upcoming election.

Kennedy's goal was to force the feuding men to ride together in presidential motorcades in Texas, making such a show of their unity that the squabble would fade from the news. Dallas was the last stop on his fence-mending trip.

With Johnson, a Texan, on the ticket, Kennedy had carried Texas by a mere 46,233 votes in 1960, but few of those votes came from Dallas. More than 65 percent of the city's 700,000 residents had voted for Nixon. Although he had to fight for the electoral votes Texas offered in the next election, Kennedy could have heeded the numerous warnings and avoided Dallas.

Politics was not the only reason he felt compelled to make the trip. When warned of a potentially hostile reception in Dallas, Kennedy said that the president of the United States should never bow to threats.

The trip did have its pleasant moments. The walls of the Kennedy's hotel suite in Fort Worth had been adorned with works of art, an acknowledgment of Jackie Kennedy's genteel sensibilities. Before departing for Dallas, the couple had phoned the gracious woman who arranged this gesture and expressed their thanks.

Unfortunately, Kennedy had been unable to prevent Jackie from seeing a poster that had mug shots of him under a headline that read: "Wanted For Treason."

After a short flight from Fort Worth, the Kennedys landed at Love Field outside of Dallas. They sat together in the back of a dark blue limousine that would take them into the city. Kennedy's schedule called for one speech there and another that evening in Austin. After an overnight stay at Johnson's ranch, they would fly home to their two children. Jacqueline Kennedy's decision to travel with him had surprised and delighted her husband; her presence would help him politically, but the trip was also part of a healing process. In August, she had given birth to a son, but the baby was born six weeks early, developed breathing problems, and died. Afterward, she told her husband, "The only thing I could not stand would be losing you."

A PINK CLOUD OF BLOOD

AT 12:30 P.M., IN THE DOWNTOWN SECTION of Dallas, Kennedy's driver made a sharp left turn in front of the Texas School Book Depository, a brick building in an area known as Dealey

Plaza. The small, grassy park was named after the father of Ted Dealey, the publisher who had so rudely insulted Kennedy in the White House.

The driver did not accelerate out of the turn; instead, he slowed to just 11 miles per hour. This was a perfect setup for murder. Armed with a rifle with a telescopic sight, a man willing to take John Kennedy's life, even with minimal shooting skills, could not miss his target.

And to the nation's horror, that is what happened. Waiting for the limousine was a 22-year-old man crouched behind a sixth floor window of the Depository. He had no connection to the fringe groups in Dallas; he was not a Bircher or a Minuteman. Instead, he concealed his insanity, having no need for the approval of his fellow madmen. It is hard to imagine him committing such a deranged act in any other American city. Lee Harvey Oswald and Dallas were a perfect fit. His contempt for life was monumental, boiling inside a tormented mind. In a barely comprehensible diary entry, he had written that he would like to "...stand up and say he was utterly opposed not only to the governments, but to the people, too [sic] the entire land and complete foundations of his socially."

From just 265 feet away, he took aim at Kennedy with a cheap, mail order rifle and fired three shots in 8.6 seconds. The last shot entered the back of Kennedy's skull at 1,700 feet-per-second, and his life evaporated in a pink cloud of blood. Jackie saw a piece of her husband's skull pinwheel in the air and climbed onto the trunk of the limousine to retrieve it. Clint Hill, the Secret Service agent assigned to protect her, the only man alert enough to act as the shots rang out, pushed Jackie into the backseat before she tumbled off the trunk of the accelerating limousine.

She later handed the piece of skull to a doctor, who fought vainly to save the president's life, and asked, "Will this help?"

President Kennedy had once visited his vice-president at his sprawling ranch near Austin. Johnson invited the president to go deer hunting the morning after his arrival. Kennedy had seen men die in war. He was not intrigued by guns and regarded the shooting of animals not as sport, but rather as unnecessary cruelty.

Thinking that turning his back on this Southern rite of passage would be rude, Kennedy killed a deer, put down the rifle, and then quickly walked away, feeling not pride in the kill but rather a sense of guilt that would haunt him for some time.

Now his body lay on a hard leather table in Trauma Room One of Parkland Memorial Hospital, four miles from Dealey Plaza, the victim of a man who had no qualms about ending life.

He had been hit twice from behind by 6.5 millimeter, round-nosed shells. The first shot hit him high up on his back, near his neck, and exited under the Adam's apple in his throat. The second shot entered the back of his head and blew out the top right side of his skull when it exited.

More than a dozen physicians, including a urologist, had rushed to the tiny trauma room, but none of them could help the president. The floor was soaked with his blood. He had no pulse. His eyes were open and his pupils were fixed and divergent, but the doctors could still detect sporadic, faint heartbeats. So they went forward with standard life-saving measures, even though to a man they knew it was hopeless.

Jacqueline Kennedy forced her way into the room. "I want to be there when he dies," she said. The doctors continued their futile work. A tracheotomy was performed and a breathing tube was inserted into Kennedy's windpipe. Measures were taken to prevent his lungs from collapsing, blood was transfused into his system, and his chest was massaged in an effort to keep his heart beating.

This charade, however, could not go on for long. The best doctors the hospital could offer tried to save the life of the leader of the free world, but the gaping wound in the president's head was clearly fatal. His vital signs went flat, and finally, at 1:00 p.m., the doctors accepted the unacceptable. Dr. Kemp Clark turned to Jacqueline Kennedy and said, "Your husband has sustained a fatal wound." Her response was a barely audible "I know."

ESCAPING PARKLAND

THE HORRORS OF PARKLAND HOSPITAL had not yet ended for Jacqueline Kennedy. She desperately wanted to flee from this place of blood and tubes and death. She wanted her husband's body to lie in state at the White House, the hallowed ground of presidents that would serve as the epicenter of the grief and ceremony that would help mute the ugliness of his death.

Nurses washed Kennedy's body, and towels were wrapped around his shattered head. He was lifted into a coffin, which was placed on a gurney and wheeled by Secret Service agents toward the exit. But Earl

Rose, the medical examiner of Dallas, blocked their way, insisting that the body stay in Dallas for autopsy.

The bodyguards surrounded the diminutive official, reminding him of the occupation of the victim and Jacqueline Kennedy's wish to leave the hospital. But his position was firm. Texas law says the body of a homicide victim must be examined to determine the cause of death, no matter whom the victim might be.

The coffin became a battering ram, shoved forward by the agents and pushed back by those trying to uphold the law. The agents pulled back their suit jackets to expose the guns on their hips, but Rose could not be intimidated. He finally stood aside only when higher-ups sent word to release the body. The dazed and angry bodyguards shoved the gurney past him and made their way to a waiting ambulance.

Her skirt and stockings stained by the insanity in Dallas, Jackie Kennedy brought her husband's body home to the nation's capital. Few who were of age at that time will ever forget the imagery she created over the next three days—Caroline Kennedy and her mother kneeling before the casket, the president's three-year-old son saluting his father, the muffled drums, the haunting funeral dirge, the riderless horse, the eternal flame at Arlington Cemetery.

The nation thought of Jackie as fragile and emotionally delicate. Few would have minded if she hid her shattered emotions from the public. Her decision to walk behind her husband's cortege for the eight blocks from the White House to St. Matthew's Cathedral for her husband's funeral mass telegraphed a sense of strength that helped people grieve. She led the president's brothers and world leaders to the mass, her grief-swollen face barely visible behind a black veil, adding dignity to the awful proceedings.

A San Francisco columnist artfully captured the mood of the country just after the assassination:

> It is less than 72 hours since the shots rang out in Dallas, yet it seems a lifetime—a lifetime of weeping skies, wet eyes and streets. Over the endless weekend, San Francisco looked like a city that was only slowly emerging from a terrible bombardment. Downtown, on what would normally have been a bustling Saturday, the people walked slowly, as in shock, their faces pale and drawn; their mood as somber as the dark clothes they wore under the gray skies.

The assassination brought the country to its knees. More than 93 percent of the televisions in the country were tuned to the three days of mourning that followed the assassination.

The public had not paid much attention to the personal side of Dwight Eisenhower; he was an aging man with a plain-looking wife, and few were fascinated by the details of his family life.

This all changed when Caroline and John Jr. and Jackie came on-stage. The White House released a steady stream of family photos and movies. They showed Caroline riding her pony or John with a basket on his head, scenes of young, vital people that charmed the nation. Republicans said this was shamefully political, but others felt that Kennedy was proud of his children and eager to illustrate the pleasures and importance of family. When he died, we felt not only our own sorrow, but also that of his wife, his children, his two brothers, his mother, and his father.

It is no wonder the nation was traumatized by the assassination. It is no wonder that it took years to heal from this trauma. In 2004, a survey found that Americans who lived through both the Kennedy assassination and the terrorist attacks of September 11, 2001, were more deeply affected by the assassination. For a long time after Dallas, their patterns of daily life were disrupted; they could not sleep, eat, or work as usual. The suddenness and brutality of Kennedy's death would remain with many Americans for the rest of their lives.

So would the horrible realization that a president was not safe in an American city. While Dallas itself could not be blamed for the actions of a single man, it had provided the diseased backdrop in which his compulsion to commit murder seemed normal and acceptable.

For those interested in the details of the assassination, and the way the shooting itself and the days of mourning that followed seeped into the consciousness of the nation, homage must be paid to William Manchester. His remarkable ability to focus on the details of this time was a triumph of reporting. He brought to life and gave larger meaning to incidents and events that lesser writers would have ignored.

Jacqueline Kennedy, for example, had decided that her husband's autopsy would take place at Bethesda Naval Hospital in Maryland. Upon hearing this news, Jackie's parents, Janet and Hudi Auchincloss, along with Kennedy friends Ben Bradlee and his wife, Toni, left the White House and were driven to the hospital to be with Jackie.

"A platoon of white-helmeted policemen," Manchester wrote:

led the car to the District line, where Maryland state troopers took over. Every officer was winding his siren, and from passing cruisers and firehouses, some of them blocks away, other sirens echoed the strident wails. It was baroque. It was Ray Bradbury. It was a perpetual fire alarm—if every house in greater Washington had been ablaze, the noise would have been identical.

Manchester said that the driver of the car, for no apparent reason other than his wish to be of service, hit speeds of 90 miles per hour. The two men sat up front while:

the four women cowering together in the back were literally frightened for their lives. "That ride was so bad," Bradlee later recalled, "that it took your mind off everything else. It was an assault on a man's senses. It added a new dimension. Before there had been sadness and the suffering with the [Kennedy] children. Now there was darkness and this unbelievable velocity. . . . I had the feeling that we were racing toward our doom.

Many in the nation on that November evening shared these feelings. We wanted to become sirens, to wail and howl our protest, and there was a palpable and disturbing sense of impending doom as the nation fought to understand what it had lost.

CHAPTER TWENTY-FIVE

TEARING DOWN AN IDOL

He will be just a flicker, forever clouded by the record of his successors.
I don't think history will have much space for John Kennedy.
-— Richard Neustadt

W ITH THE BENEFIT of a half-century of hindsight, it is possible to conclude that, during the past 50 years, John Kennedy's reputation has passed through three distinct phases: idealization, reassessment, and understanding. Exploring these phases is perhaps the best way to discover who Kennedy truly was and what he meant to the nation.

PHASE ONE: IDEALIZATION

IN THE AFTERMATH OF HIS ASSASSINATION, Kennedy was elevated to a status that is still difficult to define. He had not died for a specific cause, so he was not a martyr. His death did not fit into any category of cause and effect that our minds could construct; the reason for his assassination was beyond comprehension. If the shooting in Dealey Plaza occurred today, it would be recorded by cell phone cameras and immediately uploaded to the Internet. We would be able to watch endless replays until we became numb to the horror. In 1963, however, we could only imagine what had happened to President Kennedy. We knew only that he had been shot in the head, a fate too hideous to fully comprehend.

The only recourse for historians, the media, and the people was to wrap him in a blanket of unconditional reverence. We were not interested in his weaknesses, the mistakes he had made or the flaws in his character. There was little desire to dig too deeply into his policies or his psyche.

This idealization, of course, was the product of shock and grief, the aftermath of a national trauma unlike anything the nation had endured since the Lincoln assassination. Franklin Roosevelt had died in office in 1945. But his health had been poor and while his death was still a shock, it was not unexpected. Kennedy's death was an ugly perversion of the way we believed life should play out.

During this phase, it was impossible to say anything negative about Kennedy; the people simply would not tolerate criticism of their dead president. Kennedy had said that he would like a biography written about him at some point that "exposed the warts and all," but such objective analysis was not possible in the years after the assassination.

Aides and friends wrote sympathetic accounts of their years with him, while historians wrote reverential books conspicuously devoid of objective criticism. Countless schools and highways soon bore his name. The nation kept a close watch on his widow and two children, and each anniversary of his death brought new sadness and reflection. Then, in 1968, the assassinations of Robert Kennedy and Martin Luther King made the world seem randomly perverse.

PHASE TWO: REASSESSMENT

IT IS NORMAL FOR ICONS TO FALL, for society to tear down those it had once placed on the highest perch. Winston Churchill, who held Great Britain together with eloquence and tenacity during World War II, was voted out of office after the war ended.

Historians have written about Thomas Jefferson in reverent tones, but some also reviled him for owning slaves. The same is true of Andrew Jackson, variously a champion of democracy and a cold-bloodied man who ordered the deaths of American Indians.

Abraham Lincoln is considered the greatest president in history. A few, however, believe that he was a secret racist and morally bankrupt because he visited prostitutes as a young man.

John Kennedy was not exempt from this duality. The unqualified admiration that followed his death began to fade a decade after Dallas. In 1973, historian Arthur Link said, "As I look back now on the years '61 to '63, what seemed like great events and forward movement do not seem so great or so forward now."

That same year, writer I. F. Stone said of Kennedy, "By now he is simply an optical illusion." Richard Neustadt, who had worked as a Kennedy aide said, "He will be just a flicker, forever clouded by the record of his successors. I don't think history will have much space for John Kennedy."

These writers did not diminish Kennedy because they had discovered evidence of his misconduct or incompetence. Their criticism was most likely an emotional backlash to the depth of sorrow they felt after the assassination. When the shock of Dallas subsided, they may have felt it necessary to correct their overreaction by lashing out at Kennedy.

This rethinking of Kennedy's image actually began in small ways while he was still alive. He had inspired visions of dramatic action and change with his elevated oratory. Some felt he had let them down in this regard, and his popularity, ever so slightly, began to fade.

In the months before Dallas, his poll results were still high, but they had dipped from their highest numbers. It is difficult to believe today, but if Kennedy had lived to face a strong opponent in 1964, the election may have been a close contest.

SERIAL ADULTERY

THE FULL-SCALE DISMANTLING of Kennedy's image by historians and pundits, however, began in earnest after it became evident that he had suffered from an insatiable, perhaps pathological, need for sex.

He had committed adultery many times during his marriage. He had sex with young women in the White House swimming pool. He had sex with Marilyn Monroe in a White House bedroom. He had slept with strippers and the mistress of a mafia boss. He had sex with Jackie's friends. He had sex with the girl next door and women of high society. He contracted a venereal disease, which he may have passed to his wife. Jackie Kennedy supposedly once handed him a pair of panties she found in their bed and said, "These are not mine."

The humiliations endured by Jackie Kennedy made John Kennedy seem detestable. Some who had viewed him with high regard during his lifetime were unable to conceal their disgust and disappointment. The man who challenged us to seek personal excellence was secretly leading a life of debauchery that made him appear to be a hypocrite.

Kennedy did not live to face the consequences of his actions; we never heard him publicly confront this side of his nature, which made it difficult to forgive him after he was gone.

He may have sensed that he could not hide his personal life forever. Several Kennedy intimates observed that during the last months of his life he had been unusually withdrawn and distant.

Ethel Kennedy, his sister-in-law, recalled that she had greeted him with a sunny hello at a social function, but he did not reply. "He looked right through me, as if I was not there," she said. He seemed troubled, preoccupied with something that disturbed him.

It could have been the growing chaos in Vietnam or his fear that his support of civil rights would jeopardize his re-election.

He may also have finally realized that his sex life could be exposed. In 1962, he had watched in horror as the government of Harold Macmillan was brought down when his Foreign Secretary confessed to having an affair with a call girl. There were rumors in Washington that Kennedy himself had been involved with a prostitute from East Germany whom his brother, with the help of J. Edgar Hoover, had secretly deported.

Kennedy may have feared that all this would catch up with him, and one day his presidency would come apart at the seams.

After reading evidence of Marilyn Monroe's phone calls to the White House, Ben Bradlee, a Kennedy friend and editor of the *Washington Post*, said, "It is now widely accepted history that Kennedy jumped casually from bed to bed, with a wide variety of women. Kennedy screwed around. . . a lot."

The details of Kennedy's truly prodigious sex life bordered on the bizarre. They also raised the possibility that he was somehow unhinged from reality. There was no other way to explain his refusal to recognize the risks he took in pursuit of sexual pleasure. His affair with Judith Campbell Exner, the mistress of powerful mob boss Sam Giancana, was difficult to accept on several levels. Historian Michael Beschloss wrote of their affair:

> If Sam Giancana ever threatened, for instance, to publicize evidence
> of Kennedy's relationship, [with Exner], the president could have

been faced with a choice between giving in to whatever demands Giancana made or allowing himself to be driven out of office. What president could survive the revelation that he had knowingly slept with the mistress of a Mafia chief?

Every woman Kennedy brought into the White House or met in hotels around the country could have exploited or harmed him. A Secret Service agent during the Kennedy years said, "We didn't know if these women were carrying listening devices, if they had syringes that carried some sort of poison, or if they had Pentax cameras that would photograph the president for blackmail."

In the 1960s, the United States was a more puritanical country than it is today, and far less tolerant of sexual misconduct. If Kennedy's prolific sex life had been exposed as he campaigned in 1964, it would have been viewed as aberrant, tawdry, and unforgivable. It is unlikely that he would been re-elected.

Evaluations of Kennedy's presidency during this time were based on his weaknesses as a man. His detractors argued that if he had fooled us about his character, then by extension his presidency must have also been a sham.

He was described in books and magazines as an arrogant and reckless man whose rise to prominence had been stage-managed by a power-mad family. He had manipulated us into voting for him with the latest public relations techniques, exploiting his good looks and the appeal of his glamorous wife and young children. His idealism and eloquence were props, window dressing to enhance his image of vitality. His lust for power was inappropriate; he should have delayed his bid for the presidency until more senior Democrats had taken their turn.

In a flood of books after 1975, Kennedy was depicted as a vain, shallow opportunist. His father was described as a bootlegger, a corrupt businessman and a Wall Street manipulator, and Jack Kennedy was somehow guilty by association. The most objective observers believed that Kennedy had acted with courage after his PT boat was sunk. However, it was now argued that he had actually been negligent, that he should have been court-marshaled rather than decorated for bravery.

Another writer said that Kennedy was a cautious, mediocre elitist whose administration was no more successful than that of James K. Polk. Thomas C. Reeves, in his book, *A Question of Character,* suggested that Kennedy had used his good looks, wealth, and speaking ability to hide the fact that he was little more than a playboy. He solemnly warned that in the future we might "once more be swayed by someone who is wonderfully attractive, has a glib tongue, a bottomless wallet, and a conscience that asks little and demands even less."

In England, satirist Malcolm Muggeridge wrote, "John F. Kennedy, it is now coming to be realized, was a nothing-man—an expensively programmed waxwork; a camera-microphone-public relations creation whose career, on examination, turns into a strip cartoon rather than history."

For several years, the pundits had their say. In addition to his sexual deviance, they said Kennedy had been arrogant and abusive. He took advantage of people. In his book *President Kennedy,* Richard Reeves said of him:

> It was almost as if those around him were figures in a tableaux, who came alive only when John Kennedy was in place at the center. He was an artist who painted with other people's lives. He squeezed people like tubes of paint, gently or brutally, and the people around him—family, writers, drivers, ladies-in-waiting—were the indentured inhabitants serving his needs and desires.

These were the characteristics, Reeves noted, of one of Kennedy's heroes, Lord Melbourne, prime minister of Great Britain from 1834 to 1841. A biography of Melbourne by David Cecil, called *Melbourne,* had been one of Kennedy's favorite books. Reeves quoted Cecil's description of Melbourne as follows, implying that Kennedy had exhibited the same traits:

> The spark that should have kindled his fire was unlit, with the result that he never felt moved to discipline his intellectual processes, to organize his sporadic reflections into a coherent system of thought. He had studied a great many subjects, but none thoroughly; his ideas were original, but they were fragmentary, scattered, immature. His amateurishness was increased by his hedonism.

In the considered opinion of Richard Reeves, President Kennedy was a dilettante; he had not fully applied his skills in office because the pursuit of physical pleasure drained his energy. He was adept at playing the role of a president, manipulating others, and basking in adoration. The nation had been swept up in a frenzy of affection for a pretender.

The nation also learned that Kennedy, who had studied the life of Melbourne and invited cellist Pablo Casals to the White House, had a taste for "low-brow" entertainment. Reporters found that he had made trips while president to Las Vegas to visit Frank Sinatra and other entertainers. Their job had been to line up compliant starlets for the president to sleep with.

The political worm also turned. An older charge that Ted Sorensen had ghostwritten much of *Profiles in Courage* was recycled. It also became clear that Kennedy had lied about the extent of his health problems when he denied suffering from Addison's disease.

We also learned that he had taken amphetamines and experimented with marijuana and possibly LSD while serving as president.

PHASE THREE: UNDERSTANDING

IN THIS NEXT PHASE, historians and biographers began to move beyond the salacious nature of Kennedy's sex life and assess the factors that had made him the man he was. We learned how difficult and complex his life had been. In addition to his life-threatening health problems, he may have been the victim of maternal neglect that today could be considered child abuse.

In his 1995 book, *Reckless Youth*, Nigel Hamilton said that Jack's mother gave her nine children clinically efficient parenting, but that she was incapable of the outward expressions of love that children need.

Jack once complained that not once during his childhood had Rose held him in her arms. When he collapsed and nearly died at boarding school, he was alone, emaciated, and frightened, but his mother failed to visit her seriously ill son.

She also went on long vacations at least 17 times during Kennedy's childhood. Jack said that he had cried when his mother announced that she was departing on another vacation, until he realized that his tears caused her to become even more remote.

Finally, as she prepared to take a six-week road trip, a precocious six-year-old Jack Kennedy challenged Rose with the following: "Gee, you're a great mother to go away and leave your children all alone."

When he needed his mother the most, Kennedy said years later, "she was on her knees in some church." In 1944, when he came home from the war so weak that friends feared for his life, Rose sent a friend to greet him at the airport.

Rose died in 1995 at the age of 104. The diaries she kept were released 12 years after her death. They included the following entry:

> Why did I spend time learning to read Goethe or Voltaire if I have to spend my life telling children why they should drink their milk or why they should only eat one piece of candy each day and then after meals.

Joe Kennedy was more expressive and affectionate than Rose. He showered affection on his children, telling them stories and reading to them. He often told them how much he loved them, supporting and applauding their efforts to succeed in the world. But building a fortune was demanding and Joe was not home often.

Like many neglected teenagers, Jack Kennedy managed to get some of the nurturing he needed from outsiders, a football coach and a few special teachers at Choate, and the growing number of boys who sought his friendship. He was a student of rare intellectual ability, but he needed time to mature.

A MATTER OF SEX

BOTH JOE AND ROSE KENNEDY were terrible role models for a young man heading toward the sexual awakening of puberty. Rose was terrified of sex and used religious piety as a shield against all things sexual. She relentlessly screened the reading material and films made available to the children, hunting down anything she considered "dirty."

Joe, in contrast, had an insatiable appetite for sex and had numerous affairs during his marriage. The children became accustomed to his philandering, which he flaunted in front of them. He did little to prevent his eldest sons from following his example. Thus, Jack and his brothers received confusing messages: one parent tried to make them ashamed of sex, and the other encouraged them to sleep with as many women as possible.

For a boy in the Kennedy family, adultery was an acceptable component of marriage.

THE PEOPLE'S VIEW

THE NEGATIVE VIEWS OF KENNEDY during the years of reassessment were offered by historians, politicians, and pundits. Nothing they revealed, however, lessened the nation's high regard for Kennedy. In a 1991 poll, he ranked as the second greatest president in history, a few percentage points behind Abraham Lincoln, an astonishing statement of respect.

In 2010, long after the shock of his death had dissipated, Kennedy's public approval rating was 84 percent. His image had survived an intense period of investigation that would have ruined the reputation of any other president. In the end, the public steadfastly refused to believe, as Richard Reeves asserted in 1991, that Kennedy was an amateur pretending to be president.

Far from being amateurish, despite his questionable personal life, Kennedy's presidency was so effective that the United States is still reeling from his loss.

CHAPTER TWENTY-SIX

THE COMMON CAUSE DECAYS

Hell, those dumb, stupid sailors were just shooting at flying fish!
— Lyndon Johnson, explaining what really happened
at the Gulf of Tonkin.

WILLIAM MANCHESTER occasionally travelled to the White House to talk with President Kennedy about history and government. During one of their conversations, Kennedy mentioned that he was a reader of Thucydides, saying that one of the Greek historian's comments had so impressed him that he had committed it to memory. It said that nation's suffer when political leaders:

> devote more time to the prosecution of their own purposes than to the consideration of the general welfare... each supposes that no harm will come of his own neglect, that it is the business of another to do this or that—and so, as each separately entertains the same illusion, the common cause imperceptibly decays.

Kennedy possessed the intelligence to apply this concept to his stewardship of the United States. He promoted the general welfare rather than his own purposes.

Some of the presidents who followed him did not possess this ability. In pursuit of their own purposes, they allowed the common cause to decay, unaware of the damage that would arise from their neglect.

LYNDON JOHNSON

T HIS CHANGE BEGAN WITH THE DUPLICITOUS handling of the Vietnam War by the man who replaced Kennedy, Lyndon Johnson.

Johnson was born in a small farmhouse on the Pedernales River in Stonewall, Texas. He became a tall, awkward boy with a long nose protruding from his massive face, all arms and legs and ears. His father repeatedly failed at business, so neighbors brought food to the Johnson home.

Lyndon feared public humiliation. He ran to the boy's room to vomit when he lost a debate in high school. He brought his self-loathing with him to the White House. After viewing a likeness of himself by sculptor Jacques Lipchitz, he said, "Looks like I've been dead three weeks, and maybe ought to be."

Like Kennedy, Johnson's suffering gave him a heightened sense of empathy for others, particularly those who endured poverty and discrimination. After graduating from college, he spent a year teaching in a one-room schoolhouse on the border between Texas and Mexico. The immigrant children he taught were among the most impoverished in the nation; many went without shoes and proper nutrition.

Years later, Johnson would say,

> I shall never forget the faces of the boys and the girls in that little. . .
> Mexican School, and I remember even yet the pain of realizing and
> knowing then that college was closed to practically every one of those
> children because they were too poor. And I think it was then that I
> made up my mind that this nation could never rest while the door to
> knowledge remained closed to any American.

Johnson served for 12 years as a congressman and 12 years as a Senator. As a liberal, he was able to survive among his racist peers by becoming a chameleon. He made Republicans believe he was opposed to civil rights, while liberal Democrats thought he was an ardent supporter of them.

On November 22, 1963, Johnson suddenly had to fill the shoes of a young leader that Americans had put on a pedestal. He understood immediately that, compared with Kennedy, he would appear crude and provincial, unworthy of the presidency, and perhaps he would be subject to the public ridicule and humiliation he dreaded.

To the great benefit of the United States, Johnson rose above his fears. He handled a traumatic moment in history admirably; he took charge, convincing Kennedy's staff to cooperate with him, even though they considered him unfit for the job he inherited.

Johnson and Robert Kennedy had despised each other for years, yet, partly due to Johnson's ability to turn the other cheek, the two managed to work together for the good of the country.

Kennedy's legislative goals had been to broaden the New Deal programs started by Franklin Roosevelt. He sought a tax cut to stimulate the economy, a national program of hospital insurance for citizens age 65 and older, a massive effort to combat poverty, increased federal spending on systemic reform of the educational system, and a civil rights bill.

Kennedy did not possess the deal-making skills needed to win such radical social change, so his bills stalled in Senate committees. Johnson, however, had been a legend in the U.S. Senate, revered and feared for his ability to make his fellow Democrats and his opponents bend to his will. George Brown, Johnson's mentor and benefactor, said, "Lyndon was the greatest salesman one-on-one who ever lived."

For two years, Johnson dutifully devoted his presidency to passing the domestic legislation Kennedy had proposed. He turned Kennedy's hospital coverage bill into Medicare and Medicaid, won approval of an $11 billion tax cut, authored bills that spent billions on education, and launched the "war on poverty" that Kennedy had envisioned.

Johnson's victories, said Robert Dallek:

> can readily be seen as extensions of the avowed policies of the Kennedy Administration. The details might have been different...but historians generally agree that if Kennedy had lived out his first term and won a second, America would have witnessed something similar to the early years of Johnson's Great Society.

These achievements made Johnson a highly effective president. In many ways, he was a giant. He brought to fruition a sizable portion of Kennedy's legislative objectives for America and added many of his own initiatives.

THE SLOW UNDOING

U LTIMATELY, HOWEVER, JOHNSON BEGAN the slow undoing of everything his predecessor had accomplished. Johnson did not have Kennedy's ability to look at issues as they are, rather than relying on easy theories that do not require intellectual investigation. For him, the domino theory was beyond criticism; it was an article of faith. He would say, "If we quit Vietnam tomorrow we'll be fighting in Hawaii and next week we'll have to be fighting in San Francisco."

Before he died, as noted earlier, Kennedy had ordered an end to the nation's involvement in Vietnam. Four days after he became president, however, Johnson issued NSAM 273, which canceled the withdrawal of advisers Kennedy had mandated. In so doing, he doomed his presidency to failure and plunged the nation into a decade of turmoil.

Then he lied to the nation to justify a full-blown war in Vietnam.

On August 2, 1964, three North Vietnamese torpedo boats attacked the U.S.S. *Maddox*, a destroyer gathering intelligence in the Gulf of Tonkin off the northeastern coast of Vietnam. The *Maddox* fired nearly three hundred shells at the torpedo boats, and four U.S. jet fighters attacked them. A shell from one of the torpedo boat's deck guns struck the *Maddox*, but there were no injuries. Four North Vietnamese sailors were killed.

Johnson publicly warned that another attack would have "grave consequences." Two days later, he went on television and dramatically announced that a second attack had indeed occurred, and that he had ordered the bombing of land-based sites that supported the patrol boats.

The next day, Congress passed the Gulf of Tonkin Resolution, giving Johnson broad powers to wage war in Vietnam, without an official declaration of war.

It took decades for the public to learn that the second attack had never occurred. Jumpy sonar operators aboard a destroyer had heard what they thought were the sounds of torpedoes moving toward their ship. The destroyer opened fire in the direction of the noise. But the images on the sonar screens had been ghost images, not torpedoes. There were no North Vietnamese ships in the area. It was the type of miscalculation that Kennedy had feared could needlessly start a war.

Within days of his address to the people, Johnson learned that the second attack had not occurred. He told George W. Ball, the Under Secretary of State, "Hell, those dumb, stupid sailors were just shooting at flying fish!"

Johnson did not correct his mistake. Instead, he used the broad powers given to him by the Gulf of Tonkin Resolution to increase the American presence in Vietnam. By the end of 1965, more than 184,000 troops were stationed in the country; by 1968, that number was more than a half million.

The cost of fighting the war Johnson started, by 1968, was nearly $70 million per day. He was forced to raise income taxes and reduce spending on the programs designated to combat poverty. In a newspaper interview, Martin Luther King Jr. said, "America would never invest the necessary funds or energies in rehabilitation of its poor as long as Vietnam continued to draw men and skills and money like some demonic, destructive suction tube."

Johnson hung on year after year as the enormous cost of the war brought social progress to a halt, dooming the Great Society he had been building. He could not rise above his fear that if he ended the war, his place in history would be tarnished.

This obsession ruined Johnson's presidency and plunged the nation into turmoil. He prolonged a war Kennedy would never have fought, allowing young men to die, merely because he did not want to be the president who "lost" Vietnam.

During his presidency, Kennedy had inspired young people to learn about the power of giving to others. Now, just a few years after his death, they instead marched in the streets chanting, "Hey, hey, LBJ, how many kids did you kill today?"

With Johnson at the helm, the military industrial complex got what it wanted, an endless war fought under the pretext of protecting the people from Communists six thousand miles away. The military grew exponentially and the defense contractors made their billions.

President Kennedy would never have lied to the people to start a war. He was building a sense of unity and trust when he died. Johnson, because he was willing to lie, created an era in which the people became bitterly suspicious of their presidents and government.

After Kennedy's death, William Manchester traveled to the nation's capital reluctantly. The man who understood Thucydides was gone, and a man more concerned with his personal objectives than the common good was moving in. So... he made the trip only when necessary... sneaking into town "like a burglar."

CHAPTER TWENTY-SEVEN

NIXON SPLINTERS THE NATION

*The only place where you and I disagree is with regard
to the bombing. You're so goddamned concerned
about civilians and I don't give a damn. I don't care.*
— Richard Nixon speaking to Henry Kissinger."

I N HIS 1995 FILM, *NIXON,* OLIVER STONE PORTRAYS Richard
Nixon as a tormented man, unable to understand why the
people despised him while they loved John Kennedy. In a telling scene, Nixon asks Manolo Sanchez, his valet, why he wept
when Kennedy died. Sanchez says, "I don't know....he made me
see the stars."

Nixon was not a president who could make the people see the stars.
Instead, they suffered under his paranoia and self-absorption.

On the morning of August 9, 1974, Nixon boarded a helicopter on
the South Lawn of the White House and fled into exile. The evening
before, facing impeachment for his role in the cover-up of the Watergate burglary, he had gone before the nation to announce his resigna-
tion. He said he would rather stay and fight the charges against him,
"but the interest of the Nation must always come before any personal
consideration."

PERSONAL CONSIDERATIONS

O F ALL NIXON'S LIES, this was the most outrageous. His presidency was never about the interests of the nation. It was always about his personal considerations. Nixon was an insecure, self-destructive man who used the White House to act out a melodrama of defiance against his "enemies," the media and the Eastern intellectuals who lurked around every corner, waiting to expose him as a fraud.

Nixon did not understand that the people loved Kennedy because he would never allow personal considerations to influence his stewardship of the nation. Quite the opposite, he used the presidency to enrich the quality of their lives.

Nixon, like Lyndon Johnson, assumed that no harm would come of his self-absorption. Thus, he created a bitter, polarized society and ignored the principles that make a republic an effective form of government.

Tim Naftali, a presidential scholar, said of Nixon:

> His legacy will always be a mixture of light and shadow. There were impulses in his approach to public service that ultimately brought him down. The positive achievements, which no one can take away from him, must be put in the context of some very troubling approaches to leadership....students of the American presidency cannot walk away from them.

When he took office in January 1969, the United States was in open revolt against the war in Vietnam. More than 36,000 young men had already died, and thousands of young people were taking to the streets to demand an immediate withdrawal of combat troops. In their view, the war was unnecessary and unwinnable, prolonged by political and military strategies so maniacal that they bordered on criminality. The slaughter had to stop.

In Nixon's mind, the war was a personal issue. Those who wanted to end the fighting became his enemy. He deluded himself into thinking that ending the war would be a sign of weakness, a stain on the nation's honor. And he added anti-war activists to the list of enemies that were out to get him.

Nixon approached the war through a gauze lens of paranoia. He could not see the destruction he caused by using lies and political subterfuge to defend himself. During the 1968 campaign, he said he had a "secret plan" to end the war. This assurance contributed to his victory.

In a televised address on November 3, 1969, he announced not an end to the war, but rather a new strategy called "Vietnamization," which called for the South Vietnamese to take over the fighting as American boys were gradually withdrawn from Vietnam. Prolonging rather than ending the war, Nixon said, would allow him to achieve "peace with honor."

Near the end of this speech, Nixon did something that would have made John Kennedy, or anyone who understood the essence of a republic, sputter with rage. He divided the nation into two groups—those who agreed with him and those who opposed him—by urging the "great silent majority" to rise up and oppose the activities of antiwar protestors. This effectively divided the nation.

The next day, a White House official said the term "the silent majority" meant a "large and normally undemonstrative cross section of the country that until last night refrained from articulating its opinions on the war."

Nixon had no idea how many Americans opposed and how many approved of the war. What he asked for was blind acceptance of his position in order to soothe his fragile ego.

Almost unnoticed was that Nixon had made protest unpatriotic. It was as if George Washington had said the revolutionaries had no right to their opinions, because the majority of Americans did not agree with them.

Nixon's strategy worked as he had planned. Anti-war demonstrators, not the men who started and prolonged the war, became the enemy. In city after city, police, waded into protest marches, clubbing and beating people Nixon had said were anti-American.

On May 4, 1970, during an anti-war demonstration, four young people at Kent State University in Ohio were shot and killed by National Guard troops. Nine others were wounded, one of them paralyzed for life. A spokesman for the Ohio National Guard claimed a sniper had opened fire from a nearby rooftop, forcing the guardsmen to fire on the crowd as it began to encircle them.

Nixon condemned the killing, but in a way that tacitly blamed the victims, saying:

> This should remind us all once again that when dissent turns to violence it invites tragedy. It is my hope that this tragic and unfortunate incident will strengthen the determination of all the nation's campuses, administrators, faculty and students alike to stand firmly for the right which exists in this country of peaceful dissent and just as strong against the resort to violence as a means of such expression.

Nixon portrayed the protestors as unpatriotic sons and daughters of the liberal elite, who were using violence to get their way. A later investigation found that the protestors had been aggressive, but there had been no violence and no sniper on a rooftop.

Far from being unpatriotic, the anti-war activists Nixon despised were acting as good citizens of a republic. They had shed their apathy and embraced their civic responsibility to learn about an issue that threatened the nation's welfare. It was participatory democracy come to life.

The activists learned that draft deferments given to college students were meant to maintain support for the war among the educated middle class, while the sons of the lower classes were used as cannon fodder. They learned that the immense cost of the war was draining the nation of its economic vitality. They learned that for decades foreign policy "experts" had without question supported the domino theory, which was more of an ideology than a valid theory.

They also learned that Vietnam had unleased the type of horror and brutality that had become routine during World War II. In November 1969, it was revealed that eight months earlier U.S. Army soldiers had killed more than five hundred unarmed civilians, including men, women, and infants, in what came to be known as the My Lai Massacre. Some of the Vietnamese women had been gang raped and murdered, and their bodies mutilated.

Americans saw photos of the carnage—dead babies lying in a ditch, women begging for their lives. Years later, a survivor of the massacre, only eight years old when it occurred, said, "Everyone in my family was killed, my mother, my father, my brother and three sisters. They threw me into a ditch full of dead bodies. I was covered with blood and brains."

One of Nixon's weaknesses was his disdain for intellectual rigor. As the carnage in Vietnam intensified, he could have asked himself a simple question: Is the war in Vietnam a rational response to the threat of Communism in Southeast Asia? Or is it a senseless waste of life, a tragedy caused by our reliance on a set of beliefs rather than facts?

Rather than visit Vietnam to learn more about the true nature of the conflict, Nixon chased his demons. He dismissed the rising sentiment that America's presence in Vietnam was based on a needless fear of Communism as "liberal bullshit."

Instead of using his intellect, Nixon acted viscerally and secretly. Unknown to the American people and Congress, in 1969 he begin a secret, massive bombing campaign against North Vietnamese positions in Cambodia and Laos, using long-range B-52 bombers. It would be two years before the public learned of these attacks.

He must have realized the war could not be won, but he feared that admitting as much would confirm the intellectual superiority of his enemies.

In 1972, believing the South Vietnamese would be able to carry the burden militarily, Nixon withdrew a half million men from Vietnam, leaving only 25,000 American combat troops in the country. The South Vietnamese, however, had been unable to defeat their enemy, and Nixon's policy of intimidation and large-scale bombing attacks failed to bring the North to the peace table.

Nixon's response was another massive bombing campaign, this time against North Vietnam. This tactic eventually forced the Communists to sign, on January 27, 1973, a peace agreement that called for the total withdrawal of all American forces from Vietnam. After eight years of bloody fighting, the war was finally over.

Nixon was eventually brought down because he tape-recorded his conversations with aides and others in the Oval Office. They contained not only proof of his attempts to cover up Watergate, but also ugly indications of the hatred and anger that drove his personality. At various points, he said: "What the Christ is the matter with the Jews." "You can't trust the Jews." "Washington is full of Jews." "The IRS is full of Jews."

Writing in *The Jewish Week* in 1994, Michael Lerner said:

In a different historical period, Nixon might have acted on this hatred even more decisively. But instead he vented his hate and rage on others, including millions of young people who dared to question the wisdom of the Vietnam War and his dramatic escalation of that war. His role in supporting a military dictatorship in the Phillipines or the active role he played in over-throwing the democratically elected regime of Salvador Allende in Chile allowed fascistic forces to take power in other countries even while his campaign of dirty tricks and politically motivated indictments of political enemies subverted American democracy.

Nixon's legacy is that he allowed a personal obsession to become more important than the needs of the people. In the end, the long-haired liberals he so despised had a deeper respect for this republic than did the president of the United States.

CHAPTER TWENTY-EIGHT

REAGANOMICS: THE FINAL BLOW

Banks and corporations. . . will deprive the people of all
property until their children wake-up homeless on the
continent their fathers conquered.
— Thomas Jefferson

I N JUNE 2011, a 59-year-old man walked into a bank in a small
North Carolina town and passed a note to a teller saying he had a
gun. He demanded a $1 bill. Then, having committed a robbery,
he sat calmly in a chair and waited for the police to arrive.

As they handcuffed the man, the police discovered that he was
not carrying a weapon. He had worked for 17 years as a Coca-Cola
deliveryman, but lost his job when the economy nearly collapsed in
2008. He found a part-time job in a convenience store, but ruptured
two disks in his back and again found himself out of work. Then he
noticed a suspicious lump in his chest.

The pain in his back, he said, "was beyond the tolerance that I
could accept. I kind of hit a brick wall." He robbed the bank so he
would be sent to jail, where he would get the medical care he could
not afford as a free man.

For a few days, the story of the man who robbed a bank of a dollar to get health care was big news. Some media outlets treated the
man's plight as a depressing commentary on the nation's struggle with

the health care issue. But a reporter for the Fox Business Channel, a conservative cable television station, had another point of view. He believed it was wrong to use taxpayer money to help the man. "Better he should die," he said, "than we pay for his health care."

Two years later, reporters for the same station expressed heartfelt sympathy for a professional golfer who considered leaving the United States to avoid a proposed tax increase. The golfer, Phil Mickelson, according to *Forbes* magazine, had career earnings of $73 million and made $40 million per year in endorsements.

The Founders based this country on the notion that we are our brother's keeper. Yet, today we are a country in which many believe a man who needs our help to ease his pain should be allowed to die. On the other hand, a man who earns millions of dollars playing golf deserves our sympathy because he has to pay taxes like everyone else.

What happened? Why has there been such a dramatic shift in our national character?

AN ECONOMY BUILT ON IGNORANCE

THE ANSWER IS FOUND in the profoundly distorted thinking of two men, Milton Friedman and Ronald Reagan. Friedman, a Nobel Prize–winning economist, said the private sector of the U.S. economy, comprised of wealthy individuals and innovative corporations, can generate the wealth necessary to create jobs for all income groups in the country.

This explosive growth cannot occur, he said, if the private sector is subject to government regulations and taxes. Government, he argued, is a cumbersome and inept system that uses regulation and taxes to confiscate the wealth made by the private sector.

Standing in the room in which the Founding Fathers signed the U.S. Constitution, he said:

> The founders were a wise and learned group of people. They had learned the lesson of history—the great danger to freedom is the concentration of power, especially in the hands of a government. They were determined to protect the new United States of America from that danger. And they crafted the Constitution with that in mind.

> But in the past 50 years, we have forgotten the lesson that these wise

men knew so well. From regarding government as a threat to our freedom, we have come more and more to regard government as a benefactor from which all good things come.

What we need is widespread, public recognition that the central government should be limited to its basic functions, defending the nation against foreign invaders, mediating our disputes.

We must come to recognize that voluntary cooperation through the market and other ways is a far better way to solve our problems than turning them over to our government.

This was a gross distortion of American history, an intellectually dishonest argument used to justify anti-government sentiment. The Founders created three branches of government and an elaborate system of checks and balances to prevent the concentration of power in any one branch. Structured in this manner, they did not see government as a threat to freedom. They viewed it, in fact, as the source of our freedom and the framework for our enlightened way of life.

Nonetheless, Friedman's image of government as a fearsome, lumbering entity that hinders the private sector attracted a wide following among conservatives.

Ronald Reagan was one of them. He demonized government, portraying it as a malevolent force in America. At the Republican National Convention in 1964, seething with anger, he said:

Government has laid its hand on health, housing, farming, industry, commerce, education, and to an ever-increasing degree interferes with the people's right to know. Government tends to grow, government programs take on weight and momentum. But the truth is that, outside of its legitimate function, government does nothing as well or economically as the private sector of the economy.

The following should anger all Americans: Reagan made Friedman's narrow ideology the foundation of his economic policies, creating what came to be known as "Reaganomics." His creation, however, was based on a level of intellectual incompetence that, if it had not caused so much destruction, would be downright comical.

244 · A<small>LL</small> H<small>IS</small> B<small>RIGHT</small> L<small>IGHT</small> G<small>ONE</small>

A WEALTH OF MISINFORMATION

I N HIS EULOGY OF THE LATE PRESIDENT in 2004, Bruce Chapman, president of the Discovery Institute, said the following about Reagan, who graduated from Eureka College in 1932, majoring in economics and sociology:

> Ever since Ronald Reagan studied classical economics at Eureka College, Adam Smith was his hero. So everybody in the Administration quoted Adam Smith. Neckties with little Adam Smith busts on them festooned every male conservative chest in Washington when I was there. You had a wide range of choices: there were green Adam Smith neckties, maroon Adam Smith neckties, red, white and blue Adam Smith neckties. For a while, I didn't think [Attorney General] Ed Meese owned any other kind of tie. There were even Adam Smith scarves for the women. If Ronald Reagan had been allowed to run for a third term I imagine there would have been Adam Smith hats and Adam Smith raincoats.

Who was this man who so captivated Reagan?

Adam Smith was born in Scotland in 1723 and became one of the most influential men in history. He brought an end to mercantilism, the bizarre economic system that prevailed in Europe from the 16th to the 18th centuries. It was based on the belief that precious metals, particularly gold, were the only true source of wealth in the world.

To find this wealth, Britain, France, Spain, and the Netherlands established colonies in foreign nations, where gold and silver were mined and shipped home. Rather than being injected into the economy to stimulate economic growth, the gold was hoarded; locked away in vaults.

Every aspect of mercantilism in these countries was subject to strict government regulation. Heavy tariffs were used to discourage traders from importing goods from other nations, because this meant paying for the imports with gold, thus draining the nation's reserves.

Exporting, however, was encouraged, because it meant gold would flow into a country's vaults. The strongest nation was thought to be the one with the most gold in its vaults. "We must always take heed," said a British manifesto on trade in 1704, "that we buy no more from strangers than we sell them, for so should we impoverish ourselves and enrich them."

The only beneficiaries of this system were monarchs and the upper classes. Mercantile countries eventually became stagnant and unproductive, reduced to fighting each other for gold on land and at sea.

BUYING AND SELLING

ON MARCH 9, 1776, five months before the Declaration of Independence was signed, Adam Smith's book, *The Wealth of Nations,* was published in London. It startled the world with the radical concept that gold was not the only source of income available to nations.

Smith suggested an alternative to gold as the source of a nation's wealth. He said the money generated by those who bought and sold goods and services, from pottery makers to factory owners, could replace gold as the foundation of modern economies.

There was no need to hoard this wealth, he said; rather it should be re-invested in the economy.

It is impossible to minimize the impact this single book had on the world. People began to understand that an economic system based on hoarding gold was absurd, and that if they worked hard, they could provide for their families by selling products and services to others.

As Smith's system grew, more and more tradesmen produced a wider array of products and services. Markets were established to allow buyers and sellers to meet and conduct business. Foreign trade expanded, creating business opportunities for moneylenders, who later became bankers. They, in turn, provided the investment capital needed for business expansion. Birth rates soared as living conditions improved and workers began leaving the countryside to cluster in centers of commerce. This led to the growth of major centers, which over time became large cities.

"Adam Smith profoundly changed the world," said Lawrence Reed, president of the Foundation for Economic Education. "He brought the world out of its mercantilist days and set it on a path of individual liberty."

Smith died in 1790 at the age of 67. He had lived long enough to witness the first phase of the economic changes he inspired. In 1760, an industrial revolution began in Great Britain when businessmen developed power-driven machinery and other new devices, spawning a remarkable period of mechanization, mass production, and inven-

246 · A<small>LL</small> H<small>IS</small> B<small>RIGHT</small> L<small>IGHT</small> G<small>ONE</small>

tion. Sixty years later, this mechanization spread to the United States, eventually creating an industrialized rather than agrarian economy.

MISREADING SMITH

WHEN HE BECAME PRESIDENT in 1980, Reagan based his economic programs on what he believed Smith had said in *The Wealth of Nations*. His understanding of Smith, however, was sophomoric, disconnected, and fragmented.

Two paragraphs in the book had a strong impact on Reagan:

> Man's self-interest demands that he satisfies his wants and needs, and provides security for himself and his dependents. It is not from the benevolence of the butcher, the brewer, or the baker that we expect our dinner. We address ourselves, not to their humanity, but to their self-love, and never talk to them of our own necessities, but of their advantages.

And,

> The uniform, constant and uninterrupted effort of every man to better his condition, the principle from which public and national, as well as private opulence is originally derived, is frequently powerful enough to maintain the natural progress of things toward improvement, in spite both of the extravagance of government, and of the greatest errors of administration.

For Reagan, these paragraphs meant the following:

- The driving force behind the economy is man's self-interest. If government does not interfere with his efforts to make money, he will be able to provide for himself and his family, and he will not have to ask for handouts from others.

- This principle also applies to corporations and the wealthy. When unrestrained by high taxes and government regulations, they will produce enough wealth to create a robust economy. This will benefit those in lower economic classes in the form of plentiful jobs.

Corporate self-interest must be encouraged, no matter how selfish or petty it becomes.

- Government spends too much on programs that involve handouts for the needy, which drains the economy of money. These people should be able to provide for themselves.

Reagan believed that government is the enemy of the free market and must be controlled and marginalized. But if self-interest ruled the economy, he felt, the free market would generate enough wealth to ensure a sound economy for all Americans. This was the birth of his "trickle-down" theory of economics.

To unleash the power of self-interest, Reagan called for a $400 billion tax cut for corporations and the wealthy, including a reduction in the capital gains tax, the elimination of many government regulations, and a dramatic reduction in government spending on social programs that aided the needy.

To promote his theory that government spending on the poor is a waste of money, he made value judgments about people who rely on government assistance. He often told the following story:

There's a woman in Chicago. She has 80 names, 30 addresses, 12 Social Security cards. She's got Medicaid, getting food stamps and she is collecting welfare under each of her names. Her tax-free cash income alone is over $150,000.

The few reporters who actually fact-checked the story could not find a woman in Chicago with 80 names who was cheating the government out of $150,000 per year. They did find a few cheats among the many people who received welfare. Reagan had merged them into one woman to make his point.

The effect of this "little white lie" was astonishing. The non-existent woman in Chicago would become an enduring symbol of people, presumably black, who were "too lazy to find honest work" and greedily took advantage of hard-working white people. The media began calling this invented woman the "Welfare Queen."

Historian John Hingham said the following about Reagan's comment:

> The Welfare Queen driving a pink Cadillac to cash her welfare checks at the liquor store fits a narrative that many white, working-class Americans had about inner-city blacks. It doesn't matter if the story was fabricated, it fit the narrative, and so it felt true, and it didn't need to be verified.

Reagan also told the story of seeing a young man purchase an orange with food stamps, and use the change he received to buy a bottle of vodka. He always ended the story by saying, "This is what's wrong with America."

Most likely, Reagan had seen no such thing; he again fabricated a story to fit the stereotype he had created. He believed that, when practiced by corporations, greed produced economic growth, while poor citizens who took money from the government would bring down the nation. The colonial belief that we must be our brother's keeper had no place in Reagan's America.

Reagan believed that he was creating a modern version of the strategies conceived by Adam Smith, the great anti-government economist.

This was nonsense. Smith never advocated the type of economy Reagan devised. He did not believe that government was the enemy of the people. He simply believed that governments should abandon their practice of hoarding gold and allow the economy to benefit from the wealth generated in the free market.

Here is what Smith actually said about self-interest:

> The wise and virtuous man is at all times willing that his own private interests should be sacrificed to the public interest of his own particular order of society—that the interests of this order of society be sacrificed to the greater interest of the state.

Smith never said that government spending on the poor drained the economy of its resources. He never said that those who need public assistance should be stigmatized. That was pure Ronald Reagan.

Historian Nick Grier said the following about Smith's philosophy:

> His...objections to government intervention in the economy were directed at mercantilism and did not mean...that all government

programs are bad. Smith also believed that there was more to life than making money. For him a poor person with wisdom and virtue is far better than a rich man with neither. Admiring the rich, and aspiring to be like them, while despising and neglecting the poor is, according to Smith, "the great and most universal cause of corruption of our moral sentiments."

If he were alive today, Smith would be a liberal. He warned repeatedly that the wealthy should pay their fair share of taxes. In *The Wealth of Nations*, he wrote:

> The subjects of every state ought to contribute towards the support of the government, as nearly as possible, in proportion to their respective abilities; that is, in proportion to the revenue which they respectively enjoy under the protection of the state.

A SLEIGHT OF HAND

REAGAN ALSO ACCEPTED WITHOUT QUESTION the idea that a magical, unseen force, an "invisible hand," would ensure the success of an economy based on man's self-interest and the distrust of government.

Once again, he believed the source of this concept was Adam Smith. Smith, however, used the words "invisible hand" just once in *The Wealth of Nations,* and not in the context of man's self-interest. He used the term to encourage merchants in England to do business at home rather than in foreign countries. In vaguely spiritual language, he said this would boost the British economy and that "an invisible hand," presumably the hand of God, would guide their noble efforts.

Thus, President Reagan based his economic policies on his misinterpretation of a book written more than two hundred years earlier by a man whose objective was to promote an alternative to mercantilism. He had no comprehension of the type of economy that would exist in Reagan's time.

Adam Smith, incidentally, was one of the architects of the Scottish Enlightenment, the social reform movement that brought the concept of civic virtue to America, where, along with the concept that we are our brother's keeper, it became an underlying principle of our republic.

How could Reagan have been so wrong about Smith? It was a matter of poor scholarship. *The Wealth of Nations* is more than a thousand pages long. It was written in Old English and is difficult to read. Only the most diligent students actually wade through the entire book, mentally translating its archaic sentences into modern English.

Reagan likely learned about Adam Smith the same way students learn about him today, by listening to teachers who had read excerpts from his books. He based an entire economic system on what he *thought* Smith had said, not on what he actually said.

Can we argue that Reagan, despite his misunderstanding of Smith's concept of self-interest, still managed to implement sound economic policies that benefited the United States?

Before answering that question, we need to understand the evolution of capitalism, our remarkable economic system.

A SHORT, HIGHLY SIMPLIFIED COURSE IN ECONOMICS

WHAT EXACTLY IS CAPITALISM, this remarkable economic system that gives us an ability to work for others or start our own business, thus earning the income we need to buy a home and a car and educate our children? Capitalism means that private interests, such as corporations, own and control the means of production, distribution, pricing, and sale of the products they manufacture and sell.

It took centuries for this system to evolve. The first step in this evolution was feudalism, the economic system that prevailed during the Middle Ages. In feudal society, kings and queens controlled the overall economy, the nobility controlled farming, merchants controlled trade, priests controlled social behavior, and the working class, called serfs, controlled nothing, not even their own lives. If you were a serf during feudalism, you lived in a meager dwelling on an estate owned by a nobleman. In exchange for this shelter, you would spend your life harvesting the nobleman's crops. You were a step below those who fought the nobleman's wars in exchange for small parcels of land they could call their own. You were, in effect, not much better off than a slave; your life was a bitter, desperate attempt to avoid famine, disease, or a violent death in a war in which you had no stake. There was no reason for your existence beyond toil and misery.

Feudalism began to break down in the 12th century, when bubonic plague killed many of the serfs who ran the large estates of the nobility. The most skilled of the workers who survived found themselves in an enviable position: They could demand to be paid for their labor rather than exchange it for a meager shelter and just enough food to stay alive.

The right to be paid for labor transformed the descendants of serfs into businessmen who centuries later would be called capitalists. They used their wages to buy materials that could be turned into consumer goods and other products that could be sold at a profit. A man could buy the materials needed to make pottery, for example, and then walk from town to town selling bowls and clay utensils for more than the cost of the raw materials needed to make them.

At first, this buying and selling was practiced on a tiny scale, limited to specific towns and counties. A businessman's territory would cover about 20 miles in any direction. Ever so slowly, however, as more and more capitalists produced more and more products, local economies flourished. Birth rates soared as living conditions improved, and workers began leaving the countryside to cluster in centers of commerce, which over time became great cities.

The most industrious capitalists soon realized that they could make more money if they were able to expand their businesses. A man who walked from town to town selling pottery would dream about buying a cart and a horse to pull it, so he could travel greater distances and carry more pottery. He would even dream about buying a second and third cart and hiring others to travel the countryside selling not just pottery, but clothing and jewelry and tools...whatever he could make with his own hands and sell.

INVESTMENT CAPITAL

BUSINESS EXPANSION REQUIRED an infusion of money, a need that was eventually filled by moneylenders, the first bankers. Once he secured investment capital, a businessman had to generate enough income to pay back his loan and the interest it carried. Thus, he could not rest; he had to continually expand his business and make greater and greater profits. Success was determined by his ability to accurately predict demand for his products, to create an efficient distribution system, and to price his goods so that people could afford to buy them.

This method of doing business worked remarkably well when moneylenders charged reasonable interest rates, when there was a pool of competent workers, and when consumers had the income to buy the products sold by the early businessmen. By the time he reached old age, a man who started a business selling pottery from town to town could be the proud owner of a small business that employed several workers. He would also have the priceless knowledge that he was free to pass his wealth to those he loved.

THE BUSINESS CYCLE

FROM TIME TO TIME, THIS SYSTEM would turn sour. War, crop failures, disease, poor planning, or excessive buying and selling would turn the system upside down. Instead of expanding, local economies would contract. Bankers would charge higher interest rates for the loans that funded expansions and new businesses, making investment capital available only to the wealthy. The amount of money in circulation would decline. Sometimes, the price of goods and services would suddenly skyrocket, inducing an inflationary economy. Businessmen would warehouse unsold goods, and workers would lose their jobs. In short, the conditions that created thriving economies would suddenly disappear.

This was the beginning of what today is called the business cycle. Commerce from the Middle Ages to today has been a highly complex system that goes through cycles of boom and bust. There is a period of expansion, followed by a period of contraction, and then, somehow, growth begins anew. The early businessmen had no idea what caused these cycles; some said angry gods were punishing sinners, and others thought they were caused by changes in lunar cycles.

As man moved out from under feudalism, there were times when the economy would go bad for reasons that had nothing to do with the business cycle. Periodically, those who had attained the most wealth and property would gain control of an industry by forming monopolies. In this scenario, our pottery seller would be frozen out of the system and driven into bankruptcy by powerful merchants who could afford to produce massive quantities of pottery and sell them not only locally, but also in foreign nations.

This was an aberration of the system that had turned serfs into businessmen, and the result was always the same: The overall economy would fall out of its rhythm and collapse, the rich would get richer, and the working class would descend into the misery of inflation, unemployment, and debt. When the wealthy came under fire, their defense was always the same: The mandate of capitalism is to generate ever-greater levels of profit; they were simply meeting that objective.

Thus, our economy moves through cycles of expansion and contraction. It grows for a time, it falters for a time, and then, somehow, growth begins anew. Today, while the reason for this ebb and flow is still something of a mystery, economists have devised ways to stimulate economic growth when the economy is contracting and slowing it down when it expands too rapidly.

When the economy contracts, for example, government spending can be cut back, and individual and corporate income tax rates, and interest rates on loans for individuals and businesses, can be lowered.

Conversely, when the economy is expanding too quickly, raising the possibility of inflation, taxes and interest rates can be raised to slow the expansion before inflation takes hold.

These measures provide the economic flexibility necessary to make contractions as short as possible and expansions as long as possible.

A GOOD TEMPORARY FIX

WHEN REAGAN ASSUMED OFFICE in 1980, the economy was in a rare and terrible state known as "stagflation," which is a period of high inflation that occurs when the economy is contracting and unemployment is high. It was a time when cutting government spending and lowering taxes and interest rates was a good method of bringing the economy out of its contraction phase, slowly inducing a period of expansion.

For the first two years of his presidency, Reagan's policies did little to improve the economy. Unemployment soared, and middle and low-income Americans fell into record levels of debt. The number of homeless on the streets of America more than doubled.

But within a few years, conditions improved as the tax cuts pumped money into the economy, causing inflation to fall and employment to rise as the economy moved into a period of expansion.

As a temporary method of stimulating the economy, Reagan's policies worked. They were, however, too extreme, too draconian, and too socially divisive, to be used permanently. When the economic contraction ended, Reagan's measures should have been scaled back to fit the needs of an expanding rather than a contracting economy.

After Reagan left office, however, conservatives declared that he had been a "visionary" and that his policies should become the nation's permanent economic strategy, in good times and in bad. What should have been a temporary economic policy became instead a full-blown ideology, created by conservatives, known as "Reaganomics."

Reagan's "brilliant" strategy was not a permanent solution to the nation's economic challenges. No single, inflexible economic theory can effectively guide an ever-changing economy through its peaks and valleys.

If Reagan had been elected when the economy was expanding rather than contracting, "Reaganomics" would have been considered absurd, like throwing an anchor to a swimmer, even by members of his own party.

Conservatives realized, however, that if Reagan were elevated to the status of America's economic savior, his image could be exploited to improve the political misfortunes of the Conservative Party. Before Reagan, the party had little political influence; it had been unable to capitalize on its central belief that government is too powerful.

With Reaganomics, however, conservatives said they had proof that the government, with its meddling in big business and constant effort to raise taxes, was the enemy of the people. Touting Reagan as an economic savant gave legitimacy to their cause.

We live in this country under the flag of pluralism. It is the right of our political leaders to submit any political view, any approach to government or the economy, for public approval at the ballot box. Reagan did not break a law when he promised the people that wealth generated at the top would "trickle" down to the common man.

But his pandering to the fear of government, with the purpose of creating an economy that benefited just one segment of the population, was an egregious violation of the spirit of a republic. During and after the Reagan years, a larger segment of the population than ever before began to view government as a hostile entity that actively worked against their interests.

Another damaging product of Reagan's ineptitude was the end of civil political discourse. When it became clear that his strategy of giving free rein to special interests and promoting the fear of government was not working, the proponents of his system were forced to defend it. Instead of objectively debating the pros and cons of Reaganomics, they resorted to the politics of personal destruction. They said political leaders who called for tax hikes or disagreed with the "trickle-down" theory were not members of the loyal opposition, but rather they were "socialists," or worse, "traitors."

Today, the tactic of personal destruction is embedded in our culture. Politicians attack each other with childish abandon. We are stuck in a swamp of mindless political gridlock, and we are powerless to rectify this situation through civil political discourse...because it is a relic of the past.

Ironically, with their rigid belief in Reaganomics, conservatives have created a new form of mercantilism, one that allows 1 percent of the population to control and hoard the nation's wealth in the form of money and power.

MOTIVES

WHAT CAUSED REAGAN to harbor such powerful contempt for government? Did he really believe it was a malevolent force simply because it regulates the private sector? Why would he reverse the original intent of the Founding Fathers by promoting a system that puts personal greed above the welfare of all Americans?

Some biographers have argued that a troublesome relationship with his father was the source of Reagan's conviction that government generosity contributes to human failure.

Jack Reagan was an alcoholic who moved his family from town to town in search of work. When he was 11, returning home from a basketball game, Reagan found him lying unconscious in the snow on the front porch of the Reagan home, smelling of whiskey.

"He was drunk," Reagan remembered years later, "dead to the world...crucified." He dragged his helpless father out of view of neighbors, fighting the temptation to go to bed "and pretend he wasn't there."

Reaganomics may have been an expression of Reagan's contempt for those who, like his father, cannot fend for themselves and require a helping hand.

In *Reagan's America*, Garry Wills said of Reagan, "The needy remind him of his dependent father, from whom he has tried to separate himself all his life."

Wills also suggested that fear of authority is a hallmark of the conservative mind, saying:

> If it were possible to probe in depth the psychology of most Reaganites, I suggest that one might find a shared problem with authority stemming from childhood. I speculate that the conservative world view is based on an inner need that is satisfied by fighting against excessive power and control.

This would explain why generations of conservatives have blindly endorsed Reagan's economic policies, which coldly offered blame rather than understanding to those who were unable to support themselves without help.

Friedman and Reagan share the same legacy. They turned capitalism, the most effective economic system in the world, into an all-consuming monster that feeds on the un-American concept that greed benefits everyone.

And unwittingly, while they feared that government threatened our freedom, they created a far greater threat to freedom by concentrating power in the private sector.

THE HORRORS OF DEREGULATION

THE NEAR COLLAPSE OF THE U.S. ECONOMY in 2008 was the result of one of the more perverse tenets of Reaganomics: deregulation.

Corporations strive to create and sell an ever-growing number of products and services that will allow them to increase their profits year after year. They constantly innovate and grow, creating completely new industries in their effort to meet consumer demand and technological needs.

This process is a thing of beauty. It injects liquidity and investment capital into the economy. There would be no stock or bond markets without corporations. Collectively, they have made capitalism the most powerful economic system on earth. They are the proverbial engine of our growth.

Our history is also awash, however, with examples of the harm that results from the lack of corporate regulation, particularly in the financial sector. During the Great Depression, for example, more than

4,000 banks failed because there were no regulations to prevent them from using money deposited into savings accounts to buy securities such as stocks and bonds.

This led to chaos as bankers used depositors' funds to invest in stocks. Their value rose artificially during the wild period of speculation and excessive trading before the market crash in 1929. When prices plummeted, depositors lost more than $400 million.

Things became so bad that President Roosevelt in 1933 was forced to close all banks in the country for four days. This measure was taken to prevent depositors from withdrawing the money that remained in their accounts.

The result of this financial debacle was the most sensible effort to regulate banks ever enacted in the United States, the Glass-Steagall Act of 1933. This measure separated banks into two categories, commercial banks and investment banks. Commercial banks were limited to providing checking and saving accounts and offering loans to their customers. Investment banks could not take money from client accounts; they could only execute orders to buy and sell securities.

This separation created a long period of stability and integrity in banking. Regulations such as Glass-Steagall, as well as regulations in other areas of big business, proved to be an effective way to protect the public against corporate greed.

Government regulation, however, was anathema to conservatives, who feared the power of government, particularly its power to regulate corporations. Unfortunately, over the years, their drive for deregulation gained momentum, even among Democrats. In 1999, Bill Clinton approved the repeal of the Glass-Steagall Act, endorsing the conservative belief that markets should be able to operate without regulation in an effort to unleash man's self-interest.

Almost immediately, banks crossed the line in the sand drawn by Glass-Steagall and insanely risky investment products began to proliferate once again. In 2008, the wild, speculative trading of these products nearly brought the U.S. economy to its knees. It took a $700 billion bailout by the government under presidents Bush and Obama to prevent the economy from collapsing. Countless Americans lost their savings, their jobs, their homes, their pensions, and their health care. The crisis led to the longest recession since the Great Depression.

Another frightening result of Reaganomics has been the decline of the number of available jobs for Americans with incomes between $25,000 and $75,000. Unfortunately, the collective purchasing power of this middle-class is what creates the consumer demand that, in turn, produces jobs.

The number of Americans who identify themselves as middle-class, currently about 65 million, has never been lower in our history.

Because Reaganomics encourages outsourcing, union-busting, globalization, and automation, the number of jobs available to the middle-class has fallen dramatically. Wages for those who are still working have also declined. When adjusted for inflation, middle-class workers actually earn less today than they did in 1971.

Brian Miller, executive director of *United for a Fair Economy,* described the struggle facing the middle class as follows:

> Imagine joining friends for a late-night game of Monopoly, but in this game, there's a twist: At the start of the game, one player gets an entire side of the game board, from Pacific Avenue to Boardwalk, including the Short Line Railroad. Instead of pondering easy questions like whether to be the shoe or the thimble, you're now grappling with a more important question: Do you even stand a chance in such a lopsided game?

POLITICAL PARTY OR THUGS?

IT IS IMPERATIVE THAT THE AMERICAN PEOPLE begin to explore the damage done to the country by Reaganomics. They must question the motives of not only Reagan, but also the conservatives who later hardened his economic policies. Did they actually believe that weakening the nation's trust in government was a responsible strategy? Did they actually believe that corporations should operate without oversight?

Or was their goal to confine the ability to create great wealth to special interests, with the tacit agreement that some of it would be allowed to trickle down to conservative lawmakers and the conservative political structure in general?

Reagan was most likely guilty of ignorance. If his followers, however, deliberately created a master class of powerful citizens and special interests, they are thieves masquerading as a political party and will ultimately face the wrath of the good people in this country.

Until this issue is resolved, the following will occur: We will again endure the misery of an economic crisis like the crisis of 2008, or perhaps a series of downturns, as long as we believe that government's control of the private sector should be discarded.

As each crisis passes and the economy recovers, the public will be lulled into thinking the worst is over. But the magnitude and duration of these downturns will increase, and eventually we will be forced to accept that government is the solution to the problems created by Reaganomics.

Nowhere in the Declaration of Independence or the Constitution, or in the private writings of the Founders, does it say that our political leaders should allow special interests to dominate the economy. Yet that is precisely what has happened in the United States.

CHAPTER TWENTY-NINE

A MENTOR FOR THE AGES

It is no mark of health to be well-adjusted
to a profoundly sick society.
— John Kennedy quoting Jiddu Krishnamurti

ON THE MORNING OF NOVEMBER 9, 1960, a tall, slender young man in a gray suit climbed the steps of a hastily erected platform at an armory in Hyannis, Massachusetts. Earlier that morning, in one of the closest elections in history, he had become the 35th President of the United States. Now he would formally accept his victory and briefly outline his approach to the presidency. His wife, her face glowing from the effects of late pregnancy, stood next to him as he spoke.

For those attuned to such things, the words he spoke that morning were unusual for a newly elected president. He did not speak from a prepared text; he did not outline his plan to govern according to his party's principles. He said simply that the country faced serious challenges in the years ahead.

Then, he ended his brief remarks with the following promise: "I can assure you that every degree of mind and spirit that I possess will be devoted to the long-range interests of the United States."

Two years and eleven months later, John Kennedy was murdered in the prime of his life as his wife watched in horror. There was something, however, that could not be taken away from him that day, something that would transcend his death. He kept his promise to the American people: He devoted every degree of mind and spirit that he possessed to the long-range interests of the United States.

In polls, the American people have said they wish that Kennedy could be returned to office today. They seem to understand that we have become a different country in his absence. We have become the nation he feared we would become, lost in the fog of relentless ideological warfare, devoid of political and intellectual courage, and thus unable to resolve, or even objectively discuss, the great issues of our time.

In their collective wisdom, the people also seem to understand that Kennedy left behind a prototype for what the presidency should be in the modern era. They long for another Kennedy, a president who understands that the sole objective of government is the happiness and safety of the people. It was never meant to be used as a platform for narrow ideological beliefs.

We cannot, of course, bring Kennedy back to life. Nor should we wait for another man or woman like him to rescue us. With all the permutations and DNA sequences at its disposal, Mother Nature does not often produce political leaders as profoundly skilled as Kennedy. He was one of a kind, the product of a confluence of events and experiences that is unlikely to be duplicated.

But we can, if we have the courage, resurrect Kennedy's approach to government. We can restore Kennedy's belief that government is a noble profession. We can rid ourselves of Reagan-era anti-government attitudes. We can build a nation in which there are no Tea Party bumper stickers that read, "I love my country, but I fear my government," as if "country" and "government" are not one and the same.

Change of this magnitude will require an effort on a scale that does not seem realistic. We are dangerously comfortable with things as they are. Congress should be a place of intelligent, objective political debate that leads to policies that benefit all Americans. But that once proud body has been rendered impotent by childish bickering, and we do not rise as one to demand that civility be restored.

Thousands of adults and hundreds of children are shot and killed each year, and we have come to view this slaughter, because it involves the right to bear arms, as unavoidable.

An absurdly small number of people now control the bulk of the nation's wealth, and we do not stop to consider how badly this outrageous greed has damaged the economy and our national sense of purpose.

The media rarely ventures out of shallow water into thought-provoking coverage that helps us define and cope with issues that matter, and we do not protest as we have become accustomed to superficial reporting.

We take shelter in the shade of political correctness, the bizarre form of self-censorship that prevents us from speaking bluntly about political issues. We have lost the inclination to speak bluntly and with passion. The media endlessly repeats the sensational and the superficial, and we do not demand a closer look at issues that matter.

Despite these obstacles, there is something we must remember: We are the descendants of the men and women who created a form of government that changed the course of Western civilization. When aroused, when we work together, we can do anything. John Kennedy left this possibility behind for us to ponder when he said, "Our problems are man-made, therefore they may be solved by man. And man can be as big as he wants. No problem of human destiny is beyond human beings."

THE KENNEDY MODEL

WHAT EXACTLY IS THE PROTOTYPE for the presidency that Kennedy left behind? Let's take a final look at what we have learned about him as a man and as a president, including his general approach to the presidency, and his policies concerning the economy, war and peace, racism, and the elevation of the human spirit.

As a man, John Kennedy was far from perfect. He suffered from a narcissistic sense of entitlement, considering it his right to find sexual pleasure when and where he wanted. He did not seem to care about the impact of his behavior on those who loved him. His wife had lent intelligence and elegance to the Kennedy name, yet she had to endure the public humiliation of his tawdry infidelities.

When asked about his unremitting need for sex, he said, "They will never catch me while I am alive...and after I'm dead...who cares?"

The nation paid a steep price for this arrogance. In a remarkably short time, Kennedy had injected a healthy sense of idealism into the political system. But after his sex life was exposed, instead of celebrating and encouraging this idealism, the media spent decades reporting on the scandalous aspects of his life. The idealistic momentum he had generated disappeared and never returned.

It is ironic that the man who asked us to find the best within ourselves could have been driven out of office by his self-destructive tendencies. The United States was far more puritanical in the early 1960s than it is today, more harshly intolerant of sexual misconduct. If Kennedy's serial adultery had been exposed as he campaigned in 1964, it would have been viewed as aberrant and unforgivable, and most likely he would not have been re-elected, erasing everything he had accomplished.

While Kennedy was not a perfect man, he was a near-perfect political leader. He was a child prodigy who became an adult whose life was devoted to serving his country. Tortured by disease and pain, he threw himself into the most dangerous combat he could find, unwilling to stand aside and let healthier men fight a war that threatened the existence of the nation he loved.

Similarly, nothing could prevent him from becoming a public servant. In the years leading up to the 1960 election, before his family purchased a private plane for him to use, Kennedy traveled extensively in small, chartered planes, supporting other candidates and laying the groundwork for his run in 1960.

Ted Sorensen said of Kennedy's courage and commitment to service:

> We traveled from coast to coast. We flew in all kinds of little planes, in all kinds of weather, with all kinds of pilots—experienced and unexperienced, professional and amateur, rested and fatigued. On a flight to Rockport, Maine, the pilot could not find the landing strip, and we circled over the area as he peered out one side and the Senator, sitting in the copilot's seat, looked out the other. We were tossed for hours in a snowstorm over the Rockies and in a fog over Lake Michigan. In pelting rain we took off in an amphibious plane from a choppy, timber-filled bay in Alaska, with the Senator working the windshield wiper by hand.

GENERAL APPROACH TO THE PRESIDENCY

THE MOST SALIENT FEATURE of Kennedy's presidency was his intelligence, his scholarship. If nothing else, we should learn the following from his brief time in office: Government by ideology is a perversion of republican values. It is an effective strategy for presidents who lack the competence or the inclination to do the hard work required by high office. It frees them from the rigors of making decisions based on intellectual effort, and disguises their lack of knowledge of history, economics, world affairs, or any number of important issues. All that is needed is a gift for using the theatrical aspects of politics to exploit anger and resentment toward government. The public understands ideological arguments more readily than the finer points of policy, and opponents can be swept aside without objective debate by simply labeling them as un-American.

Kennedy welcomed the intellectual demands of the presidency. He made decisions based on his analysis of facts, not according to the blanket dictates of a rigid ideology. When asked a question about policy, he would often preface his answer with the phrase, "In the final analysis." This meant that he had considered both sides of the issue and made a decision based the merits of the respective arguments, not according to a predetermined view.

As noted in the first chapter, Kennedy governed as if the future of the United States was always in doubt. Somewhere in the world, and somewhere in the country itself, were the seeds of problems that could eventually threaten the safety of the country he was sworn to protect.

To prevent these seeds from growing, he reasoned, the people must be informed about important issues and involved in their resolution, almost as if they were a separate arm of government. This was a form of preventative government, which much like preventative medicine, was designed to confront problems head on, before they could fester and grow.

In his speeches, Kennedy heightened the nation's awareness of civic responsibility and participatory democracy, two virtues that form the heart and soul of this republic. He challenged the American people to shed their complacency and learn about the issues that determine the quality of their lives. He believed that a government that allowed its people to become complacent, uninvolved in their future, would someday become dangerously divided and unable to face its problems honestly.

It was vitally important, Kennedy believed, for the people to receive unbiased information about major issues, unaltered by what he called "doctrinaire beliefs." He understood that rigidly held opinions make rational government impossible. Important issues, he believed, should be addressed with flexibility and objectivity, not with a predetermined conservative or liberal solution.

Thus, as mentioned in the first chapter, Kennedy's general approach to the presidency can be expressed in three simple principles:

1. It is the president's responsibility to identify threats to the nation's welfare.
2. It is the president's responsibility to inform the people about these threats truthfully, so they are prepared to react to them effectively.
3. It is the president's responsibility to provide the people with facts, not biased information clouded by "predetermined beliefs."

Kennedy most likely developed these views during his intense study of American government. Years after her father's death, Caroline Kennedy found among his possessions a copy of the *Federalist Papers,* the articles and essays written by Alexander Hamilton, James Madison, and John Jay in support of the ratification of the U.S. Constitution.

A passage in the papers said:

> It has been frequently remarked, that it seems to have been reserved to the people of this country, by their conduct and example, to decide the important question, whether societies of men are really capable or not, of establishing good government from reflection and choice, or whether they are forever destined to depend, for their political constitutions, on accident and force.

Kennedy wanted us to use reflection and choice to establish good government. He made us believe that we are a great people, that we live in a great country, and that we are indeed capable of establishing a strong, responsive government through our conduct and example to others.

KENNEDYNOMICS

KENNEDY'S PRO-GOVERNMENT, non-ideological strategy allowed him to create economic policies that addressed the needs of all Americans. During his time in office, no one group of Americans was favored over another. He told his economic advisers to "see things as they are" rather than fall back on economic doctrines determined by a belief system.

Using this approach, he created an economy capable of flexing with the expansions and contractions of the business cycle, which is an eminently sane economic policy.

Kennedy's warning about allowing partisan fervor to determine economic policy, quoted in chapters 1 and 20, deserves to be repeated here. He said economic policies should never be made according to:

> some grand warfare of rival ideologies which will sweep the country with passion...but with the practical management of a modern economy. What we need are not labels and clichés but more basic discussion of the sophisticated and technical questions involved in keeping a great economic machinery moving ahead.

During his battle with executives over the price of steel in 1962, Kennedy made it clear to the nation that corporations that conduct business in the United States have the obligation to contain their greed in the name of the common good. He said:

> Price and wage decisions in this country, except for a very limited restriction in the case of monopolies and national emergency strikes, are and ought to be freely and privately made. But the American people have a right to expect in return for that freedom, a higher sense of business responsibility for the welfare of their country than has been shown in the last two days.

This reminder of our heritage, considering the growth of corporate greed after Kennedy was gone, was an important moment in our history. He publicly declared that he would not allow the people to become victims of corporate greed. No president since Kennedy has possessed the courage, or the commitment to our welfare, to make a similar declaration.

WAR AND PEACE

KENNEDY FOLLOWED THE SAME PATTERN in matters of war and peace. He rejected the prevailing belief that the only acceptable method of fighting Communism was military intervention. We tend to forget that he literally saved the world from a nuclear holocaust during the Cuban missile crisis because he resisted the generals who favored a preemptive strike against Cuba.

Instead of a rigid policy that called for war, he relied on his understanding of the universality of the human condition to seek peace with the Soviet Union. On June 10, 1963, at a speech at American University, he said:

> So, let us not be blind to our differences…but let us direct attention to our common interests and to means by which our differences can be resolved…For, in the final analysis, our most basic common link is that we all inhabit this planet. We all breathe the same air. We all cherish our children's future. And we are all mortal.

RACISM

IN A SINGLE SPEECH, speaking not as a politician but rather as a human being, Kennedy challenged Americans to rise above long-held perceptions about racial equality. He urged white Americans to imagine what it would be like to be black in America. How would they feel if they were on the receiving end of the misery racism inflicts upon blacks? "Who among us," he asked, "would be content to have the color of his skin changed and stand in their place?"

Having a president capable of this non-political, humanistic view of race relations elevated the nation's sense of right and wrong, which ultimately led to landmark legislation that at least attempted to bring equality to blacks.

No president since Kennedy has been able to rise to this level of innate understanding and generosity toward people who so badly needed compassion rather than condemnation. This style of government was not a requirement of the presidential oath of office or tradition. It was a gift from an intelligent, idealistic young leader to his country. Until the day he died, Kennedy saw himself as a public servant, a chivalrous protector of the people, not as a go-between for an ideology.

THE HUMAN SPIRIT

KENNEDY HAS NOT BEEN GIVEN due credit for the following: He taught us that a president who refuses to engage in unproductive ideological warfare could instead turn his attention to pursuits that allow the American people to live on a higher plane.

This is not a small matter. Instead of expending his energy demonizing those who disagreed with his policies, Kennedy spent his time trying to make the United States "one of the great schools of civilization." With the Peace Corps, he taught us the power of giving, making us a better country and better people. When he quoted Jefferson and Adams, he was urging us to embrace our history. When he quoted the poets, he was encouraging us to find meaning in culture and intellectual pursuits. He once said:

> When power leads man toward arrogance, poetry reminds him of his limitations. When power narrows the area of man's concern, poetry reminds him of the richness and diversity of existence. When power corrupts, poetry cleanses.

In 2014, the United States landed a spacecraft on a comet 311 million miles from earth. The information it gathers may help us understand how life on earth began. This and countless other technological advances would not have occurred if Kennedy had not opened our eyes to the wonders and possibilities of space exploration. If someday we must flee this planet and start a new civilization elsewhere, the rockets that propel us will be the product of Kennedy's ability to govern with the long-term health of the country in mind.

EVERYTHING HE GAVE US IS GONE

TODAY, MORE THAN 50 YEARS after Dallas, Kennedy's carefully crafted strategies to nurture this republic have all but vanished. The mindless partisan warfare that he warned us to avoid has become the organizing principle of our government, ending some of the time-honored traditions that knit us together.

When John Kennedy was president, for example, there was a mood of excitement and unity in the United States. The people sensed that their president viewed the country as more than just a collection of liberals and conservatives, that it was the creation of remarkable men with the wisdom to create an enlightened form of government. As a result, they felt a deep sense of respect for the presidency.

On May 20, 1962, more than 12,000 people jammed into Madison Square Garden in New York. They were on their feet, alive with the electric sense of anticipation you would find at a rock concert today. The president of the United States was coming.

The buzz and excited chatter turned to wild applause when a band began to play the four sets of ruffles and flourishes that precede "Hail to the Chief," the Presidential Anthem that has signaled the arrival of the president since it was first played in 1815 to honor the memory of George Washington.

President Kennedy emerged from a darkened portion of the stage and walked to the podium. The Garden erupted in cheers, and Kennedy had to wait until it died down before he could speak.

He was in New York to support legislation that would create the establishment of a national program of hospital insurance for those 65 and older, a program that later would become known as Medicare.

When the cheering stopped, Kennedy began his speech by urging his audience to honor our republic by educating themselves about the health care issue. This process, he said, was part of the civic responsibilities implied in the principles of a republic. He said:

> I come from Boston, Massachusetts, near Faneuil Hall, where for a whole period of years meetings were held by interested citizens in order to lay the groundwork for American independence. While there may be some who say that the business of government is so important that it should be confined to those who govern, in this free society of ours, the consent, and may I say, the support, of the citizens of this country is essential if this or any other piece of progressive legislation is going to be passed. Make no mistake about it…make no mistake about it.

The three major television networks of the time broadcast the speech live. A young woman told a reporter, "It meant something that Kennedy came here. When that song [Hail to the Chief] came on, I had goose bumps all over. I saw my president."

Ceremonies that pay homage to the office of the president are important. They reinforce the respect that should exist between the people and their chief executive, no matter which party he represents.

Today, respect for the presidency no longer exists. When President Obama takes the stage, a piano player somewhere offstage plays a Cole Porter tune. He has been portrayed as an ape in cartoons. During his State of the Union speech in 2009, he was interrupted by a conservative congressman who shouted, "You lie," making a mockery of tradition with his blatant disrespect for the nation's highest office.

A more important breakdown of Kennedy's style of government began with Lyndon Johnson and Richard Nixon. They did something that Kennedy would never have done. They lied to the people about vitally important issues. Both men failed to comprehend Kennedy's maxim that for the United States to succeed, "its leaders must tell the truth."

Johnson lied about events in the Gulf of Tonkin to encourage Congress to approve what became a vicious, nation-shattering war. Nixon perpetuated this war with lies and deception, and finally was brought down by the lies he told to avoid prosecution for a petty crime, splintering the bond of trust Kennedy had built with the people.

Then, in 1981, Ronald Reagan began demonizing government itself, telling the American people it was their enemy, the source of the nation's problems. His objective was to render government incapable of challenging the supremacy of special interests.

Reagan was too parochial to understand that our Founding Fathers, after assessing the future needs of the newly created United States of America, transformed it into the most effective form of government ever known, a republic.

He also failed to understand that civic virtue and participatory democracy will eventually disappear in a country that fears its government. Without these values, a republic cannot survive.

Kennedy told us that government and public service are noble professions. Reagan told us that greed is good. He wanted an America in which special interests flourish while those without the capacity to generate wealth are stigmatized and shunted aside in disgrace. Instead of elevating the human spirit, this policy made us meanspirited and bitter.

Reagan said that big government was bringing down America. Kennedy argued that government, no matter how cumbersome it becomes, is still what makes America a great country. The remedy is not to reject it, but rather to make it more effective. He invited the people to join him in this effort.

In the years after Reagan left office, conservatives used his antigovernment philosophy to build a political stronghold based on the concept that the private sector is more important than government. They used the politics of personal destruction to silence those who disagreed with this concept.

The infantile political bickering that resulted from this approach has become so extreme that our government is no longer capable of responding to threats to the quality of our lives.

HOW LONG CAN WE SURVIVE?

THIS LEADS inexorably to the following question: How long can we survive as a counterfeit form of the most enlightened and effective form of government ever devised by man?

There is no clear answer. No one knows how long the United States can exist in this fractious environment. Never before has our government been so ineffective for so long. We could go on for another hundred years, or we could come unglued in the near future. But at some point, the confusion and inefficiency created by anti-government ideology will bring us down.

Is this far-fetched? Perhaps, but history is filled, as Kennedy knew, with examples of wars and economic downturns that began due to the confusion, complacency, and greed that arises when leaders fail to confront reality.

Imagine that it is 2035 and the economy is coming apart at the seams. Following the near collapse of 2007–2008, Congress enacted measures to lessen the impact of trading risky derivative products in the stock market. But as the economy improved, the lessons of 2008 were forgotten and these products again began to proliferate.

Now, in 2035, it is happening again; the market, driven to preposterous new highs by derivative trading, is crashing. This time, banks and insurance companies cannot be rescued, the cost would be too great, and they are going under.

Attempts to slow the decline bog down in childish bickering. No matter how bad the situation becomes, conservatives will not admit that greed has ruined the economy. To do so would be to trash the sacred memories of Milton Friedman and Ronald Reagan. They blame the disaster on meddling by liberal presidents who tried to tame the free market.

Soon, billionaires and corporations, who had an iron grip on the nation's wealth for so long, are in danger of losing it all. The economic decline threatens to ruin not only our economy, but the world economy as well. We are on the brink of a global economic meltdown that will lead to a dark age of misery around the world.

Then, while the economy teeters on the edge of ruin, an even more dangerous situation arises. Due to petty ideological bickering, lawmakers in the United States never developed an adequate plan to eliminate the threat posed by the terror group ISIS, and it gradually became more powerful.

Now, in 2035, to our horror, ISIS announces that it has acquired two nuclear devices, and that it plans to set one off in the United States, and one in Israel.

Panic and confusion engulf Congress. Hard-liners, reactionaries who believe that war solves all our problems, insist that both Israel and the United States should launch immediate preemptive nuclear strikes on ISIS. But exactly where should they attack? ISIS groups are embedded in several countries. Nuclear strikes will kill millions of innocent people.

Both sides in Congress hurl invectives at each other, and an already dysfunctional government becomes impotent. Amid the chaos, as the countdown to Armageddon begins...the global economy collapses.

TURNING BACK THE CLOCK

THE TIME HAS COME TO ACKNOWLEDGE that Kennedy's approach to government was eminently sane. We do indeed face a seemingly endless series of threats to our well-being, and there is no guarantee that these threats will unfold in favorable patterns. They may come home to roost all at once.

Returning to the rational and productive form of government Kennedy established will require a heroic effort. It will be a matter of finding the courage to change entrenched attitudes and perceptions.

With each passing year, for example, as the nation falls deeper into political gridlock, it becomes more apparent that presidents and political leaders should be evaluated according to the quality of their support for republican values. A single question should become the yardstick by which they are judged: Did they nourish our faith in republican government, or were they ideologues who ignored our founding values in order to promote their individual beliefs?

Kennedy did not try to put out fires after they started. His methodology was to use intelligence and scholarship to "prevent the fire from starting in the first place." But as he understood, this is not possible unless we maintain a smoothly functioning government that has the support of its people.

Today, we seek simple, immediate solutions to complex problems. We judge those who run for office by their ability to participate in the trivial melodrama that politics has become. We do not seek leaders who have acquired a sound understanding of American history, government, economic theory, and the social institutions that shape the way we live. Perhaps we have come to believe that because the Internet offers immediate answers to questions, human beings need not be capable of intellectual scholarship.

POLITICAL CORRECTNESS

A CRUCIAL PART OF THE EFFORT to bring back Kennedy's style of government will involve the following: There is something that badly needs to be said in this country, but it makes us uncomfortable. So rather than saying it out loud, we retreat behind our smartphones and iPads and let the matter slide.

It is this: One of the nation's political parties, the Conservative Party, has become a danger to our well-being. Individually, its members have become ridiculous figures, pandering to fear and the narrow-minded beliefs held by people who, in the name of the common good, should be educated rather than encouraged to sink deeper into ignorance. They do not act as the loyal opposition, balancing liberal ideas with conservative ones, with the objective of producing commonsense legislation. Their sole concern is electing political leaders and presidents who will preserve Reaganomics.

Science, for example, appears to have confirmed that climate change is real. Corporations that pollute the atmosphere should be working to lessen the problem. Lawmakers should impose a carbon tax on polluters. This, of course, would require them to dip into their profits and spend money, something Conservatives cannot abide. Thus, they argue that climate change does not exist; it is an invalid theory devised by those who want to dictate what the private sector can and cannot do.

Similarly, Conservatives work against regulations that would halt the spread of guns, because the powerful gun industry is part of the private sector, which they believe should operate without regulation.

To win popular support for this concept, Conservatives have pandered to the fear of government, telling their constituents that liberals are plotting to take away their guns. They accept contributions from gun manufacturers, essentially becoming lobbyists, paid to prevent lawmakers from enacting laws that will hurt the sale of firearms. Meanwhile, mass slaughters in schools, malls, and movie theaters across the country have become routine.

THE BIG STING

FOR THE PAST THREE DECADES, the Conservative's agenda has focused on enhancing the ability of the private sector to generate wealth. They have demonstrated a startling lack of respect for the ideal that the public good is more important than the accumulation of wealth.

How would Kennedy react if he knew that in 2010 the Supreme Court ruled that corporations are people, in effect, citizens of the United States? He would likely call this ruling an extension of Reagan's sophomoric economic policies.

According to the Founders, Kennedy might argue, citizens of the United States are obligated to meet their civic responsibilities in the name of the public good. Corporations, however, cannot meet this mandate. They exist only to make ever-increasing profits, which they have used to exploit government through campaign contributions and other forms of political blackmail. If they were indeed virtuous citizens of this republic, they would not use their immense wealth to corrupt lawmakers and influence policy; they would instead use it to promote the common good.

Using anti-American philosophy, Conservatives have pulled off one of the greatest heists the world has ever known: They funneled the bulk of this nation's massive wealth into the hands of an absurdly small number of corporations and wealthy individuals. The Founders did not design the United States to be a plutocracy, a country controlled by the wealthy, yet that is precisely what has happened in Kennedy's absence.

If he were alive today, Kennedy would tell us that when politicians pursue a personal agenda rather than the public good, laboring under the illusion that no harm will come of their neglect, the welfare of the average citizen becomes secondary.

AVOIDING UNPLEASANT TRUTHS

There is a tendency among historians and media pundits to resist probing too deeply into the changes that occurred in America after it lost a leader with Kennedy's determination and skill.

Some try to prove that he was overrated, that the nation's high regard for him is naive, so they hunt for facts, events, and nuance that make him seem petty or fraudulent. There is ample material in Kennedy's personal life to fuel their efforts.

This exercise, however, is cynical and self-destructive. Minimizing Kennedy allows us to avoid the realization that we thrive on the type of political idealism he gave us, that it brought out the best aspects of our government and our human nature.

We can also sidestep the disturbing truth that, after Kennedy was gone, we allowed our political leaders to drive underground the time-tested form of government the Founders gave us, creating the political, economic, and social problems we face today.

That we have lost touch with our past has been noticed by no less a figure than Pope Francis. During his visit to the United States in 2015, he said something that John Kennedy would have appreciated: that our faith in good government is the source of human dignity. Specifically, he said the following:

> One of the highlights of my visit is to stand here, before Independence Hall, the birthplace of the United States of America. It was here that the freedoms which define this country were first proclaimed. The Declaration of Independence stated that all men and women are created equal, that they are endowed by their Creator with certain inalienable rights, and that governments exist to protect and defend those rights.

> But history also shows that these or any truths must constantly be reaffirmed, re-appropriated and defended. The history of this nation is also the tale of a constant effort, lasting to our own day, to embody those lofty principles in social and political life....This shows that, when a country is determined to remain true to its founding principles, based on respect for human dignity, it is strengthened and renewed.

John Kennedy spent his life fighting to maintain the respect for human dignity that comes alive when this country remains true to its founding principles. He made us a better country and a better people, he gave us a tantalizing glimpse of how good life in a republic can be, and in the process…he made us see the stars.

Kennedy's flag-draped coffin in the East Room of the White House in November 1963. He had served just 1,036 days in office, but he nonetheless created a prototype for the way the presidency should be conducted in a republic. Photo by Abbie Rowe

ADDENDUM

CONSPIRACY

THOSE WHO BELIEVE THAT JOHN KENNEDY DIED at the hands of conspirators will be dismayed that Lee Harvey Oswald has been identified as his assassin in this book. Conspiracy advocates believe that in 1963 there were industrialists, criminals, or men in government so evil that they were capable of murdering a president.

This could be true; Kennedy had enemies. He angered military and civilian hard-liners when he refused to start a nuclear war with the Soviet Union or escalate the war in Vietnam. He defied big business and tried to do away with loopholes they used to avoid taxes and amass incredible wealth. The level economic playing field he wanted for America would have muzzled the obsessive corporate drive to make ever-greater profits. And his brother Robert had launched a campaign to rid the nation of organized crime.

The author is gratified that skeptics are actively searching for evidence of more than one gunman in Dallas. He does not dismiss their research out of hand and acknowledges that they have raised disturbing questions about the assassination that have yet to be answered.

The test of conspiracy in the Kennedy assassination, however, rests on a single issue. Two government investigative bodies have concluded that three shots were fired from the sixth-floor window of the Texas School Book Depository. The Warren Report said the first shot missed, and the second shot hit the president in the back of his neck, and emerged to hit Texas Governor John Connally, who was seated in front of him. The third shot struck the president in the head and killed him.

It is the second of these shots that makes or breaks the case for conspiracy. Critics have ridiculed the official government conclusion that one bullet passed through Kennedy and hit Connally. Calling it a "magic bullet," they believe that, to hit Connally, the bullet had to make an impossible change in direction after exiting Kennedy's throat, thus its magic qualities. They claim a bullet was fired instead from a grassy area in Dealey Plaza or a sewer drain or a building other than the Depository.

Numerous studies and computer re-creations of the shooting have found that Kennedy and Connally were in position to be struck by the same bullet; no such impossible change of direction occurred. Also, repeated analysis of the trajectory of the shots show they all came from the sixth floor of the Depository.

The critics dismiss these studies and re-creations, saying they are flawed, but they have been unable to produce a computer analysis of their own that refutes the single-bullet theory. If they were to meet this challenge and prove the single-bullet theory wrong with unshakable forensic evidence, then John Kennedy would have been the victim of conspiracy and the world would change overnight. The author would then fiercely support their efforts to expose the assassins, he would shout from the rooftops.

It is possible, although not likely, that Oswald did not fire the shots, and that, as he maintained, he "was just a patsy." But to date it is beyond argument that all three shots came from the sixth-floor window of the Depository and that both men were hit by one bullet.

Why do the conspiracy theories persist? In a letter to *The New York Times* in 1992, William Manchester offered the best explanation:

> Those who desperately want to believe that President Kennedy was the victim of a conspiracy have my sympathy. I share their yearning. To employ what may seem an odd metaphor, there is an aesthetic principle here. If you put six million dead Jews on one side of a scale and on the other side put the Nazi regime, the greatest gang of criminals ever to seize control of a modern state, you have a rough balance: greatest crime, greatest criminals.

But if you put the murdered President of the United States on one side of a scale and that wretched waif Oswald on the other side, it doesn't balance. You want to add something weightier to Oswald. It would invest the President's death with meaning, endowing him with martyrdom. He would have died for something. A conspiracy would, of course, do the job nicely. Unfortunately, there is no evidence whatever that there was one.

Ironically, the death of a president who asked us to believe in government has added to the distrust of government that is holding this country back today. It is not unreasonable to suggest that Kennedy himself would wish for an end to the speculation and a renewed interest in the type of leadership he provided before Dallas.

BIBLIOGRAPHY

Bernstein, Irving. *Promises Kept: John F. Kennedy's New Frontier.* New York: Oxford University Press, 1991. Print.

Beschloss, Michael R. *The Crisis Years: Kennedy and Khrushchev, 1960-1963.* New York: Edward Burlingame, 1991. Print.

Bradford, Sarah. *America's Queen: The Life of Jacqueline Kennedy Onassis.* New York: Viking, 2000. Print.

Campbell, R. H., and Andrew S. Skinner. *Adam Smith.* New York: St. Martin's Press, sixth-floor, 1982. Print.

Caro, Robert A. *The Years of Lyndon Johnson.* New York: Alfred A. Knopf, 1982. Print.

Collier, Peter, and David Horowitz. *The Kennedys.* New York NY:: Encounter, 2002. Print.

Dallek, Robert. *Lyndon B. Johnson: Portrait of a President.* Oxford, England: Oxford UP, 2004. Print.

Dallek, Robert. *An Unfinished Life: John F. Kennedy, 1917-1963.* Boston: Little, Brown, 2003. Print.

Douglass, James W. *JFK and the Unspeakable: Why He Died and Why It Matters.* Maryknoll, NY: Orbis, 2008. Print.

Elkins, Stanley M., and Eric L. McKitrick. *The Founding Fathers: Young Men of the Revolution.* Washington, DC: Service Center for Teachers of History, 1962. Print.

Fiske, John. *The American Revolution.* Boston: Houghton Mifflin, 1891. Print.

Frank, Robert H. *The Darwin Economy: Liberty, Competition, and the Common Good*. Princeton: Princeton, NJ, 2011. Print.

Fries, Charles W., Irv Wilson, and Spencer Green. *"We'll Never Be Young Again": Remembering the Last Days of John F. Kennedy*. Los Angeles: Tallfellow, 2003. Print.

Galbraith, John Kenneth. *The Good Society: The Humane Agenda*. Boston: Houghton Mifflin, 1996. Print.

Gibson, Donald. *Battling Wall Street: The Kennedy Presidency*. New York: Sherdian Square, 1994. Print.

Golway, Terry. *JFK Day by Day: A Chronicle of the 1,036 Days of John F. Kennedy's Presidency*. Philadelphia: Running, 2010. Print.

Goodwin, Richard N. *Promises to Keep*. Toronto: Times, 1992. Print.

Goodwin, Richard N. *Remembering America: A Voice from the Sixties*. Boston: Little, Brown, 1988. Print.

Hacker, Jacob S., and Paul Pierson. *Winner-Take-All Politics: How Washington Made the Rich Richer–And Turned Its Back on the Middle Class*. New York: Simon & Schuster, 2010. Print.

Hamilton, Nigel. *JFK, Reckless Youth*. New York: Random House, 1992. Print.

Kennedy, John F. *Prelude to Leadership: The European Diary of John F. Kennedy, Summer 1945*. Washington, DC: Regnery Publishers, 1995. Print.

Kennedy, John F. "Profiles in Courage - John F. Kennedy - Paperback." *HarperCollins US*. Harper & Brothers, n.d. Web. 06 Oct. 2015.

Kennedy, John F., and Maureen Harrison. *John F. Kennedy in His Own Words*. New York: Barnes & Noble, 1996. Print.

Klein, Edward. *All Too Human: The Love Story of Jack and Jackie Kennedy*. New York: Pocket, 1996. Print.

Mahoney, Richard D. *JFK: Ordeal in Africa*. New York: Oxford, 1983. Print.

Mahoney, Richard D. *Sons & Brothers: The Days of Jack and Bobby Kennedy*. New York: Arcade Publishers, 1999. Print.

Manchester, William. *The Death of a President*. New York: Harper & Row, 1963. Print.

Manchester, William. *Portrait of a President*. Boston. Little, Brown, 1962. Print.

Markmann, Charles Lam, and Mark Sherwin. *John F. Kennedy A Sense of Purpose*. New York: St. Martin's Press, 1961. Print.

Matthews, Christopher. *Jack Kennedy: Elusive Hero*. New York: Simon & Schuster, 2011. Print.

Matthews, Christopher. *Kennedy & Nixon: The Rivalry That Shaped Postwar America*. New York: Simon & Schuster, 1996. Print.

McCullough, David G. *John Adams*. New York: Simon & Schuster, 2001. Print.

McPherson, James M., and David Rubel. *"To the Best of My Ability": The American Presidents*. New York: Dorling Kindersley Publishers., 2000. Print.

Nasaw, David. *The Patriarch: The Remarkable Life and Turbulent Times of Joseph P. Kennedy*. New York: Penguin, 2012. Print.

Newman, John M. *JFK and Vietnam: Deception, Intrigue, and the Struggle for Power*. New York, NY: Warner, 1992. Print.

O'Brien, Michael. *Rethinking Kennedy: An Interpretive Biography*. Chicago: Ivan R. Dee, 2009. Print.

O'Donnell, Helen. *A Common Good: The Friendship of Robert F. Kennedy and Kenneth P. O'Donnell*. New York: William Morrow, 1998. Print.

Patterson, James T. *Grand Expectations: The United States, 1945-1974.* New York: Oxford, 1996. Print.

Pfiffner, James P. *The Character Factor: How We Judge America's Presidents.* College Station, TX: Texas A&M University Press, 2004. Print.

Pitts, David. *Jack & Lem: John F. Kennedy and Lem Billings: The Untold Story of an Extraordinary Friendship.* New York: Carroll & Graf, 2007. Print.

Reeves, Richard. *President Kennedy: Profile of Power.* New York NY: Simon & Schuster, 1993. Print.

Reeves, Thomas C. *A Question of Character: A Life of John F. Kennedy.* New York: Free, 1991. Print.

Reinhart, Carmen M., and Kenneth S. Rogoff. *This Time Is Different: Eight Centuries of Financial Folly.* Princeton, NJ. 2009. Print.

Rubin, Gretchen. *Forty Ways to Look at JFK.* New York: Ballantine, 2005. Print.

Schaller, Michael. *Ronald Reagan.* New York: Oxford, 2011. Print.

Schlesinger, Arthur M. *A Thousand Days: John F. Kennedy in the White House.* Boston: Houghton Mifflin, 1965. Print.

Schneider, Gregory L. *Conservatism in America Since 1930: A Reader.* New York, 2003. Print.

Shaw, John. *JFK in the Senate: Pathway to the Presidency.* New York.: St. Martin's Press, 2013 Print.

Smith, Adam, and James R. Otteson. *Adam Smith: Selected Philosophical Writings.* Exeter, UK: Imprint Academic, 2004. Print.

Sorensen, Theodore C. *Counselor: A Life at the Edge of History.* New York, Harper, 2008. Print.

Sorensen, Theodore C. *Kennedy*. New York: Harper & Row, 1965. Print.

Sorensen, Theodore C. *Why I Am a Democrat*. New York: Henry Holt, 1996. Print.

Stockman, David Alan. *The Great Deformation: The Corruption of Capitalism In America*. New York, 2013 Print.

Talbot, David. *Brothers: The Hidden History of the Kennedy Years*. New York: Free, 2007. Print.

Whalen, Richard J. *The Founding Father; The Story of Joseph P. Kennedy*. New York: New American Library, 1964. Print.

Widmer, Edward L. *Listening In: The Secret White House Recordings of John F. Kennedy*. New York: Hyperion, 2012. Print.

Wofford, Harris. *Of Kennedys and Kings: Making Sense of the Sixties*. Pittsburgh: University of Pittsburgh, 1992. Print.

Woodward, Bob. *Maestro: Greenspan's Fed and the American Boom*. New York: Simon & Schuster, 2000. Print.

INDEX

PHOTO CREDITS

Front Cover: *portrait of President Kennedy;* by Jacques Lowe

Back Cover: *Eternal Flame at President Kennedy's gravesite, Arlington National Cemetery;* by Larry Downing

Page 2: *President Kennedy on the beach in Hyannis Port;* by Mark Shaw

Page 18: *Ambassador Joe Kennedy and sons on passenger liner;* courtesy JFK Library; photographer unknown

Page 86: *Presidential candidate, Senator Kennedy talks with miners in West Virginia;* by Hank Walker

Page 134: *President Kennedy at press conference;* courtesy JFK Library; by Abbie Rowe

Page 196: *President Kennedy greeting supporters;* by George Tames/*The New York Times*/Redux

Page 196: *President Kennedy lies in state;* courtesy JFK Library; by Abbie Rowe

LETTER CREDITS

All letters written by John Kennedy; courtesy of John F. Kennedy Presidential Library and Museum

ACKNOWLEDGMENTS

THE CONTRIBUTIONS OF SEVERAL PEOPLE helped this book become a reality. The author is indebted to Robert Lascaro, the book's designer, for his inspired design and his unwavering belief in the thesis of the book. Jeffrey Vogel was a keen observer who helped shape ideas and supplied critical thinking. Martha Tomich and Robert Morin offered warm and much appreciated support. A special thanks to Claire Gerus, my literary agent, who listened when so many others would not.

ABOUT THE AUTHOR

PETER MCKENNA IS A JOURNALIST who has devoted the last five years to understanding how the assassination of John F. Kennedy changed America. Prior to this endeavor, he worked as the editor of financial publications in New York. He is a graduate of Columbia University School of Journalism. In 1978, he started his own weekly newspaper that specialized in environmental and social issues. Mr. McKenna has written articles for *The New York Times, Newsday,* and other publications. His previous book, *The Event Trading Phenomenon,* offered the average investor a way to profit in a manipulated stock market. He is an avid ocean sailor and lives in New York with his wife and his little brown dog.

ALL HIS BRIGHT LIGHT GONE

The Death of John F. Kennedy
and The Decline of America

If you wish to discuss this book with the author,
please visit **http://allhisbrightlightgone.com**